THE ROMANCE OF
FORGOTTEN MEN

STATUE OF DANIEL BOONE

The ROMANCE of FORGOTTEN MEN

By JOHN T. FARIS

Thomson

Profusely Illustrated

Essay Index Reprint Series

BOOKS FOR LIBRARIES PRESS
FREEPORT, NEW YORK

STANDARD BOOK NUMBER:
8369-1033-8

LIBRARY OF CONGRESS CATALOG CARD NUMBER:
68-58787

PRINTED IN THE UNITED STATES OF AMERICA

CONTENTS

[vii]

ILLUSTRATIONS

[ix]

ILLUSTRATIONS

·

ILLUSTRATIONS

[xi]

ILLUSTRATIONS

[xii]

FOREWORD

The most satisfactory way to study history is by reading biography. As Emerson said, "All history resolves itself very easily into the biography of a few stout and earnest persons."

But it is a mistake to feel that all the biographies studied must be those of famous men, men who are the acknowledged leaders of their day. What would Green's "History of the English People" have amounted to if the author had confined himself to telling of the lives of kings and nobles? Because he saturated himself with the stories of the common, ordinary people the book he wrote became a classic, at once the beacon and the despair of historians who have followed him.

The real story of the development of our country has not been told by any historian. This story cannot be told within the compass of a single volume or series of volumes. Those who would reconstruct the story of the United States, taking the best history as a mere outline, should fill in the blanks and give character to the whole by seeking for the life stories of those who played their part—perhaps a very humble part—in the dramatic events of the years, remembering, with the Sage of Concord, that while "king and lordship, power and estate, are a gaudier vocabulary than private John and Edward in a small house and common day's work, . . . when private men . . . act with original views, the luster will be transferred from the actions of kings to those of gentlemen."

Where are we to find the stories of these men who

threw their glorious light on our country's past? Now and then a second-hand bookshop yields a quaint biography that is treasure trove. Volumes are buried in the archives of historical libraries; perhaps the cards show that no one has taken these from the shelves for a decade, perhaps a generation. Hints of the story of some man may be given in an old magazine article, and the only way to recover the record of his life is to yield to the time-consuming but wonderfully fascinating sport of piecing out the tale from documents here and there.

In these and other ways the author of *The Romance of Forgotten Men* has found the stories of the obscured makers of history who have been chosen for the volume. The Bibliography gives the titles of many of the volumes read, but this cannot give even a hint of the delightful search of old records, diaries, and letters which have made possible some of the most pleasing additions to stories already published.

Of course the author realizes that to few readers will all the names of characters chosen for the book be unfamiliar. Many times the comment will be made by readers, "That man is not forgotten; his name is as familiar to me as that of my own father." Undoubtedly! Yet the thought that the majority of those whose stories are told have been forgotten by most readers, in spite of the important part they played in the history of their country, has been the author's reason for including them.

JOHN T. FARIS.

Philadelphia
April, 1928

THE ROMANCE OF
FORGOTTEN MEN

CHAPTER I

THIRTY YEARS OF COMEDY AND TRAGEDY IN THE LIFE OF "BARON" HENRY W. STIEGEL

ROSES

A SHORT distance above Columbia, Pennsylvania, a town that came dangerously near to choice as the permanent Capital of the United States, the beautiful Susquehanna River receives the waters of picturesque Chickies Creek. At least that is the short name given to the creek in these days when the musical title bestowed by the Indians seems too long for common use. Chickieswalungo is its proper name, but this has been broken in two, half being retained by the creek, while half is given to the town Salunga, some miles west of Lancaster on the Lincoln Highway. North of Salunga the creek reaches back towards its source in the fertile lands of Lancaster county, which was so long looked upon as "the Granary of the United States."

Perhaps half way between Salunga and the beginning of the stream is the pleasant old town of Manheim, a typical prosperous village of the Pennsylvania Germans, on the road between Lancaster and Lebanon.

Along the road, on the second Sunday in June, may be seen travelers in all kinds of vehicles bound for the Baron Stiegel Memorial Church at Manheim. Each wayfarer hopes that he may arrive in season to receive a seat for the annual Feast of Roses.

This feast is kept in memory of Baron Henry William Stiegel who, on December 4, 1772, conveyed a lot to the Trustees and Wardens of the German Lutheran Congregation settled and established in the town of Manheim. The consideration stated was five shillings. But there was provision also for the "Yielding and Paying therefor unto the said Henry William Stiegel his Heirs and Assigns at the said Town of Manheim in the month of June yearly forever hereafter the Rent of One Red Rose if the same shall be lawfully demanded."

There is record of the payment of the nominal ground rent twice only, during the lifetime of the donor of the land. But after the erection of the new church building in 1891, when a red rose was placed in the conspicuous rose window, a descendant of the man who asked for the annual red rose arranged to present himself for the stipulated payment. And every June since then members of the Stiegel family are on hand to receive the rose. Naturally the chosen day has become the chief yearly festival of the old church at Manheim.

Who was this Baron Stiegel? And how did he come to make such a delightful stipulation in his deed of gift? Of course it is possible to agree with Frederick William Hunter that the call for the annual rose was not the indication of a poetical strain in the makeup of a business man who at the time of his gift made people think that he was a wizard of finance and industry. Mr. Hunter calls attention to the fact that Stiegel lived in a day when it was the very general custom to sell property for a cash consideration plus an annual ground rent in perpetuity. In the case of a free gift of land, "it was the custom to specify, in addition to a nominal cash consideration, a purely nominal substitute for the annual rental"—one grain of wheat, or one peppercorn, or, as in this case, a June rose.

But why yield the point that Baron Stiegel, with all his devotion to business, had a bit of the poetical along with the strange mixture of the practical and the impractical which showed itself in the comedy and the tragedy of his busy life? There are other evidences than this historic rose of the poetical quality.

IMMIGRANTS

Now for the Baron. When the ship *Nancy* reached Philadelphia on August 31, 1750, there were on board two hundred and seventy immigrants. Among them was a young man who called himself Heinrich Wil. Stiegel, together with his mother and his eleven-year-old brother Anthony.

Immediately after landing the passengers went to the Philadelphia Court House, where the older brother signed his name to the declaration required of him:

"We subscribers, natives and late inhabitants of the Palatine upon the Rhine and places adjacent, having transferred ourselves and families into this province of Pennsylvania, a colony subject to the Crown of Great Britain, in hope and expectation of finding a retreat and peaceful settlement therein, do solemnly promise and engage that we will be faithful and bear true allegiance to His Present Majesty King George the Second and his successors, Kings of Great Britain, and will be faithful to the proprietor of this province and that we will demean ourselves peaceably to all his said Majesty's subjects and strictly observe and conform to the laws of England and of this province to the utmost of our power and the best of our understanding."

Many people have believed the tradition that this young man of twenty-one, who agreed so promptly to these requirements, was in possession of a fortune of forty thousand pounds. However, subsequent events reveal the fact that if he could command one thousand pounds he would have thought himself fortunate. He was an adventurer, determined to make his fortune in the new land, but uncertain, evidently, just how he was to do this.

There is no evidence, either, that he was overwhelmed by the attentions of the Quaker City which might have been showered upon him if at that time he had been known as Baron. The title does not appear in any document, nor was any claim to noble birth made by him or in his behalf. The story of his later years will indicate how he came to be given a distinction that his neighbors would have been quick to declare was no elevation, though the weakness of some Americans for a title was as apparent then as it is, to-day.

LOVE

Young Stiegel must have felt that Philadelphia was not the place to make his fortune. At any rate he turned his steps westward very soon, going to Lancaster county, where so many German immigrants were going that the sturdy character of the population—Pennsylvania Dutch, they are called—persists to this day.

Lancaster county is gridironed by many creeks, whose waters fall so rapidly, in places, that mill sites suggested themselves to the first settlers. Not far away were de-

ON THE HIGHWAY NEAR MANHEIM, PENNSYLVANIA

OFFICE OF BARON HENRY WILLIAM STIEGEL,
MANHEIM, PENNSYLVANIA

RARE SPECIMENS OF STIEGEL GLASS IN THE METROPOLITAN MUSEUM OF ART,
NEW YORK CITY

posits of iron, as well as vast forests. What more natural, then, than the building of primitive forges on the creek, to which iron was supplied from mines opened for the purpose, while fuel was provided by gangs of men who cut the trees and hauled the wood? Ruins of a number of these forges may be found in Lancaster, Lebanon and Berks counties.

Among these iron furnaces one of the oldest and most prosperous was near the site of the later town of Bricker-ville, which nestles amid the green hills on the Horse Shoe Road, a highway of the pioneers built in 1752 along the route of a road still older, and an Indian trail that dates back hundreds of years. The proprietor, Jacob Huber, owned also four hundred acres of woodland for the fuel whose smoke went up a stack on which was carved a boasting couplet, after the manner of his day and his people. The lines, which seem to refer to another member of the family, perhaps a son, have been translated with accuracy more of the spirit than of the letter:

> Johan Huber, the first German man
> To turn out iron work thus spick and span.

But young Stiegel was more interested in Huber's daughter than in his furnace. For, on November 7, 1752, he became the husband of Elizabeth Huber, a buxom girl of eighteen. Probably interest in the furnace succeeded the marriage; probably father-in-law Huber made the iron work so attractive that Stiegel paid enough attention to it to learn the business. Evidently, too, he spent some time in Philadelphia—at least enough to make a good impression on men who were destined to play a large part in his eventful life.

The young wife died in February, 1758. Did the death

[5]

of his daughter make Huber willing to give up his activities at the furnace? At any rate, in less than three months, the furnace with its lands was sold to Stiegel, and to Stiegel's partners, Charles and Alexander Stedman, Philadelphia merchants. At the time of Stiegel's arrival in Philadelphia these men were the agents for the *Nancy*. Possibly at that time their attention was attracted to the sturdy immigrant. They seem to have watched his progress with such approval that they were glad to risk some of their savings in a great venture.

So many matters moved with deliberation in those pioneer days that a hasty action like Stiegel's second marriage seems quite startling. Eight months after the death of Elizabeth the first, and less than six months after his father-in-law parted with the family business, Elizabeth the second, whose name was Holz, was led to the altar. Probably the compelling reason for the hasty marriage was the presence of two young children in the Stiegel home.

IRON

To the furnace which was in the possession of Stiegel and his partners the name Elizabeth was given, perhaps at once. This was a natural name, for it was located in Elizabeth township. But, in view of the fact that many a furnace of the pioneers bore the name of some woman of the proprietor's family, does it not seem likely that Elizabeth furnace was either a memorial to the first wife, or a compliment to her successor? This would be in accord with the poetical temperament of the visionary young proprietor.

Attention to business brought prosperity. The demand for the products of the Elizabeth Furnace led to the pur-

chase of thousands of acres more of woodland. Within
a few years the partners owned more than ten thousand
acres, and the furnace was securing an enviable reputation
for the making of various products of iron, especially the
primitive iron stoves for combined heating and baking,
and, finally, the stoves called "six-plate," and "ten-plate,"
because they were made of that number of pieces of iron.
On some of these stoves, at a later period, the iron-
founder cast the inscription:

Baron Stiegel ist der Mann
Der die Oefen giessen kann.

This rude couplet Frederick William Hunter, with his
ability to change crude poetry into expressive vernacular,
has translated:

Baron Stiegel is the cove
That can cast your iron stove.

Thus the founder used the title Baron. But the fact
is worthy of note that he did not call himself so in any
formal documents; in these he was always simple Henry
William Stiegel. Evidently he was making use of a name
bestowed on him, perhaps affectionately, certainly with
admiration, by neighbors who watched his meteoric rise
and the baronial magnificence of his home and the habits
of the man who lived there.

The variety of the work done at Elizabeth Furnace is
revealed by an advertisement dated March 27, 1769, in
the *Pennsylvania Chronicle and Universal Advertiser*:

"Iron Castings"

"Of all dimensions and sizes, such as kettles or boilers
for pot-ash works, soap boilers, pans, pots, from a barrel

to 300 gallons, ship-cabooses, Rachels, and sugar house stoves, with cast funnel of any height for refining sugars, weights of all sizes, grate bars and other castings for sugar works in the West Indies, &c, are all carefully done by Henry William Stiegel, iron master, at Elizabeth Furnace, in Lancaster county, on the most reasonable terms."

In a single year the receipts from orders from the West Indies were £418.4.4, while the total receipts of the furnace for ten years were £10,636.10.7, of which nearly £3000 was clear profit.

In the midst of the first prosperous years at Elizabeth Furnace, Henry William Stiegle, as his name was given in the records, appeared in Philadelphia, to take the oath of allegiance to the King. This was in accordance with the Act of Parliament which gave the privilege to every man "having inhabited and resided the space of seven years and upwards and not having been absent out of said Colonies for a longer space than two months out of the said seven years, and having produced to the Court a certificate of their having taken the Sacrament of the Lord's Supper in some Protestant or Reformed Congregation in the Province within three months." The certificate granted to those who fulfilled this condition declared them "natural born citizens of Great Britain."

From Philadelphia Citizen Stiegel went back to the management of the Elizabeth Furnace. That he had no simple task is evident from the fact that sometimes as many as two hundred men were needed to care for a Lancaster county furnace, the gathering and hauling of the iron ore, and the cutting and transporting of wood. Several hundred acres of the best woodland had to be denuded of timber each year.

EXPANSION

The modest buildings at Elizabeth Furnace were not enough to satisfy the ambitious manager. He removed the old buildings and put up others. Then he erected a score or more of houses for his workmen, as well as a mansion for himself. This house is still standing, close to the old furnace. And a sturdy house it is.

But Elizabeth Forge was not sufficient to satisfy the young ironmaster. If one establishment was good, why not have another? So he looked for a second opportunity. This he found when he crossed the spur of the Blue Ridge which separated Elizabeth Forge from the Lebanon Valley. There he wandered up Tulpehocken Creek until he found a promising furnace which dated from 1749. This he bought in 1760, together with 88 acres of woodland. Within three years the land belonging to the furnace totaled more than 3100 acres. A half interest in the new venture was sold to his partners at the Elizabeth Furnace, the Stedmans, for £3132. The joint property was called Charming Forge. Once again the poet was in evidence.

In the meantime, however, the Stedmans had bought 729 acres of land in Manheim township, not far from Elizabeth Furnace. And they persuaded Stiegel to buy an interest of one third in the land, on which they proposed to lay out a town.

Charming Forge proved a profitable venture, for the bar-iron produced there was marketed, to quote the words of Hunter, "at prices calculated to make any present-day iron-smith rub his eyes in an incredulous envy." On one occasion 69½ tons of the product went to London, and £1839.4.5 was the payment for the shipment.

Prosperity led, naturally, to a rather unwise increase

in expenses at the ironmaster's home near the Elizabeth Furnace. One of Stiegel's own papers shows a summary of his resources at this period:

Servants Retinue	£208. 7.6
Musical Instruments	375.12.4
Household Furniture	483. 0.5
Clothing	206.16.3
Negro Cyrus	80. 0.0
Debts due me	2028. 4.4

In these days, when the amounts thus set down in a very off-hand manner would be worth ten times as much as when Stiegel maintained his establishment, a banker would be apt to shake his head in disapproval. The love of ease, of pomp, of making an impression on his neighbors and associates, was leading him into troubled waters. Soon the simple mansion at Elizabeth did not content him; he built two rather extravagant homes, one on the land in which the Stedmans had sold him an interest, another at Schaefferstown, some miles from Elizabeth Furnace. Some of the funds spent so prodigally were raised by a mortgage on Elizabeth Furnace. In both establishments he lived in baronial magnificence, maintaining a large retinue of servants, driving to and from the houses in a coach and four, and arranging that cannon mounted for the purpose should be fired to welcome him on his return to either house.

Then on a platform above the roof of one of the houses he had a private band which played for him during the evenings and added its din to that of the welcoming artillery. Is it any wonder that the people called him Baron?

Such a man could not enjoy his grandeur unless there were people who could see it. Provision was made for them when the land he owned with the Stedmans was laid out in lots. To this town the name Manheim was given. A tavern—the "King of Prussia"—was the center of life in the new town, and of this Stiegel was the proprietor.

Not even yet, however, is the tale of Stiegel's activities and vision fully unfolded. Iron was too prosaic; he would be known for something much more spectacular.

GLASS

So he became a manufacturer of glass. At Elizabeth Furnace he had made a beginning in 1763, probably the year when he began his Manheim mansion. There, bottles and window-glass were manufactured. But he wanted to be a glassmaker on a larger scale. Probably his trip to Europe, made in 1763 and 1764, was undertaken for the purpose of studying methods of making glass. This trip, like all his other expeditions, was made on a princely scale; the books of Charming Forge show that he drew £600 for the purpose.

The Manheim Glass House, into which he incorporated, probably, some of the ideas gleaned through his trip to the Rhine country, cost £1600.

On October 8, 1765, it was possible to fire the ovens. For a time bottle- and window-glass were the chief product, but, in spite of the depression of colonial trade due to the Stamp Act and the subsequent non-importation agreement, the program was enlarged. In the *Pennsylvania Chronicle and Universal Advertiser* on March 27, 1769, the announcement was made:

"The said Stiegel begs leave . . . to inform the public, that his Glass Manufactory in Manheim town . . . is again at work, where are made all sorts of bottles, window glass and sheet glass; also retorts and other glasses for doctors and chymists."

Still more indicative of Stiegel's enlarging program was the advertisement in the *Pennsylvania Journal and Weekly Advertiser* on July 5 of the same year. After a preliminary paragraph, the announcement read:

"As the proprietor has been at an immense expense in erecting said works, and engaging some of most ingenious artists in said manufacture, which is now arrived at perfection, and above all, as at this crisis it is the indispensible duty, as well as interest of every real well wisher of America, to promote and encourage manufacture among ourselves; they hope from the glorious spirit of patriotism at present voluntarily and virtuously existing here, to receive the approbation and encouragement of the public, which they expect to merit a continuance of, by selling their goods on much lower terms than such imported from Europe are usually sold."

Among the products of what took on, eventually, the title, The American Flint Glass Manufactory, were bottles, jugs and mugs of Nile green, olive and red-brown, sweetmeat jars, blue flint mugs and egg glasses, sugar bowls of amethyst flint, vases of many tints, bowls, decanters, wine-glasses, and flasks and mugs of flint, decorated with ambitious designs.

Distributing stores were located in New York and Philadelphia, and, in general, there were many developments which only a growing business would justify.

DIFFICULTIES

But the business did not grow. Difficulties increased. The buying power of the colonists decreased. Stiegel's

JOHN BARTRAM

OLD COURT HOUSE, TOWN HALL AND MARKET,
PHILADELPHIA, IN THE DAYS OF JOHN BARTRAM

WHERE JOHN BARTRAM WENT TO MEETING. DARBY MEETING,
NEAR PHILADELPHIA

partners, the Stedmans, were in trouble; they longed to
get out of their various investments with Stiegel, instead
of going in deeper, as he would have chosen to have them
go. He was right in thinking that financial salvation lay
in concentrating his efforts in one direction, but he made
the mistake of choosing glass instead of iron. He tried
to dispose of his interests in the forge. In May, 1767,
he offered for sale both Elizabeth Forge and Charming
Forge, with the lands attached, "as well as the present
Estate belonging to the said Maker, for the Manufacturing of Pig Iron, Cast Iron, & pots &c, also the Making
of Barr Iron. Together with all the Tools, Utensils,
Teams, Horses, &c to the said Company belonging, that
is to say, one third part therein at Elizabeth Furnace, and
one half therein at Charming Forge, the said Henry William Stiegle proposes to sell at the low price (for ready
Cash) for Eight thousand pounds, Pennsylvania Currency . . ."

"Ready Cash" was sorely needed, but it could not be
secured. The next best thing seemed to be a mortgage.
This was secured, on March 9, 1768, from Daniel Benezet, of Philadelphia. For £3000 Stiegel pledged all his
property at Elizabeth Furnace and Charming Forge, as
well as at Manheim.

A second and larger glass manufactory was built at
Manheim. Desperate efforts were made to capture trade.
Instead of taking in sail, he loosed all canvas, and so invited destruction from a wind that was already becoming
a typhoon. His biographer, Hunter, says of his vain efforts after financial salvation:

"Like a football player, ducking down the slippery field
with the ball tucked tightly under one arm and the other
extended to ward off the tacklers of the opposing side, he

carried his glass project desperately forward, ducking and dodging amid judgments, foreclosures and sheriff's sales, with an effective though unavailing mixture of desperate courage and naïve effrontery."

Stiegel's feeling that the country owed much to him because of his self-sacrificing efforts to bring his glass factory to perfection, led him, on March 10, 1773, to advertise in the *Pennsylvania Journal and Weekly Advertiser* his purpose to have a lottery, the resort of governments, political subdivisions, schools, and churches, as well as of private individuals when money was to be raised, and it was not known how to secure the funds in other ways. So he announced:

"The Proprietor of the American Flint Glass Manufactory at Manheim in Lancaster County, with the advice of many gentlemen in the city, his friends, has offered a Scheme of a Lottery to the patronage of the public, to enable him to carry on a manufactory of public advantage and to raise a sum of money for that and other beneficial purposes in the scheme mentioned."

There were two drawings. A third was advertised, but the sale of tickets was insufficient. The result was disappointing. The glass factory made but £83.3.10, although £638.12.11 was put out in prizes and expenses. According to the plan the sale of tickets should have brought a handsome return of hundreds of pounds.

CRASH

The lottery was the final vain attempt of the financial wizard of Lancaster county to help himself. Next he turned despairingly to his friends. On February 15, 1773, he resolved to write to John Dickinson at Fair Hill, who had been his patron for many years, telling him of his dire necessity and appealing for aid. The letter he sent is among the manuscript treasures of the Historical Society of Pennsylvania:

Dear Sir—

Last Saturday night I was informed by Mrs. Stiegel that the Sheriff of Lancaster County hath been at my House and in pursuance of Mr. Isaac Coxe's Execution Levied all of my Effects, toke an Inventory of all my Household furniture, &c.

What Mr. Coxes Design is by this Step God knows, but it is impossible for me to Express Dear Sir the Effect this Step has already had on me and the dreadful Stroke I am aprehensive it will produce from my other Creditors without I can find a Human friend to assist me.

It surely gives me pain that I am under the Disagreeable Necessity of Troubling you so often, but as I Rely on your Goodness I have made Bold to send you inclosed an Exact Estimate of all my Estate and the Debts I owe which I pray you to Look over and Consider also my Situation and Circumstance. Sure I am if I obtain no Assistance I shall be in Danger of being Ruined. But if on the other hand assisted I have not the least Doubt of saving all my Manheim Estate and of making money fast as my Glass houses are in fine order and the last addition thereto finished.

If therefore I now could obtain the favour of you Dear Sir to take up Mr. Coxe's morgage and Lent me £2000 to Discharge the Judgments and Debts I could retrieve me Self in a short Time and repay you as will apear to you by the Estimate.

The Satisfaction Dear Sir that will arise in your Breast will be Great when you Reflect That by Assisting a Man Struling with Difficulties and one who is doing all in his power to pay his Debts with the Strictest Honour, you may prevent the Ruin of a Family. I Remain in Expectation of your Kind Answer,

Your Most afflicted and Distressed Servant,

HENRY WM. STIEGEL.

But John Dickinson felt that he could do no more for his friend. Seeing that he must help himself, Stiegel issued a broadside on June 1, 1773, in which he announced that there will "be Sold by the Subscriber, by way of Public Vendue," on a day appointed, "an half part of Charming Forge, and lands thereto belonging: situated at Tulpehocken Township, in the County of Berks, also at Manheim, in Lancaster County, one of the best mill-seats for custom, in Lancaster County, adjoining the said town, on Chiciesalongoe Creek, there is 14 feet fall."

Not yet was he utterly cast down. On August 4, 1774, he wrote to a friend:

"Let them give me time and I will pay every dollar. Can it be that my former friends in Lancaster County will drive me to ruin when I have increased the wealth of the county by at least £150,000?"

All efforts to stave off ruin amounted to nothing. Execution followed execution, and on August 13, 1774, the Supreme Court of Pennsylvania issued a "writ of Levari Facias" (an order for public sale) of "one capital messuage and furnace, called or known by the name of Elizabeth Furnace," together with some ten thousand acres of lands, "being late the Estate of Henry William Steigle, Seized and taken in execution." The sale was to take place on September 16, 1774.

Ten days after the order of the Supreme Court was issued, the harried man humbled his pride and sent an appeal more fervent than ever to John Dickinson. In the letter he said:

". . . Mr. Cox having entered up his Judgment Keeps me Tied hand and feet that I can make no sale . . . All this might be altered if I hath but one friend to assist me and take my part . . . Suffer me once more to Entreat

[16]

and Beg your Assistance. Depend on it you will not suffer.
I remain after my Humble Compliments, with Great Esteem . . ."

With this letter was enclosed a statement of assets and
liabilities. Liabilities, including mortgages of £4000,
came to £10,402.12.1, while assets were set down at
£10,970.14.2.

In addition, Stiegel would have the Manheim estate,
the Manheim ground rents of £240 per year, a large brick
house, 92 acres of the best land, the glass house, and all
other buildings adjacent; in all, about £9000 in value.

If Dickinson sought to do anything for his associate, his
efforts accomplished nothing. Everything was sold. And
still there were debts.

PRISON

In accordance with the stern laws then on the statute
book, when the possessions of the bankrupt were insufficient to pay his creditors, Stiegel's body was seized, and
he was imprisoned in Philadelphia, probably during the
last week of November, 1774.

But the prisoner did not lose all hope. Still he figured
how he might pay his debts and resume his place in the
manufacturing business. He found consolation in God,
for he was a faithful Christian. Once he wrote on the
fly-leaf of one of his books a prayer in which he said, in
part:

"Save me from stumbling stones and traps of the
wicked which they have prepared for me . . . Turn from
me disgrace and contempt . . . Deliver me from the bad
people . . . Let my innocence come to light . . . Grant
unto me strength and patience that I may through dis-

grace or honour, evil or good, remain in the good, that I may follow in the footsteps of Thy dearly beloved son, my Lord and Saviour who had to suffer so much for my sake. . . ."

On December 15 he sent to his creditors word that he had appealed to the Honorable House of Assembly "for a Law to relieve my Person from Imprisonment." He asked them if they had objections, to appear "at the Gaol in the city, before the Committee of Grievances."

Evidently there was no opposition to the request of the prisoner in the jail, for when the Assembly adjourned later in December, 1774, it had ordered the release of Stiegel. Probably the act took effect at once, so that on Christmas day the bankrupt was a free man.

The deliberate method of doing business in those days is shown by the fact that the official document authorizing the release was not issued until April 28, 1775. Then "The Honourable John Penn, Esq. Governor and Commander in Chief" authorized "Edmund Physick, Keeper of the Great Seal," to certify to the passage of the "act for the relief of Henry Wm. Stiegel, a languishing prisoner in the Gaol of Philadelphia County with respect to the Impressment of his Person."

ECLIPSE

In 1777, when the British were threatening Philadelphia, Robert Morris bought the Manheim mansion which Stiegel had occupied with so much pride, and in September of that year he took his family to it for a refuge.

During the early months of their occupancy, when Congress was in session at Lancaster, the new proprietor entertained royally various men of prominence, who marveled at the comforts provided in the great brick house, which contained three large rooms on each floor, separated by great halls. Wainscotings and cornices were marvels of the woodworker's art. "The fireplaces were adorned with tiles, samples of which are still preserved by the Historical Society of Pennsylvania," says Hunter. "The parlor walls were painted with scenes of falconry; handsome tapestries were hung there. . . . The second floor contained a private Chapel, with arched ceiling, pews and a pulpit, where, when no clergyman was available, Stiegel himself conducted services for his neighbors and workmen."

Just before entering the house, Mrs. Morris wrote to her mother, asking her to visit her "at the once famous place where were yet vestiges of the last owner's folly and may prove a useful lesson to us, his successors."

At that time Morris was looked on as one of the richest men and greatest land-owners in America, and was the dependence of Washington for the financing of his campaigns. Yet only a few years later he followed Stiegel into bankruptcy, then into the very jail in Philadelphia where Stiegel had languished. Moreover, at the time of his financial difficulties, he was building a wonderful mansion. This he was unable to finish; for a long time the staring building was known as "Morris's Folly." What an echo that name was of Mrs. Morris's reference to "the vestiges" of Stiegel's "folly" which did not prove a salutary lesson to his successors!

In the meantime Stiegel was trying to pay his debts and recoup his fortunes. His efforts were unavailing. Ruinous sales robbed him of all his savings, and he was compelled to take employment as caretaker of Elizabeth Furnace. In 1776 he became foreman for Robert Coleman, the new proprietor, whose descendants still own and live in the old house near by which was once occupied by Stiegel.

During the Revolution the Furnace, under Stiegel's direction, manufactured cannon balls for Washington. After the Battle of Trenton, Washington showed his interest in the furnace by sending there a force of Hessian prisoners, who were to dig a canal for a larger water supply.

When the war orders fell off, there was no further need of the foreman's services, so the broken man returned to Brickerville, where he made a precarious living as a teacher of music. For a time he lived in the parsonage of the church at Brickerville, of which he was a member, where for many years he had been a leader.

"This, to my mind," says Hunter, "is the most pathetic thing in the entire record of Stiegel's life. One can see him, stranded and penniless . . . doubtless sitting by the light of a single candle, after trudging along the Horse Shoe Pike, from giving a lesson to some farmer's brat, and figuring on a blank page of the Day Book of his first successful venture how many pounds it would take to retrieve his ruin."

When the coming of a pastor to the Brickerville church made necessary his removal from the parsonage, he turned his steps sadly to the Thurm Berg, or Castle, which he had built near Schaefferstown in 1769. The property was owned by the brother who had come with him to America.

But not even in the old Castle was he permitted to remain long. A wanderer, he went out, once more to teach school, later to eke out a miserable existence by doing clerical work and even menial tasks.

In 1785, when he died, he was not much more than fifty years old. But he was a broken, disappointed man. No one knows where he was buried. Those who knew him must have felt that he had gone into total eclipse.

FAME

The Manheim Glass Factory was torn down in 1812. The bricks were used later in the erection of the Neffsville Hotel at Neffsville, Lancaster county. This seemed to be the end of Stiegel and his glass.

But it was not the end. For many years specimens of the glassware made at Manheim were treasured by old families. Some of those who saw the pieces, even collectors of fine glass, made fun of those who declared there was anything of value in the relics.

But in recent years there has been a rapid change of sentiment. Eager connoisseurs have bent every effort to discover what was so long despised. Those who know real art have come to the conclusion that in the green glass and the flint glass that came from Manheim there was something individual and graceful, "having the unmistakable personality of handwork done with love." Tumblers and mugs, salts and cruets, smelling bottles, wine bottles, glasses, phials, toys, mustard pots, candlesticks and flower jars! With remarkable patience farmhouses and other likely places have been searched, sometimes with success. And often the choicest specimens have come from most unlikely places.

Occasionally the papers report such a sale as that made in New York, in February, 1926, when three simple pieces of Stiegel glass brought $2070. "The first is of clear white flint with a bird on the cover and lovers' knot handles, 6.75 inches in height," a reporter of the sale wrote. "This piece brought $1000. The next is 8.5 inches

[21]

high, of clear white flint, diamond-mold pattern and sapphire-blue rim and knob. Its price was $700. The third is 6.25 inches high, emerald green, and sold for $370."

Other prices at the same sale were similarly fabulous:

"A pair of sapphire-blue Stiegel vases, 13.5 inches high, brought $1150; a sapphire-blue Stiegel vase, 7⅞ inches, $690; a blue-violet cream pitcher, $255; a light-amethyst pocket flask, $160; and a New Jersey emerald glass pitcher, 6.5 inches, with ball stopper, $360."

Many of these masterpieces became museum specimens. In the Metropolitan Museum of Art, in New York City, an honored place is given to scores of specimens of the work of Henry William Stiegel, the glass manufacturer of Lancaster county. Some of the most beautiful of these specimens were decorated with vitrifiable enamels. The expert of the Metropolitan Museum, in telling of the points in which these pieces differ from similar pieces made abroad, has explained:

"The Stiegel workmen used six opaque enamel colors, a white, a yellow that ranged from light to chrome, a Nile green that I have never seen used on any other glass thus decorated, a cobalt blue used in a light and a dark shade, a black, and, finally, a brick red that will remind students of Japanese prints of the reddish color so successfully employed by Horonobu and Korinai in 1768 in reprinting undecorated woodwork. These colors, as seen in the Stiegel pieces, show a true vitrified surface, except in some instances where the darker shades of red have not been fused properly and lack the proper glossy and brilliant finish. They have remarkable purity of tone; were applied with considerable thickness; and, as a consequence, the edges of the designs are cleaner cut than in any similar pieces."

"BARON" HENRY W. STIEGEL

And so it happens that as, each June, Stiegel's descendants receive the Red Rose in the Stiegel Memorial Church at Manheim, they rejoice that, after so long a time, their ancestor is honored in the land where he suffered dire humiliation.

CHAPTER II

HOW JOHN BARTRAM LEARNED NATURE'S LESSONS

A FEW rods from the bank of the Schuylkill River, in West Philadelphia, stands an ancient stone house beneath one of whose windows is a rudely carved stone with this inscription:

> It is God Alone, Almyty Lord,
> The Holy One By me Ador'd.
> Iohn Bartram 1770.

This confession of faith was added to the house many years after the earnest Quaker owner built it. For another stone, set in the south wall, has this record:

> Iohn : Ann : Bartram : 1731.

The quaint house was built by John Bartram's own hands in the midst of a tract of land which he transformed from a wilderness into a garden, bearing all manner of trees and fruits and plants, gathered from up and down the Atlantic coast and as far into the interior as the Alleghany Mountains.

SELF-TAUGHT

The plain Quaker gardener, who was born March 23, 1699, had little opportunity to attend school, but he made up for the lack by teaching himself. He learned Latin and Greek in the intervals of his farm work. He was a diligent farmer, and his crops were abundant, but he was not content to plant the seed and reap the grain; he wanted to know more of the wonders of God's world. His son William wrote of him: "While engaged in plowing his fields and mowing his meadows, his inquisitive eye and mind were frequently exercised in the contemplation of vegetables, the beauty and harmony displayed in their mechanism, the admirable system of order which the great Author of the universe has established throughout their various tribes, and the equally wonderful powers of their generation, the progress of their growth, and the various stages of their maturity and perfection."

As he studied, there came to him the desire to plant his garden; so he bought a piece of ground at a tax sale, built his house, hewed out of stone a great watering trough, which is still shown to visitors, contrived a wonderful cider-mill in a ledge of outcropping rock on the bank of the river, and proceeded to lay out a five-acre garden, the first botanical garden in America.

JOURNEYS OF A PIONEER

Eager to include in his garden specimens from all parts of the country, he occupied a portion of each year in laborious journeys. "Neither dangers nor difficulties impeded or confined his researches after objects in natural history. The summits of our highest mountains were ascended and explored by him. The Lakes Ontario, Iroquois and George; the shores and sources of the rivers Hudson, Delaware, Schuylkill, Susquehanna, Allegheny and San Juan were visited by him at an early period, when it was truly a perilous undertaking to travel in the territories, or even on the frontiers of the aborigines."

His son William wrote in regard to these trips: "He travelled several thousand miles in Carolina and Florida. At the advanced age of near seventy years, embarking on board of a vessel at Philadelphia, he set sail for Charleston, in South Carolina. From thence he proceeded, by land, through part of Carolina and Georgia, to St. Augustine in Florida. When he arrived at the last mentioned place, having been appointed botanist and naturalist for the king of England for exploring the provinces, he received his orders to search for the sources of the great river San Juan (or St. John). Leaving St. Augustine, he travelled by land to the banks of the river, and embarking in a boat at Picolata, ascended that great and beautiful river (near four hundred miles) to its source, attending carefully to its various branches and the lakes connected with it. Having ascended on one side of the river, he descended by the other side to its confluence with the sea."

The notes made on the trip were later sent to England, and were received with gratitude by his royal employer.

THROUGH THE EYE OF AN ENGLISH VISITOR

A delightful glimpse of life at the Bartram home is given in these extracts from a letter from a visitor to America, written in 1769, and published in London in 1782 in *Letters from an American Farmer:*

"I was received at the door by a woman dressed extremely neat and simple, who asked me who I wanted. I answered, 'I should be glad to see Mr. Bartram.' 'If

thee will step in and take a chair I will send for him.'
'No,' I said, 'I had rather have the pleasure of walking
through his farm.' After a little time I perceived the
Schuylkill, winding through delightful meadows, and soon
cast my eye on a new-made bank, which seemed greatly to
confine its stream. I at last reached the place where two
men were at work. An elderly looking man, with wide
trousers and large leather apron on, looking at me, said:
'My name is Bartram. Dost thee want me?' 'I should
be glad to spend a few hours in your garden,' I said. 'Our
jaunt into the garden must be postponed for the present,
as the bell is ringing for dinner.' We entered into a large
hall, where there was a long table full of victuals; at the
lowest part sat his negroes; his hired men were next; then
the family and myself, and at the head, the venerable
father and his wife presided. Each reclined his head and
said his prayers . . .

" 'Pray, Mr. Bartram, what banks are those which you
are making; to what purpose is so much expense and so
much labor bestowed?' I asked. 'No branch of industry
was ever more profitable to any country, as well as the
proprietors,' he replied. 'The Schuylkill in its many wind-
ings once covered a great extent of ground, though its
waters were but shallow even in our highest tides; and
though some parts were always dry, yet the whole of this
great tract presented to the eye nothing but a putrid,
swampy soil, useless either for the plow or the scythe.
The proprietors of these grounds are now incorporated;
we yearly pay to the treasurer of the company a certain
sum, which makes an aggregate superior to the casualties
that generally happen, either by the inundations or the
musk squash (musk-rat). It is owing to this happy contrivance that so many thousand acres of meadows have

been rescued from the Schuylkill which now both enricheth and embellisheth so much of the neighborhood of our city.'

" 'Pray, sir, what expense are you at ere these grounds be fit for the scythe?' I asked. 'The expenses are very considerable, particularly when we have land, brooks, trees and bush to clear away; but such is the excellence of these bottoms, and the goodness of the grass for the fattening of cattle, that the produce of three years pays all advances.'

THE FARMER AT WORK

"We went into the garden, which contained a great variety of curious plants and shrubs; some grew in a greenhouse, over the door of which was written these lines:

'Slave to no sect, who takes no private road,
But looks through nature, up to nature's God.'

"We went to view his favourite bank; he showed me the principles and method on which it was erected; and we walked over the grounds which had been already drained. The whole store of nature's kind luxuriance seemed to have been exhausted on these beautiful meadows; he made me count the amazing number of cattle and horses now feeding on solid bottoms, which but a few years before had been covered with water. . . . He next showed me his orchard, formerly planted on a barren, sandy soil, but long since converted into one of the richest spots in that vicinage. 'This,' he said, 'is altogether the fruit of my own contrivance. I purchased, some years ago, the privilege of a small spring, about a mile and a half from hence, which at considerable expense, I have brought to this reservoir; therein I throw old lime, ashes, horse dung, and so forth, and twice a week I let it run, thus impregnated. I regularly spread on this ground, in the fall, old hay, straw and whatever damaged fodder I have about my barn. By these simple means, I mow, one year with another, fifty-three hundreds of excellent hay per acre, from a soil which scarcely produced five fingers (that is, cinquefoil) some years before. . . . Within the banks of my meadow ditches, I have greatly enriched my upland fields; those which I intend to rest for a few years, I constantly sow with red clover, which is the greatest meliorator of our lands. For three years after, they yield abundant pasture. When I want to break up my clover fields, I give them a good coat of mud, which hath been exposed to the severities of three or four of our winters. This is the reason that I commonly reap from twenty-eight to thirty-six bushels of wheat an acre; my flax, oats and Indian corn I raise in the same proportion.' "

THE MAKING OF A BOTANIST

The curious visitor asked Mr. Bartram how he learned to love botany. Thoughtfully the answer was given:

"One day I was very busy in holding my plow (for thou seest, I am but a plowman), and being weary, I ran under the shade of a tree to refresh myself. I cast my eye on a daisy; I plucked it mechanically, and viewed it with more curiosity than common country farmers are wont to do, and observed therein many distinct parts, some perpendicular, some horizontal. 'What a shame,' said my mind, or something that inspired my mind, 'that thee shouldst have employed so many years in tilling the earth, and destroying so many flowers and plants, without being ac-

quainted with their structure and their uses.' I returned
to my team, but this new desire did not quit my mind; I
mentioned it to my wife, who greatly discouraged me from
prosecuting my new scheme, as she called it; I was not
opulent enough, she said, to dedicate much of my time to
studies and labors which might rob me of that portion of
it which is the only wealth of the American farmer. However, her prudent caution did not discourage me; I thought
about it continually—at supper, in bed, and wherever I
went. At last, I could not resist the impulse; for on the
fourth day of the following week, I hired a man to plow
for me, and went to Philadelphia. Though I knew not
what book to call for, I ingenuously told the bookseller my
errand, who provided me with such as he thought best,
and a Latin grammar beside. Next I applied to a neigh-
bouring schoolmaster who, in three months, taught me
Latin enough to understand Linnæus, which I purchased
afterwards. Then I began to botanise all over my farm.
In a little time I became acquainted with every vegetable
that grew in my neighbourhood, and next ventured into
Maryland. In proportion as I thought myself more
learned, I proceeded forth and by a steady application of
several years, I have acquired a pretty general knowledge
of every tree and plant to be found in our continent. In
process of time I was applied to from the old countries
whither I every year send many collections. Being now
made easy in my circumstances, I have ceased to labour,
and am never so happy as when I see and converse with
my friends."

In his work in the garden, Mr. Bartram was assisted
by a company of negroes to whom he had given liberty.
Each man received £18 a year wages, with board and
clothes. The oldest of the number was his master's busi-

ness man, going frequently to Philadelphia, and arranging
the shipments of plants and trees and insects which were
sent to England by almost every vessel leaving the port of
Philadelphia. The grave of this faithful servant is still
pointed out to visitors to Bartram's Gardens.

Bartram's fame was carried to England with his journals. These fell into the hands of Peter Collinson, of
London, who was devoted to science. The perusal of the
diaries showed the Englishman that he had found a kin-
dred spirit, and he wrote to Bartram. This was the beginning of a correspondence that continued for years. "The
two helped each other, rallied each other, loved each
other, for nearly fifty years without ever meeting face to
face!" one historian has said. "Through Peter Collinson, John Bartram's correspondence extended to all the
distinguished naturalists of his time. It was he who engaged, first Lord Petrie, then Philip Miller and the dukes
of Richmond and Norfolk, to subscribe an annual allowance of thirty guineas to meet the expenses of Bartram in
procuring for them American plants to adorn their gardens."

THE LEGACY

The monuments of John Bartram are an old volume
of correspondence with his English friends, and the garden, neglected, cut in two by the railroad from Philadelphia to Washington, but still the old estate wrested from
the river by the hands of the lover of nature nearly two
hundred years ago.

Many of the trees have perished, and have left no sign.
One relic of the past still stands, though it may not last
many years longer—the great trunk of a cypress which was

planted about 1735. On one of his trips into Delaware the botanist procured the cypress slip, which he carried home in his saddle-bags. It grew to be one hundred and fifty feet high and twenty-seven feet in circumference. In 1899 it still bore a few live twigs. But now the trunk stands in the midst of the garden, gaunt, huge, crumbling into dust.

The Lady Petrie pear tree is still bearing fruit, after more than a century and a half. In 1763 Bartram wrote to Peter Collinson: "The Pear raised from her (Lady Petrie's) seed hath borne a number of the finest relished fruit. I think a better is not in the world."

Box trees planted by the botanist are yet green. There is a jujube tree, planted in 1735, which waves above the old house. Elsewhere are a ginkgo tree from Japan, a holly, a tulip tree, a silver-bell tree, a cucumber tree, of the species brought from Ontario in 1743, and a horse-chestnut, grown from seed received from England in 1746. These are among the old trees that are still green. Over the arbor grows a trumpet vine which was sent from North Carolina in 1749.

Bartram's Gardens were looked upon as one of the wonders of colonial days. Here Washington and Franklin and Jefferson used to come for rest and refreshment, and here tens of thousands of others have had that intimate communion with nature that the proprietor of the gardens made possible for them by his years of loving toil.

When he was dying he feared that his pride would be laid waste by the British army, which was advancing from the Brandywine. He died, September 22, 1777, before the soldiers came to Philadelphia. But when they came it was not "to lay waste his darling garden, the nursling of almost half a century," but to pass it by unharmed.

The botanist's son John succeeded him as proprietor. With him lived his brother William, whose fame as a nature lover was second only to that of his father. After his death, in 1823, the garden passed to other hands. To-day it is a park belonging to the city of Philadelphia. It should have a constant stream of visitors. Yet comparatively few go there. Many old residents have not thought it worth their while to visit it; many more do not know of its existence. But some day it will take its proper place as one of the spots that everyone must see.

CHAPTER III

THE STORY OF THREE BRADFORDS, COLONIAL
PUBLISHERS AND PRINTERS

WHEN mention is made of early printers in the colonies, especially in Philadelphia, most people are apt to think, among the first, of Benjamin Franklin. Yet it is a fact that if the versatile Franklin had not won fame in other fields, his place as a printer and publisher, in the thought of people of to-day, would be much less prominent than that of a family devoted to "the art preservative" whose connection with Penn's colony began more than forty years before Franklin made his famous entry into Philadelphia, and nearly fifty years before the return from the sojourn in London which was followed by the real beginning of his professional career in the city by the Delaware.

This pioneer in the printing industry in the Quaker City was William Bradford, the founder of a line of printers and publishers of the same name who were prominent for one hundred and forty years, either in Philadelphia or in New York, or in both cities. In his Autobiography Franklin makes a number of references to the second of the line, Andrew. Unfortunately, these are rather uncomplimentary; they give the impression that the Sage of Pennsylvania was restive under the competition of the pioneer printers of the colony. Horatio Gates Jones, a careful student of history, in an address before the Historical Society of Pennsylvania, on February 8, 1869, called attention to some of these references in the Autobiography, and added:

"When Franklin established his paper, the *Pennsylvania Gazette,* the Bradfords had been for nearly half a century before him leading the way to literature and art. And it was only after their well-planned and indefatigable labors had cleared away the obstructions which proved impossible to all less generous enterprise, that the celebrated representative of their common art appears on the field, to gather, along with them, the fruits of their long-continued toil."

A SOBER AND CIVIL GIFT TO AMERICA

William Bradford was born in England in 1660, within a year after Oliver Cromwell resigned as Protector. In his youth he was apprenticed to Andrew Sowle of London, in whose office he learned the printer's trade, and in whose home he found his wife, Elizabeth Sowle.

Among the intimate friends of Andrew Sowle was William Penn. To him the apprentice was introduced. What wonderful hours young Bradford must have spent in listening to the glowing plans of the Quaker Proprietor for the "Holy Experiment" he was to try in America! Among other things, Penn told of his desire to have a printer in the new colony, from the beginning. The thought appealed to William, and William appealed to Penn, so when the *Welcome* sailed from Deal on September 1, 1682, bearing Penn to his sylvan possessions, Bradford also was a passenger.

After the landing at New Castle, Delaware, on November 28, 1682, the young printer remained long enough

[35]

to look over the ground and to decide on his needs for the life venture he was to make there. Then he returned to England. But in 1685 he was in Philadelphia once more, this time prepared to cast in his fortunes with the Proprietor and his infant city by the Delaware River.

Not least in the tale of his equipment for business was a letter from George Fox, the eminent Quaker. Addressing many leaders among the Friends of America, Fox said:

"This is to let you know that a sober young man, whose name is William Bradford, comes to Pennsylvania, to set up the trade of printing Friends' books. And let Friends know of it in Virginia, Carolina, Long Island, and Friends in Plymouth Patent and Boston. So his settling to print at Philadelphia may serve all these countries, namely: Pennsylvania, East and West Jersey, Long Island, Boston, Winthrop's Country, Plymouth Patent, Pisbaban (where was Pisbaban?), Maryland, Virginia, and Carolina . . . He is a civil young man, and conversant of truth."

AT THE BEGINNING OF HIS CAREER

Evidently, Bradford was looked on as a Friend. His connection with the peculiar people gave him valuable introductions, and made easier some of his plans to work in a community where Friends dominated the colony for many years. But he was too self-reliant to depend on even such good customers as the Quakers; before a great while he was doing work for all the Middle Colonies. Within a few years he was recognized by patrons not only in Pennsylvania, but as well in New York, New Jersey, Connecticut, Rhode Island, and Maryland.

And the beginning of this extensive work was less than

IN THE GARDEN OF SIR WILLIAM HAMILTON, PHILADELPHIA.
INSPIRED BY BARTRAM'S GARDENS

OLD SCHOOLHOUSE WHERE ALEXANDER WILSON TAUGHT. DEMOLISHED IN 1875.
NEAR BARTRAM'S GARDENS, PHILADELPHIA

three years after the arrival of Penn and the beginning of
Philadelphia and Pennsylvania! The marvel of this may
be seen from the fact that in Massachusetts no printing
was done until eighteen years after the settlement of the
province. In Maryland and Virginia, the leaders were so
afraid of printers that a ban was put on them and their
work.

When John William Wallace spoke of Bradford before
the Historical Society of New York, he could not resist
painting a word-picture of this pioneer printer:

"The figure of this enterprising youth as he labored at
his press in the early days deserves, I think, to make a
picture on the canvas which shall perpetuate the history of
American civilization."

Then he called attention to the fact that "in all other
countries the typographical art had been cultivated beside
the supporting walls of palaces; within the protecting
closes of religious houses, or under the fructifying air of
patronage and wealth. Where rank and wealth and learning have not been its cheerful supporters, the press has languished, or has had to wait for happier times."

But William Bradford was an exception. "He crossed
the ocean a thousand leagues away from the genial influence of education and taste." He had no "assistance of
the learned," nor any "patronage of the great." Very
soon he was "printing the wisdom of Francis Bacon for
the rough trader whose soul is absorbed in schemes of
gain, or for the poorer colonist, anxious only to build himself a shelter from the storm, or to provide for the day
that is passing over his head. His patrons are the ignorant
Finlanders and Swedes and Hollanders."

In his own words he had "laid out the greatest part of
that small stock he had on materials for printing (which

are very chargeable) and coming here found little encouragement, which made him think of going back." Yet he decided to fight on, setting his own type, correcting his own galleys, making up his own forms, and "applying the full vigor of his arm to turning the crank," that he might lift from the press the printed sheet.

The self-reliant printer was soon planning to print books. These he bound himself, in a workmanlike manner. Three years after setting up his shop, when he was less than twenty-eight years old, he told the Friends at Burlington, New Jersey, of his purpose to print a folio Bible, with marginal notes, together with the Book of Common Prayer. He asked the support of subscriptions, "because it will be a very great charge insomuch that I cannot accomplish to do it myself without assistance." He told of his purpose to complete the work in eighteen months, and said that the twenty shillings he would have to charge for the book should be paid "half silver money, and half country produce at money prices." A thoughtful provision was made in addition: "But they who really have not money yet are willing to encourage the work," would be permitted to pay in goods alone.

While the ambitious plan was not carried out, it is worthy of note that this was made in good faith full seven years before Cotton Mather proposed to print the Bible in Boston.

Another ambitious plan was carried out. In 1690, in partnership with the Hollander, William Rittenhouse, he built, near Philadelphia, on a branch of the Wissahickon, the first paper-mill in the colonies. This was placed on land secured by the Sowles from their friend Penn, which had passed to Bradford.

Six years after the building of the paper-mill John

Holme, in his poem, "The Flourishing State of Pennsylvania," wrote:

> Here dwelt a printer, and, I find,
> That he can both print books and bind.
> He wants not paper, ink, nor skill;
> He's owner of a paper mill.
> The paper mill is here, hard by,
> And makes good paper, frequently.

TROUBLES AND TRIALS OF A PRINTER

To-day printers and publishers sometimes think that they have to steer carefully if they would avoid the reefs of libel and the rocks of fine and imprisonment. Perhaps it helps them to recall the fact that more than two hundred years ago the dangers in the path of the unwary printer were infinitely greater; he had to be as careful as an automobile driver of to-day as he ventures within the bailiwick of a squire who acts as if he were the divinely appointed regulator of road traffic.

William Bradford's first sorrow came in 1686, after his publication of an almanac which soon became the expected annual product of Philadelphia printers. This almanac, which was called *Kalendarium Pennsylvaniense,* or *American Messenger, an Almanack,* seemed innocence itself. But the sensitive foes of William Penn were also eagle-eyed; when they turned to the anniversary of the date on which the Proprietor assumed control of Pennsylvania, they discovered the awful statement, "The beginning of Government here by the Lord Penn."

To provincial magistrates the use of the handle to Penn's name gave grievous offense. So Bradford was called before them and was warned "not to print anything

[39]

but what shall have lycence from ye council." William Penn must not under any circumstances be called "The Lord Penn"! Had they not come away from England to escape the domination of nobles?

The Almanack for 1687 was entirely innocuous. To present-day readers it would seem strange, not only because it called January the eleventh month of the year, in strict accord with the Old Style calendar, but because its astronomical calculations were given with special reference to Burlington, rather than Philadelphia. For a time the New Jersey town was the more important of the two places.

But the publication of the Almanack for 1688 brought renewed trouble. The Friends were displeased by reason of the presence of what they called "unsavoury matter." It would be difficult for a reader to-day to discover anything offensive, but the Friends, like the magistrates, were supersensitive, and they insisted on the suppression of the entire edition. To their credit be it said, however, they reimbursed Bradford for the loss thus caused.

The year 1688 brought still greater anxieties. It seems that the Annual Fair, which was already an institution in which Philadelphia took much pride, had been held down near the center of population, close to the Delaware. But that year the Governor and Council decided that it was to be held "at the Centre," or Centre Square, the City Hall Square of to-day. This was too far from the fashionable quarter of Water Street to suit the people, so a number of influential men wrote a remonstrance and circulated this for signature. Bradford, sympathizing with the remonstrants, printed "a paper touching ye keeping of the Fair at the Centre."

The Provincial Minutes tell the rest of the sad story:

"A Summons was sent . . . for the Summonising of ye Subscribers of a Contemptuous Printing paper touching ye keeping of ye Fair at ye Centre; where it was ordered by ye Governor and Council to be kept."

When, next day, "ye 16th of ye 3d Month, 1688, it was Reported that all had been Summoned, the Deputy Governor and Council, after Reproving them, did pardon all those who subscribed to what was indorsed on the back of one of the printer papers." But provision was made that it would be contempt if any "printer paper" remonstrated against the wise doings of the Governor and his Council.

The printer was not cowed. Convinced that he had a duty to perform, he resolved to be faithful to the people in their struggle against the authorities. He had a vision of the freedom of the press, and this he would maintain.

In 1689, when a question arose between the Governor and the people as to their rights under the charter given to William Penn, Bradford printed the charter, for the information of the citizens. While there was no imprint on the document, the Council felt sure as to Bradford's responsibility, since he was the only printer in the colony. Therefore he was sent for, and was examined as to his action. He decided that the Council had no evidence, and he said he would not incriminate himself. But let the minutes of the examination tell the tale:

Governor. "Why, sir, I would know by what power or authority you thus print? Here is the Charter printed."

Bradford. "It was by Governor Penn's encouragement I came to the Province, and by his license I print."

Governor. "What, sir, had you license to print the Charter? I desire to know from you, whether you did print the Charter, or not, and who set you to work."

Bradford. "Governor, it is an unspeakable thing for any man to accuse himself; thou know'st very well." . . .

Governor. "Can you deny that you printed it? I do know you did print it, and by whose direction, and will prove it, and make you smart for it, too, since you are so stubborn."

In the course of the examination it was agreed that the charter was the groundwork of the laws of the province. Bradford said the people should be familiar with it. But the Governor proposed to bind him over in £500 "to print nothing but what I allow."

This was too much. Bradford felt that he must go to a more liberal community. So he asked for his *Bene Decissit,* or certificate of character and letter of introduction. According to the minutes of the Friends to whom he belonged, "William Bradford laid before the meeting his intention of transporting himself to England." In accordance with his request, a certificate of good behavior was ordered made ready for him.

But his associates were not ready to see him leave. What would Friends do without his printing press? The next Quarterly Meeting asked him if he could not remain. He was promised all the business Friends could throw in his way. They agreed to pay him a yearly salary of £40, and to take at least two hundred copies of all books "printed by the advice of Friends."

All was satisfactory until 1692, the year of the split among the Friends, when some sided with George Fox and some with Governor Keith. Bradford took his stand with the latter, for he felt that thus he was espousing the cause of the people against those who were using their authority unjustly. He printed an appeal to the people. For this grave offense he was arrested, and the obnoxious pamphlet was seized by the sheriff, as well as his printing office.

When he was placed on trial before his Quaker judges, the sheriff presented as evidence the very type from which the offending pamphlet had been printed, which was still locked in the form, exactly as it had come from the press. Gravely the jurors examined the form, holding it close to their eyes, making vain efforts to read the type. But they did not know with what care it was necessary to handle the chase with its contents. While one unfortunate juror was squinting at the strange-looking form, the quoins which fastened the type within the chase became loosened, and in a moment the thousands of pieces of type were falling. Vainly the juror grasped at the rain of metal, and sorrowfully he looked at the pi on the floor and at the empty metal container in his hand.

Thus the evidence against Bradford vanished!

When the judges found against him, the printer appealed to Governor Keith and the Council. The case was heard on April 23, 1693, but the result was a triumph for the appellant. The order was given that the sheriff of Philadelphia "do return to William Bradford, Printer, his tools and letters taken from him in September last."

But the straw that broke the camel's back was the order by the Friends, adopted in meeting, "that William Bradford the Printer do show what may Concern Friends of Truth before Printing, to the Quarterly Meeting of Philadelphia."

No wonder the harassed Bradford was ready to listen to proposals made to him from New York. In March, 1693, it was "Resolved in Council in New York":

"That if a Printer will come & settle in the city of New York for the printing of our Acts of Assembly and Public

Papers, he shall be allowed the sum of £40 Current Money of New York per annum for salary."

In addition, of course, he was to be free to serve the public.

The bait was too attractive to be resisted. The same year, 1693, found Bradford in New York, where he became Royal Printer, an officer of the Crown. Within two years his salary was £60.

One of his early issues was entitled "A Letter of Advice to a Young Gentleman leaving the University,—Concerning his Behaviour and Conversation on the World."

However, not all his issues gave as little offense to the authorities. He had his difficulties with Governor Cornbury, who more than once held up his pay. In spite of this fact, he was ready to print the discourse preached in Trinity Church in 1706 at the funeral of Lady Cornbury. A copy of this pamphlet still in existence bears a delicious manuscript note which shows that Cornbury was obnoxious not only to Bradford, but to many others:

"On the death of Lady Cornbury, who was a young and beautiful woman, distinguished too by rank, her husband asked the Legislature to allow her a publick funeral. That body with decorous expressions of regret, declined the Earl's request; but added with *empressement,* that they would, at any time be most happy in granting one to his Lordship."

Bradford was a vestryman of Trinity. That church was interested in his work, not only the Prayer Book, but other later projects. In 1704 the church records tell of an order to lend him thirty or forty pounds for six months, on security but without interest, the money to be expended for printing paper "to print the Comon Prayer Book."

CONTRASTED METHODS OF FRANCE AND ENGLAND IN DEALING
WITH INDIANS

BATTERY OF ASSOCIATORS OF 1747 ON THE DELAWARE, NEAR PHILADELPHIA.
WILLIAM BRADFORD WAS A LIEUTENANT HERE

The New York printer lived in honor until May 23, 1752, when he was ninety-two years old. He was buried in Trinity churchyard. The original stone which marked his grave, accidentally broken when the new church was built, is in the possession of the New York Historical Society.

PENNSYLVANIA'S FIRST NEWSPAPER PUBLISHER

Now for the second Bradford, printer. His name was Andrew, and he was the son of the William who went to New York in 1693. At that time Andrew, who was born in Philadelphia, was seven years old. When he was able to take his place as an apprentice, he went into his father's office to learn the business. This was in pursuance of the ex-Philadelphia printer's plan to keep the plums and the incidental thorns in the family. He did not, therefore, lose his grip entirely on Philadelphia and its trade, but had matters in such shape that when Andrew was fitted for independent work the Quaker City was waiting to receive him.

It was not strange, then, that a proposition made in 1709 from Rhode Island was not looked on with favor, though this had been invited by the ambitious Andrew. The General Assembly at Newport resolved that "whereas there is one Bradford, son of Bradford the printer of New York, who has offered himself to set up a Printing Press in this Place, and to find paper and print all things that may relate to the Colony and Government for £50 a year," overtures be made to him to undertake the work. The Friends of Philadelphia were still on good terms with William Bradford, in spite of his preference for Trinity Church. They indicated their willingness to secure young Andrew a press, of which they were to be the proprietors, and in 1712 he began work there. Thus entered the City of William Penn a man who has been called "the less gifted, but not less respectable or successful Son"— the second in the long line of Bradfords who were printers in Philadelphia from 1685 to 1825, without interruption, save for the years between the departure of William the First and the arrival of his son Andrew, and the brief period of the British occupation of the city. The successive holders of the honor were a father, his son, a grandson, a great-grandson, and a great-great-grandson.

Until 1720 Andrew was the only printer in Pennsylvania. His first work of any consequence was the book containing the Laws of the Province. This he offered to print, the paper being furnished by the province, for £100. Of this amount £50 was paid out of the stock of the province, while it was arranged that the balance should be a charge on the province; 500 copies were to be supplied to the authorities. The edition carried the cumbrous title:

"The Laws of the Province of Pennsylvania, collected into one volume, by order of the Governor and Assembly of the said Provence, Projected and Sold by Andrew Bradford in Philadelphia, 1714."

Unfortunately the copies remaining in the hands of the printer soon became unsalable because some of the laws were repealed by Queen Anne and her advisers, whose jealousy of colonial legislation was evident in many instances.

It is of interest to note that when the Assembly learned of this misfortune of the printer, for which he was not responsible, it provided for a supplementary grant of £30 to reimburse him.

Later he was made official printer of the province. During his term of office, in 1728, he printed a creditable revision of the laws—352 pages, folio. This work was done at his establishment, "at the Sign of the Bible," the designation adopted by his father before him. There he conducted also a store where, according to an early advertisement, he sold:

"Jesuit's bark, very good Bohea tea, chocolate, molasses, new rec. pickled sturgeon, Spanish snuff, dried deer skins, and beaver hats (some with silk linings)."

The advance of culture and wealth in the province is evident from the fact that, in 1730, he was selling also:

"Choice parcels of stationery, lately imported from London, Dutch quills, blank books, royal, medium and post papers, good Slates, choice ink, powders and japanned ink, sealing-wax and wafers, including crown and half-crown wafers for officers, folio letter cases, very good paper in royal, demy, superfine large post, foolscap, gilt paper for letters, fine glass ink fonts, very nice ink stands of various sorts, and several kinds of stationery ware."

The people who patronized such a stationery store, where books also were sold, were ready for a newspaper. So, on December 22, 1719, Andrew Bradford issued the first number of the *American Weekly Mercury,* a paper which was published for twenty-three years. The initial number of this first paper in the Middle Colonies announced that it was planned for the encouragement of trade. Local news and personal gossip were absent from the first, for the feeling was that the space should be devoted to "foreign news, Commercial statistics, custom-house entries, including those of all considerable ports along the Coast, and especially of New York and Boston." There were also occasional literary communications, as well as extracts from the English classics.

A study of the files of the paper shows that, mechanically, it was in advance of the standards of that day. The type from which it was printed, as well as the paper, was manufactured at the Rittenhouse Paper Mill, of which mention has been made already.

A second weekly newspaper was started in Philadelphia by a printer named Keimer, in 1723. This he called *The Universal Instructor*. A comparison of the two papers shows how vastly superior was Bradford's work, both as editor and as printer.

When this Keimer, a few years later, was about to depart for Barbados, he gave utterance to a rather jealous appreciation of the prosperous Bradford. He said:

> In Penn's Wooden Country type feels no disaster,
> The Printer grows rich: one is made Post Master.
> His father, a printer, is paid for his work,
> And wallows in plenty just now in New York.
> Though quite past his labors and old as my Grannum,
> The Government pays him forty pounds per annum.
> But alas! your poor type prints no figure like Nullo;
> Cursed, cheated, abused, by each pitiful fellow.
> Though working like slaves, with zeal and with courage,
> He can scarce get, as yet, salt to his porridge.

Before long the son found himself beset by difficulties like those which had driven his father from the province. On January 2, 1721, he was honest enough to say:

"Our General Assembly are now sitting, and we have great expectations from them, at this juncture, that they will find some effectual remedy to revive the dying credit of the Province, and return us to our former happy circumstances."

Such flagrant disregard of the rights of the powers that be could not be brooked. So, on February 2, 1721, Andrew was called before the Provincial Council. To them he explained that he had no knowledge of the offending paragraph; it was inserted by the journeyman who set up the paper, entirely without his knowledge. On this plea he escaped punishment, but he was straitly charged by the Governor that for the future he must publish nothing concerning the affairs of the Government, or that of any other of Her Majesty's Colonies, without the permission of the Governor or Secretary.

THE TALE OF TWO RIVALS

The *Mercury* was young when, in 1723, another budding printer came to Philadelphia. This was Benjamin Franklin, who had learned the trade at the office of his brother in Boston. He first stopped in New York, where he applied for work to William Bradford. By him Franklin was urged to go to Philadelphia. There he sought work from Andrew Bradford. There was no work in the office of the *Mercury,* so Bradford sent him to Keimer whose *Weekly Instructor* needed a man to take the place of a printer, Acquila Rose, who had just died. Andrew showed his friendship by providing lodging for Franklin until Keimer intimated that he thought it hardly fitting that his printer should live with his rival.

But the rivalry between Keimer and Bradford was as nothing to the rivalry between Franklin and Bradford. This enmity—which may have been more professional than personal—had many undignified expressions as long as Bradford lived.

[49]

Franklin was an open critic of Bradford's work. In his Autobiography, he says of the *Mercury:*

"The only paper we had in Philadelphia at that time, and which Bradford printed, was a paltry thing miserably printed, in no respect amusing, and which yet was profitable."

Again he wrote, after he had left Keimer and had set up an establishment with Hugh Meredith:

. "The public printing, always a profitable matter, was in the hands of Andrew Bradford. He printed the usual 'Speech of the Governor at the Meeting of the Assembly,' in a coarse, blundering manner; we reprinted it elegantly and correctly and sent one to every member. They were sensible of the difference; it strengthened the hands of our friends in the House, and they voted us their printers for the year ensuing."

Bradford took a hand in these charges, which indicated that the rivalry was not merely professional but political as well. When Franklin was awarded the printing of the money of the colony of New Jersey, at higher prices than were asked by another, he said:

"Its no matter, its the countrys money, and if the Publick cannot afford to pay well, who can? Its proper to serve a Friend when there is opportunity."

Another episode in the rivalry, as related in the Autobiography, tells of Franklin's desire to marry the daughter of a relative of his landlady, Mrs. Godfrey. According to his own account, this was, to say the least, more discreditable to Franklin than to Bradford.

"The parents encouraged my addresses, by inviting me continually to supper, and leaving us together, till at last it was time to come to an explanation. Mrs. Godfrey undertook to negotiate our little treaty. I gave her to

understand that I expected to receive with the young lady
a sum of money that would enable me at least to discharge
the remainder of my debt for my printing material. It
was then, I believe, more than a hundred pounds. She
brought me for answer that they had no such sum at their
disposal. I observed that it might easily be obtained, by
a mortgage on their house. The reply to this was, after
a few days' interval, that they did not approve of the
match; that they had consulted Bradford, and found that
the business of a printer was not lucrative; that my letters
would soon be worn out, and must be supplied by new ones,
that Keimer and Harris had failed, and that probably, I
should do so too. Accordingly they forbade me the house,
and the young lady was confined. I know not if they really
changed their minds, or if it was merely an artifice, sup-
posing our affection to be too far engaged for us to divert,
and that we should contrive to marry secretly, which would
leave them at liberty to give or not as they pleased. But,
suspecting their motive, I never went again to their house."

In 1728 Franklin, probably unintentionally, involved
Bradford with the authorities of the colony. This came
about through a deep-laid scheme by Franklin which professed itself to be anything but what it was in reality.

Again the story is told in the Autobiography. A printer
who had left Keimer's employ, asked Franklin for employment.

"We could not employ him immediately; but I foolishly
told him, under the rose, that I intended shortly to publish
a new parochial paper, and that we should thus have work
for him. Webb betrayed my secret to Keimer, who, to
prevent me, immediately published the prospectus of a
paper that he intended to institute himself, and in which
Webb was to be engaged. I was exasperated at this pro-

ceeding, and, with a view to counteract them, not being able at present to institute my own paper, I wrote some humorous pieces in Bradford's, under the title of the Busy Body . . . I thereby fixed the attention of the public upon Bradford's paper; and the prospectus of Keimer, which was turned into ridicule, was treated with contempt. He began, notwithstanding, his paper; and after continuing it for nine months, having at most not more than ninety subscribers, he offered it to me for a mere trifle. I had for some time been ready for such an engagement; I therefore instantly took it upon myself, and in a few years it proved extremely profitable to me."

"FOR THE GOOD OF MY COUNTRY"

Now note how the ingenious Franklin approached Bradford in his first Busy Body paper:
"Mr. Andrew Bradford: I design this to acquaint you that I, who have long been one of your Courteous Readers, have lately entertain'd some Thoughts of setting up for an Author my Self; not out of the least Vanity, I assure you, or Desire of showing my Parts, but purely for the Good of my Country.
"I have often observ'd with concern that your *Mercury* is not always equally entertaining. The Delay of Ships expected in, and want of fresh Advices from Europe, make it frequently very Dull; and I find the Freezing of our River has the same Effect on News as on Trade. With more concern have I continually observ'd the growing Vices and Follies of my Country-folk; and their Reformation is properly the Concern of every Man. . . . Yet 'tis true in this case, that what is every Body's business is Nobody's Business; and the Business is done Accordingly. I

[52]

Thurſday, *October* 31, 1765.   **THE**   NUMB. 1195.

PENNSYLVANIA JOURNAL;

AND

WEEKLY ADVERTISER.

EXPIRING: In Hopes of a Reſurrection to LIFE again.

BRADFORD'S DOLEFUL DIRGE BECAUSE OF THE STAMP ACT

THE BROKEN TOMBSTONE OF
WILLIAM BRADFORD

THE LONDON COFFEE HOUSE, PHILADELPHIA. BUILT IN 1752.
BRADFORD'S BOOKSTORE TO THE RIGHT

therefore, upon mature Deliberation, think fit to take
Nobody's Business wholly into my own Hands; and, out
of zeal for the Publick Good, design to erect myself into
a kind of *Censor Morum,* proposing, with your allowance,
to make use of *The Weekly Mercury* as a Vehicle in which
my Remonstrances shall be convey'd to the World."

That sounds fair enough. But the reader of the passage already quoted from the Autobiography cannot help
wondering if "zeal for the Publick Good" was interpreted
by Franklin to mean the downfall of Keimer's paper that
his own plans might succeed.

Now these Busy Body papers proved—as Franklin intended—helpful to the *Mercury.* Their unusual literary
quality was noted and approved. In fact, the favor ac-
corded them was so great that, when Franklin ceased to
contribute weekly papers, they were continued by other
hands.

All went well until Busy Body number thirty-one appeared. This was on a political subject. In these days
it would be counted very mild, but in the fevered days of
1728 it was loaded with dynamite for Bradford. For it
appeared just before the annual election, and was devoted
to the reflection that there was always a tendency in the
party in power to perpetuate itself, though rotation in
office was necessary for the public good.

Lieutenant-Governor Patrick Goode called the Council
in special session to lay before them Editor Bradford's
derelictions. The offender was arrested and examined by
the Mayor and Recorder of the City. His dwelling and
his office were searched for the written copy of what was
held to be a libel on the Government. The Attorney-
General was commissioned to prosecute the editor of the

Mercury for the publication. Accordingly Bradford was bound over to court.

When the next issue of the *Mercury* appeared, the readers were astonished to see, in addition to a statement of regret that the Busy Body in question had given undesigned offense, a second paper on the same subject, which, it was announced, was ready for printing before the effect of the first had been seen. This was printed exactly as it was.

Apparently that ended the matter. The case was not pushed. The career of the paper was not interrupted.

Perhaps the incident was responsible for added reputation for the bold editor. At any rate he became a Councilman, and continued to hold office to the close of his life. He was already a vestryman of Christ Church, as his father was a vestryman of Trinity Church in New York.

It is a matter of history that from the date of this clash between Bradford and the authorities the freedom of the press became greater, not only in Pennsylvania, but throughout the colonies.

The rivalry between Editor Bradford and Editor Franklin—for Franklin became an editor when he secured Keimer's paper for a song—was evident when Bradford was Postmaster, from 1728 to 1731. One of Bradford's privileges, as given by Deputy Postmaster Spottswood, was the free carriage of his own paper to the subscribers. Franklin says that his paper was refused admission to the mails, though, as he says, "I really procured other papers and distributed my own, by means of the post, . . . by bribing the post boys who served me only by stealth."

In time Bradford was deprived of his office, owing to his dilatoriness in sending in his accounts. Franklin became his successor. Then he remembered the resentment excited by Bradford's action in excluding his paper from the mails. "My disgust was so rooted that, . . . I took care to avoid copying his example." At least that is the story given in the Autobiography, though there is not lacking evidence that the problem was not solved so simply and magnanimously.

The rivalry between Bradford and Franklin continued. There was notable evidence of it in 1740, when Franklin planned to begin a literary monthly. Bradford anticipated him by a short time. The result was a rather unseemly series of charges and countercharges in the papers of the two men.

Both magazines were premature; the public was not ready for them. Franklin's publication ceased very soon. So did that of Bradford, though this was revived by his nephew, Colonel William Bradford, in 1757. It seems that almanacs only could look for success in 1740. Of these booklets Bradford published seven. One of these was called *Poor Will's Almanac*, and was a rather unworthy rival of *Poor Richard*.

It is good to know that in later life Franklin recognized the folly of such undignified charges and countercharges as these of himself and Bradford. For, from Paris, he wrote to a friend in America:

"You do well to avoid . . . the . . . personal abuse so scandalously common in our newspapers. . . . Such things subject us among strangers to a reflection like that made by a gentleman in a coffee-house to two quarrelers, who, after a mutually free use of the words rogue, villain, rascal, scoundrel, etc, seemed as if they would refer the dispute to him. 'I know nothing of you or your affairs,' said he; 'I only perceive that you know one another.'"

The probability is that Franklin's opposition to Bradford was for business purposes only. For when his rival died, on November 24, 1742, Franklin's *Pennsylvania Gazette* spoke respectfully of the man who had done so much for Philadelphia and Pennsylvania.

The body of the printer was laid in the burial ground of Christ Church. He is remembered still as one of the most liberal contributors to the erection of that church.

In Thomas's *History of American Printing,* the comment is made:

"He increased his property, became easy in his circumstances, and preserved, in a considerable degree, the confidence of his fellow citizens."

WILLIAM BRADFORD THE THIRD

Before the death of Andrew Bradford came his nephew, William Bradford, from New York. He was the grandson of the William Bradford who came over with William Penn. His father, too, was named William Bradford, while his mother was Sytje Santvoort. In their New York house he was born on January 19, 1721 (old style).

Andrew Bradford of Philadelphia had no children, so he was glad to take his nephew as an apprentice. And when the years of learning the trade were over, William Bradford became the partner of Andrew. This was long enough before the death of Andrew to make possible the printing of a number of tracts which bore their joint imprint. One of these read: "Printed by Andrew and William Bradford, at the Sign of the Bible, in Front Street, 1740." Another little volume, printed in the same year, was a book of Hymns and Sacred Poems by John and Charles Wesley, which was sold "for the Benefit of the Poor in Georgia."

Within a year of the formation of the partnership, William withdrew, and announced his purpose to go to England for the purpose of securing the best possible materials for carrying on his trade when he returned to Philadelphia.

In London he conferred with his great-aunt, Mrs. Tace Sowle Raylton, daughter of the Andrew Sowle who had taught the original William Bradford his trade. To her the ambitious printer told his desire to be a publisher and bookseller. She helped him by introductions to the best publishers in the city.

In 1742 William found himself once more in Philadelphia, in possession of the finest equipment for a printing office and bookstore in all the Middle Colonies. On July 8 he announced in Franklin's *Pennsylvania Gazette* that he had set up a printing office "where Mr. Andrew Bradford formerly lived in Second Street." There he planned to issue very soon the initial number of *The Weekly Advertiser* or *Philadelphia Journal* "in which paper, gentlemen may have extracts of their letters published, containing matter fit to be communicated to the Public."

The first number of the new paper was issued on December 2, 1742. It has been called "one of the best printed, best edited, and most widely circulated papers of the last century in our country." It was published by himself, or by one of his sons for sixty years.

John William Wallace, after careful comparison of the files of the *Journal* with those of the *Gazette,* says that "as an editor and printer of a newspaper, Bradford was not behind Franklin in any respect, and in the department of news—the only department which the intelligence of that day was able to conceive of, as one fit to engage the efforts of a *Gazette* or a *Journal,* at all—Bradford was perhaps in advance of him."

Not only by his paper, but by a number of books, Bradford "established his title to be regarded as among the best printers in America." His primacy was recognized, probably in 1744, by his appointment to be "Printer to the King's Most Excellent Majesty for the Province of New Jersey."

Until 1780 he continued his active work as a printer and publisher. He issued many books, published a magazine, and was a tower of strength to Pennsylvania and her sister colonies by reason of his readiness to reflect, through his publications, the kaleidoscopic changes in the thirty-eight years from the first issue of the *Journal* to the time of his retirement.

The fortunate possessors of a file of the *Journal* have at their command a record of days of war and peace that is invaluable. "A Journal which embraced the times of both the French wars, the Indian war, the epoch of the Stamp Act, Revolution, Constitution, and, the crowning glory of them all, the administration of Washington, must always remain a historical monument," says Wallace. "From 1764, when the Stamp Act was proposed, till the occupation of Philadelphia by the British, when the *Journal* was temporarily suspended, it is probably the most valuable of the American journals."

One reason for its great value was stated by the editor of the Germantown *Telegraph* in 1852:

"There breathed throughout it a sentiment of patriotism, a detestation of oppression, a hostility to tyranny, and a love of liberty and freedom of the press as deep and fervid as exists anywhere at the present day."

The great reason for this value of the *Journal* as a patriotic record and a patriotic investigator is that the editor and proprietor was himself, from the beginning of his paper to the close of the Revolution, an active patriot. "He is not to be numbered among the greater military characters of our Revolutionary War, nor as a scientific soldier of any kind. His profession was not arms. He was a printer, a publisher, a bookseller, a man of business; eminent, too, in his own day, in all those vocations; and leaving, in all, records so creditable that they come down to ours. He took up arms only in self-defense, or in defense of what was dearer than self; his country. His military attainments, however, were respectable, and of his bravery no one ever doubted."

THE CAREER OF A PRINTER-PATRIOT

Because the career of William Bradford—or Colonel Bradford, as he was known after the Battle of Princeton—was so typical of the patriots who won the freedom of their country, it is worth while to stop to review the widely divergent service which he rendered to Pennsylvania and the colonies, in the days of struggle, while, at the same time, he continued the business that not only made possible his patriotic service, but also extended that service to leaders of the colonies as well as to the rank and file of the country's supporters. To read the subscription list of the *Journal* is to call the roll of statesmen and warriors, of liberty-loving patriots and self-effacing heroes.

The year 1744, when France was warring against England, marked the real beginning of Bradford's patriotic service. Spain also was at war with the Mother Country. Therefore privateers authorized by both countries looked on the commerce of England and her colonies as lawful prey. Philadelphia and the Delaware River invited attention from these privateers, by reason of her location and her large trade. The danger was pointed out to the Friends who were in authority in Pennsylvania, but they refused either to see this danger or to make appropriation in the time of need. But business men of the Quaker City, inspired by Bradford, associated themselves together for the defense of the city, and erected a battery on the Delaware River, just below the city. Of this association Bradford was a leader.

Twelve years later, in 1756, Bradford had a vision of a great Philadelphia Exchange, "a place of resort where our chief citizens in every department of life could meet each other and converse upon subjects which concerned the city or the state." The result was the establishment of "The Coffee House for Merchants and Traders." Its headquarters, at the corner of Front and Market Streets, soon became the best-known place in Philadelphia. During the days before 1760 it was the resort of those who were loyal to the king, but after the troubled days of the Stamp Act it became a rallying place for patriots. During the Revolution it was the meeting-place for the "Committees of Safety and other public bodies, which were called into existence by the emergencies of the crisis."

During the lull before the storm of Revolution, Bradford was at the head of those who formed the Colony in Schuylkill, the quaint old fishing club which became the State in Schuylkill when the Declaration of Independence was signed. This hot-bed of patriotism had much to do with the success of important events in the War of Independence.

Bradford was an early, active, and uncompromising opponent of the Stamp Act; as one of the Sons of Liberty.

COLONEL WILLIAM BRADFORD
THE PATRIOT PRINTER OF 1776

he w s interested in seeing to it that no tea was landed in Philadelphia. The morning issue of the *Journal* on October 31, 1765, the day before the Act was to take effect, is familiar through reproduction to students of history. And he sent from his press the "Journal of the Proceedings of the Congress held at Philadelphia September 5th, 1774." In 1775 a similar journal of the next Congress was printed. "The sale of both books was unprecedented," says his biographer. "On the title-page of the former was a vignette—twelve hands grasping a column based on Magna Charta, and surmounted by a Cap of Liberty; on the other, a like vignette—patriot-soldiers swearing upon the altar of their country."

In June, 1776, he was sent by John Hancock, President of Congress, with six boxes of money, for delivery to General Washington in New York.

In July, 1776, when he was fifty-six years old, Bradford joined the army, though by law he was exempt from military service. He was wounded at Princeton. After this battle he was made chairman of the Pennsylvania Navy Board, which did so much to defend the Delaware against the enemy. With this body he served until its discharge in 1778.

"Thus"—to use the language of his son, William—"forsaking all private interests he followed the Standards of his country to the field," and in the field he remained until, broken by the rigors of service he was compelled to retire and see others complete the winning of independence.

When the war was over, he lived in retreat in the country near Philadelphia, until September 25, 1791. Before he died he assured his children that, though he bequeathed to them no fortune, he left them in the enjoyment of liberty.

His body was laid to rest in the churchyard of the Second Presbyterian Church of Philadelphia, more than one hundred years after the coming to Philadelphia of the first of the Bradfords, printers and patriots.

CHAPTER IV

CALEB WALLACE, PIONEER IN "THE DARK AND
BLOODY GROUND"

YEARS OF PREPARATION

HOW America drew for settlement and development
on the sturdiest people of Europe was never better
illustrated than in the case of Caleb Wallace, descendant
of emigrants from Scotland who came from the clan made
famous by Sir William Wallace. Caleb Wallace's second
wife looked for her ancestry to the Isle of Man, where
for generations the Christian family had been prominent
among those who ruled the little island that is father of
so many intrepid seamen and fishermen.

Among other events that made the year 1734 notable
for the colony named in honor of Queen Elizabeth was
the coming of the first of the Wallaces to "the back parts
of Virginia." They settled in Woods' Gap in Albemarle
county. There they knew they would be lonely, but they
wished to be far enough removed from the places where
the Established Church was strong, that they might worship God according to the ideas in which they had been so
thoroughly grounded in Scotland.

The people of Woods' Gap were not content to be deprived of their privileges. When these were denied them,
they sent a petition, in 1755, to the Presbytery of Hanover, "representing their destitute circumstances." They

had plenty to eat, and they could secure ample clothing and shelter. But destitution, to Scotchmen, meant something far different. They were not satisfied until a minister was sent to them. The minister proved to be the Rev. Samuel Davies, who, four years later, became president of the College of New Jersey. Not only did they want a minister, but they wanted the best to be had!

Scotchmen were notable pioneers, so not even good preaching could keep Samuel Wallace, son of Peter Wallace, of Woods' Gap, from listening to the luring appeal of the Cub Creek Community, one hundred miles farther south, in what is now Charlotte county. This community was founded by John Caldwell, Scotch-Irishman of Lancaster, Pennsylvania, who did not wait until he was in the new home before taking steps to insure proper moral and religious surroundings. In May, 1738, he persuaded the Synod of Philadelphia to make overtures to the colonial authorities in Virginia "in behalf of himself and many families . . . who are about to settle in the back parts of Virginia." So two representatives of the Synod were sent on the long and difficult journey "to wait on the Governor and Council of Virginia with suitable instructions in order to procure the favour and countenance of the government of the province to the laying of foundations of our interest in the back parts thereof."

From the community for which preparations were made so carefully came at least two famous men, in addition to Caleb Wallace. These two were John Caldwell Calhoun, the South Carolina statesman, and James Caldwell, whom the British called "the Fighting Chaplain" of the Revolution. They hated him because of his zeal for the cause of the patriots. His life was always in danger. The enmity of the British led to the burning of the chaplain's church at Elizabeth Town, New Jersey, where he numbered among his parishioners William Livingston, Governor of New Jersey, Elias Boudinot, Commissary-General of Prisons and President of Congress, Abraham Clark, one of the signers of the Declaration of Independence, as well as more than forty commissioned officers of the Continental Army. A few months after the burning of the church, Mrs. Caldwell was murdered by the British, while in 1781 the chaplain himself was shot by a Continental soldier who was thought to have been bribed by those whose enmity Caldwell had earned during the conflict.

In the atmosphere of religion and patriotism which nurtured such men as Caldwell and Calhoun, Caleb Wallace was born in 1742 in the home of Samuel and Esther Wallace. His early education was received, in all probability, in the home, and possibly from some minister who, as was customary in those days, added instruction of the children of his people to his duties as minister. Very likely the memory of the days when there were such limited opportunities for schooling later influenced the man Wallace to become a founder of colleges and a devisor of plans for making education easy for all.

Caleb was drawn to his pastor, Robert Henry; the man had a sense of humor that appealed to the lad. It is not strange, then, if the knowledge of Henry's graduation from the College of New Jersey, in the class of 1751 attracted the boy to that institution. What a wonderful thing it would be if he could go there! His desire was strengthened by the presence in the community, in 1756, of the Rev. Samuel Davies, who, in 1753, as a trustee of the college, had gone to England to secure funds for its use. Very likely the boy Caleb heard him tell of some of his experiences on that notable journey. Probably the boy was one of the company of two thousand who gathered in the forest to listen to the great preacher who was so soon to go to Princeton. Then when Caleb was seventeen years old, he came in contact with James Caldwell, listened to his burning eloquence, and talked to him of the New Jersey college.

Yet ten years more passed before the son of Samuel Wallace was able to go in search of a higher education. He was needed at home to help carve a farm out of the forest; as the oldest son he would feel much responsibility to help in the support of the family. Then, money was a very scarce article in the mountain regions of Virginia before the Revolution. And how could he, whose advantages had been so slender, hope to satisfy what seemed the tremendous requirements of the College of New Jersey, which he knew so well by reason of his talks with men who had been there? Think of his dismay as he thought that "none may expect to be admitted but such as, having been examined by the president and tutors, shall be found able to render Virgil and Tully's oration into English; to turn English into true and grammatical Latin; and so well acquainted with the Greek as to render any part of the four Evangelists in that language into Latin or English, and give the grammatical construction of the words."

Those were the days when no one thought of questioning the soundness of a definition of education in classical terms! What would Davies and Calhoun have thought of these twentieth-century days when many educators refuse to enter into an argument as to the advisability of including the classics in a liberal education, saying there are too many other things of greater importance?

Finally, in 1767, when Caleb was twenty-five years old,

he was able to undertake with ardent hopes the journey to Princeton. To-day a Virginia student is able to reach the New Jersey town between breakfast and dinner, but in 1767 ten days or two weeks, full of hardships, separated Charlotte county, Virginia, from Mercer county, New Jersey.

The physical equipment of the eager student on his journey, was meager, according to present-day standards. But one of the most important things he carried with him was a letter from his pastor:

"These are to Certifie all Christian people to whom these Presents shall come, that I have been acquainted with Caleb Wallace, since he was a Boy, and he hath always sustained a Moral character, & is going from home Free from any publick Scandal or liable to any Church Censure known to me. . . ."

YEARS OF EDUCATION

The journey led, not to Princeton, for Wallace was not yet ready for the exacting requirements of the College of New Jersey, but to Elizabeth Town, to the home of his friend, Rev. James Caldwell. There he lived for two years, while he was attending the grammar school.

That he made good use of his opportunities is evident from a certificate dated "1768, Novembr 2nd," which tells of his membership in the literary society of the school, and of his departure with a good character. "We do hereby recommend him to all Persons as an Agreeable Member of Society," was the conclusion of the letter. In addition to this testimonial, the student carried with him to Princeton a letter signed by no less a person than Elias Boudinot, telling of his "Publick good character," and "his Personal merit and Worth." Not only so, but the signer testified to the "Regard and affection" in which he was held by the *Socialis Societas* of Elizabeth Town.

At Princeton he found that the work of instruction at Elizabeth Town was so well done that he was able to enter the junior class, after examination, and to undergo the period of two weeks' trial required of all students. Evidently he made good in the subjects required for that year: "Algebra, Geometry, Trigonometry, Practical Geometry, Conic Sections, Natural Philosophy, English Grammar and Composition. Thus he would be ready for the studies of Senior year; Natural and Moral Philosophy, Criticism, Chronology, Logic, and the Classics."

During his residence, the president was Dr. John Witherspoon, who came from Scotland in August, 1768. President Davies, the friend of Virginia days, to whose teaching he had looked forward, had died suddenly after serving but eighteen months.

Among his fellow students were many men who later won distinction. Chief among them was the sophomore, James Madison. Frederick Frelinghuysen, who was to be a member of the Continental Congress, then United States Senator for New Jersey, was a classmate. Aaron Burr, the brilliant but erratic son of a glorious father, was a freshman when he was a senior.

These men enjoyed the best that could be given by a school that did wonders with the £2,800 of endowment, of which but £950 was productive. Yet the trustees felt able to pay to the president £350 a year. Of course this was in Proclamation money; the equivalent in sterling was but £206. And during the early life of young Wallace the trustees made a remarkable venture of faith. For it is written that "The Board, having taken into consideration the great want of Philosophical apparatus for the use of the students in the college in Natural Philosophy," appropriated £250 for the purchase of apparatus. That budget enabled them to buy, among other things, the wonderful orrery of David Rittenhouse, the ingenious mechanical contrivance by which he illustrated the movements of the heavenly bodies. In spite of the efforts of the University of Pennsylvania to secure this, Princeton was successful, and the machine became the wonder of students who saw it in the place provided for it in Nassau Hall, where it reposes to this day.

At the time of Wallace's residence, Nassau Hall was the only building of the college. There was room in it for 147 students, provided they crowded three into a room. There were sixty rooms, including those used for recitations, the refectory, the kitchen and the library. The building, which was occupied in 1756, though not completed until 1762, has been called "one of America's finest examples of colonial architecture." Robert Smith, one of the two designers, was also the designer of Independence Hall, the Old State House, in Philadelphia. At the time of its erection it was the largest stone building in the colonies, and it retained this distinction for some years.

College students feel that the provisions made for eating are among the matters that give them greatest concern. This was probably so in the days of Wallace, as well. So he would be much interested in Jonathan Baldwin, whose duty it was to "victual" the college, and to collect for the food from the students. Then he had to secure the tuition and room rent of these students, and the pew rent from the residents of the town who attended services on Sunday in the college chapel. This important man was expected also to buy college furniture, to hire the servants, to pay the tutors, to sell books, to call trustees to their meetings, and to clean the chimneys!

To him, too, was probably given authority to enforce the rules adopted during the days of President Aaron Burr, which were still in force. When damage was done in a college room, and the author could not be discovered, the cost was to be levied "on those that live in the room or in the gallery where it is done." He could permit students to smoke tobacco, provided they paid the college, through him, five shillings. Five shillings must be paid each quarter for sweeping the bedroom of a student and making the beds.

Edward M. Norris, in *The Story of Princeton*, tells of other rules. "It is decreed that 'Every scholar shall keep his hat off about 10 rods to the President and 5 to the Tutors'; that 'Every Freshman sent on an errand shall go and do it faithfully and make quick return'; that 'Every scholar shall rise up and make obeisance when the President goes in or out of the Hall or enters the Pulpit on days of religious worship'; that an 'inferior,' when walking with a 'superior,' 'shall give him the highest place'; that 'inferiors,' when they first come into the company of a 'superior' or speak to him, 'shall show respect by pulling their Hats'; that when meeting at a door or entrance, an 'inferior' shall 'give place to a superior'; that an 'inferior,' overtaking or meeting a 'superior' going up or down stairs, 'shall stop, giving him the banister side'; that an 'inferior' . . . 'shall never intrude himself upon a superior'; that an 'inferior' 'shall never be first in any undertaking in which a superior is engaged or about to engage'; that an 'inferior' 'shall never use any indecent or rude language in a superior's presence, such as making a noise, calling loud or speaking at a distance, unless spoken to by him, and if called or spoken to by him, if within hearing, shall give a direct pertinent answer concluding with Sir.' "

In the course of his rambles about Princeton Wallace would become familiar with places that were to be famous —for instance, the beautiful banks of Stony Brook, where, in 1777, the Battle of Princeton was to be fought; the house near the banks where General Mercer, mortally wounded in the battle, would be carried; and the Berrien house, three miles from town in another direction, where, after the surrender of Cornwallis, Washington would live for some months during the session of Congress in Nassau Hall. Thus the young patriot made acquaintance with scenes that were to be historic shrines. At the same time he was living in an atmosphere that was calculated to develop his love of country and hatred of tyranny. For gradually the students at the College of New Jersey were making ready for the day when the Declaration of Independence was sent out from the Old State House in Philadelphia. An indication of these changing views is the fact that, in 1761, an orator on Commencement day talked on "The Military Glory of Great Britain." One year after Wallace's graduation another orator spoke of "The Rising Glory of America." And at Wallace's own graduation exercises the entire class, by earnest choice, was garbed in garments manufactured in America. Not for them were cloths imported from England, on which an odious tax was paid!

Probably, if there were record of the fervid oratory on the rostrum of the American Whig Society—one of the two oldest literary societies in America, of which Wallace was a founder—this would tell the same story as the changing Commencement themes and the homespun clothing.

YEARS OF SERVICE IN VIRGINIA

A little while before Wallace was graduated, there was quickened religious interest at Princeton. "Revival" is the name usually given to such quickening. The students were in two camps with reference to this great event. Wallace was a leader of one party; he was interested, vitally, in the "awakening." The leader of the other party was Aaron Burr, always an "aginer" of everything moral and religious. "Fanatics!" was the cry of Burr's followers as they looked on Wallace and his associates. But their sneers did not disturb those at whom they were cast; they were not men who could be dismayed by cheap words.

Wallace proved that he was dead in earnest in his purpose to do the most he could for his people when he went back to Virginia, by asking the approval of the Presbytery of New Brunswick on his plan to enter the ministry. After a year of post-graduate study, probably either under Dr. Witherspoon, or under Pastor Caldwell of Elizabeth Town, he asked the Presbytery's authority to begin the work which he planned. While he was in Princeton for this extra work, he was thrown into close contact with James Madison, who, likewise, was doing post-graduate work. Madison did not plan to be a minister, yet during that year he was busy with theological subjects. The intimacy of that year was responsible for the interest of the two men in one another during the decades that followed.

Soon after leaving Princeton the young minister had an opportunity of doing something for the institution that had done so much for him. Not far away, but over the line in Pennsylvania, was the historic Neshaminy (now Neshaminy of Warwick) Presbyterian Church, whose people still use the building they occupied at that time. The pastor, Rev. Charles Beatty, was planning to go to Barbados and elsewhere in the Windward Islands, there to solicit funds for the needy institution. The church needed a supply, and Caleb Wallace stepped into the breach. Payment for his services was received from the board of trustees of the college to which, so recently, he had been paying money for benefits received.

But the heart of Wallace was with his people in the Southland, so he was glad of the appointment given him to visit the Southern Provinces, especially Virginia, South Carolina and Georgia. With him went John Simpson, a man from New Jersey, who settled in South Carolina, and soon showed his temper by keeping company with men who many times bore themselves bravely in the face of attacks by the British. During the war he lost his house, his library, his sermons, and all else that he possessed.

After fulfilling his commission to points farther south, the young minister listened to the call of his home congregation of Cub Creek in the beautiful Valley of Virginia, and settled among the people he knew. This speaks well for him; not often is a man desired by the people who know him to live among them as their minister.

But young Wallace did another difficult thing, for at the same time he married a church, he married a wife, and that from the community in which both were to live! This, it has been said, is a very risky thing for any minister to attempt. But the husband and wife kept their heads and won the hearts of the people who knew them both.

The father of the bride, Samuel McDowell, had much to do with the future career of his son-in-law. For just at that time he was a member of the Virginia Legislative Assembly, which was in that year, 1774, having its time of conflict with Governor Dunmore. Angry because he could not bend the legislature to his will, the Governor sent them back home, where they called their people together in a service of "fasting, humiliation, and prayer, to implore Heaven to avert from them the evils of civil war, to inspire them with firmness in support of their rights, and to turn the hearts of the King and Parliament to moderation and justice. . . ."

It is altogether likely that to Wallace must be conceded the authorship of an epoch-making paper which grew out of this state of affairs, the appeal of 1774 to the House of Burgesses, sent by the Presbytery of Hanover, "in behalf of themselves and all the Presbyterians in Virginia in particular, and all Protestant dissenters in general." This paper requested that the denomination be not placed at a disadvantage in doing their work. They were ready to observe all reasonable restrictions, but they asked leave to itinerate and to preach through various parts of the country. They asked that night meetings be made legal, for them, as for others. Willingness was expressed to keep doors open during service; "yet we would humbly represent that such a requirement implies a suspicion of our loyalty, and will fix a stigma on us in after ages." Request was made that the penalty for disturbing the worship of dissenters be the same as that for disturbing worship in the Established Church.

This self-respecting petition said, further:

"We are petitioning in favour of a Church that is neither contemptible nor obscure. It prevails in every province to the Northward of Maryland, and its advocates in all the more Southern Provinces are numerous and respectable. The greatest monarch in the North of Europe adorns it; it is the established religion of the populous and wealthy States of Holland; it prevails in the wise and happy Cantons of Switzerland, and is the possession of Geneva, a State among the foremost of those who at the Reformation emancipated themselves from the slavery of Rome; and some of the first geniuses and writers in every branch of literature were sons of our Church."

But the House of Burgesses was too much occupied with other matters to listen to this spirited appeal of the dissenters. Soon the legislature was dissolved, and the Conventions of 1775 and 1776 followed. The latter body asked the delegates representing the colony in General Congress to request that body "to declare the United Colonies free and independent States." Wallace was probably the author of this, the first paper of the kind in Virginia.

When the first legislature of the new State of Virginia met at Williamsburg, Mr. Wallace presented to it a memorial on the subject that had received such scant consideration from the House of Burgesses. For this duty he was appointed by Hanover Presbytery. Modestly he says that the reason for his appointment was that "none of the ministers who were older in the ministry and better qualified could undertake it." In this memorial he emphasized the fact that "in the frontier Countries, which are justly supposed to contain a fifth part of the inhabitants of Virginia, the dissenters have borne the heavy burdens of purchasing glebes, building churches, and supporting the established clergy." The declaration was made that these dissenters asked no ecclesiastical establishments for themselves, as they could not approve them when granted to others. They did ask that all be treated alike, and that all should be exempted from taxation for the support of any church whatsoever.

[75]

Both Madison and Jefferson were members of the body before which came this memorial. Jefferson was a friend to be counted on, and Madison was sure to he a helper because of his previous insistence on an amendment to the Declaration of Rights in June, 1776. The story of this amendment is told by Bancroft in his *History of the United States:*

"Only one clause received a material amendment. Mason had written that all should enjoy the fullest toleration in matters of religion. . . . A young man, then unknown to fame . . . proposed a change. He was James Madison, the son of an Orange County planter, bred in the school of the Presbyterian Dissenters under Witherspoon at Princeton, trained by his own studies, by meditative rural life in the Old Dominion, and by an ingenious indignation at the persecution of the Baptists, by innate principles of right, to uphold the sanctity of religious freedom. He objected to the word 'toleration' because it implied an established religion which endured dissent only as a condescension. . . . His motion, which did but state with better dialectics the very purpose that Mason wished to accomplish, obtained the suffrage of his colleagues. This was the first achievement of the wisest civilian of Virginia."

Unfortunately, Thomas Jefferson was called away, and there was fear that the Act about which the memorial was protesting would be passed during his absence. But he was sent for, and on his return he managed to amend the bill in such manner that many of the desires of the Protestants were heeded.

In a letter to his friend James Caldwell at Elizabeth Town, Mr. Wallace expressed his satisfaction with the result. He had not secured all he wished, but there was on the statute-books "an Act exempting dissenters for all time to come from supporting the Church of England, declaring all penal or persecuting laws against any mode of worship, etc, null and void," and for the present left all denominations to support the clergy by voluntary contribution.

In the letter to Mr. Caldwell, the Virginia patriot, who had been contending for the very things that characterized the struggle for independence, expressed sorrow that New Jersey, "the seat of learning and the garden of America, should become a field of blood, a barren desert, a Theatre in which Tyranny is acting more horrid scenes than were ever represented in fictitious Tragedy." Then he added his view "that at this distance from the scene of action and of danger" he still persevered in the sentiment that "an American ought to seek an emancipation from the British King, Ministry and Parliament, at the risk of all earthly possessions of whatever means."

The brief period of Wallace's residence in Virginia was remarkable also for his vital connection with two notable educational institutions, which, in his day, were given the start that has enabled them to continue to this period. In 1775 he assisted in organizing Hampden-Sidney College, on a beautiful location on a tributary of the Appomattox River. The first president of the institution was Samuel Stanhope Smith, who, later, was president of the College of New Jersey. Among the early trustees were James Madison and Patrick Henry. In 1777 the minister of Cub Creek said that it flourished beyond the most sanguine expectations of its founders. "It is furnished with excellent Tutors, and the great number of students has become a real grievance, so that it wants no human help to make it a miracle, considering its age and remote situation, but a few thousand pounds to furnish buildings. Although money has become very plenty in our country, yet we are discouraged at present from finding subscriptions for the purpose by a popular sentiment which prevails, that we should secure our Independence before we pay our regards to the Muses."

At first this institution was known as Prince Edward Academy, and was not incorporated until 1782, eight years after the opening of the second, and even more famous institution, Liberty Hall, which began its existence at Cub Creek. Later this became Washington College, and, as Washington and Lee University, it still flourishes, after nearly a century and a half of usefulness. As trustee of the college, Mr. Wallace gave much of his best thought to its welfare, until he removed from its territory. And then, as will appear, his genius as a leader in education was even more in evidence.

YEARS OF SERVICE IN KENTUCKY

When the ancestors of Caleb Wallace went to "the back parts of Virginia," they thought they were seeking the frontier. But about 1764 there was some talk of a farther frontier—the Kentucke country, the unknown part of Virginia's charter lands. No Indians lived there, but the tribes from south of the Ohio liked to make periodical hunting trips there. After Daniel Boone ventured there in 1769, other white hunters followed him, but not until 1774 did settlement begin. Then progress was so rapid that in 1784 there were 30,000 people in the new land, attracted there at first by the glowing promises of the Transylvania Company, for whom Richard Henderson bought 18,000,000 acres from the Indians for merchandise valued at, perhaps, £10,000. The Company's power

CALEB WALLACE

was broken in 1776 when George Rogers Clark succeeded
in persuading the Virginia Legislature to establish the
county of Kentucky, and to include the lands claimed by the
Transylvania Company, in the region bounded by the Kentucky, Cumberland and Ohio rivers. Emigration became
even greater when the lands were administered for Virginia, by men charged with taking care of her interests.

In 1781 the Legislature of Virginia asked that the Governor "call to an account every officer, agent, commissary,
quartermaster, and contractor, or other persons concerned
in the disbursement of public monies, who have been or are
in service in the western country belonging to this State,
for all their proceedings, and to appoint others to manage
the business, if necessary, in the meantime."

Though the Governor was willing to appoint the commission, he found difficulty in persuading men of influence
to serve, because of the alarm due to the transfer of Cornwallis' operations to Virginia. So not until October, 1782,
was the commission able to start. Of the four men who
served, Caleb Wallace was one. He welcomed the opportunity to go to Kentucky, where his brother-in-law, Stephen
Trigg, had lived for three years, remaining there after
the conclusion of his service as a commissioner to adjust
conflicting land titles. But Wallace was not to see his relative, for he was killed by Indians in the Battle of the Blue
Licks nearly three months before the departure from Virginia. This battle was fought after the siege of Bryant's
Station by savages under the command of the Irish rene-
gade, Simon Girty. When the Indians, as a feint, raised
the siege, they were followed by settlers, who were reën-
forced by Colonel Trigg's troops from Lincoln county.
Daniel Boone, too, was one of the leaders whose men were

[79]

massacred by the Indians. The terror of the people as a result of this disaster was told picturesquely by a prisoner in his letter to the Governor:

"Through the Continued service of a Seven Years' vicissitude nothing has happened so alarming, fatal & injurious to the Interest of the Kanetuckians in Particular & all its votaries in General, as the present concatenation of Hostilities, wherewith I am now to acquaint Your Excellency. . . . To experience the feelings of the Inhabitants of both the Counties at this Ruefull scene of hitherto unparalleled barbarities Barrs all words & cuts Description Short."

This was the time when Daniel Boone made his plea:

"I know, Sir, that your situation at present is something critical. But are we to be totally forgotten? I hope not. . . . I have encouraged the people here in this county all that I could, but I can no longer Encourage my neighbours nor myself to risque our lives here at such Extraordinary hazzards."

Such perfervid appeals had their influence. The people of Kentucky must not feel that Virginia was indifferent to them. Even the appointment of a commission for such a purpose as that of which Wallace was a member would help to reassure them.

The journey of the men from Virginia was made over the Wilderness Road, the track hewn out of the forests and through Cumberland Gap by the stalwart aides of Daniel Boone, who had been commissioned for the task by the Transylvania Company. By this route tens of thousands of settlers found their way from Virginia and North Carolina to Kentucky. By no means least among these were the little company of Wallaces—Caleb, his

[80]

AN OVERSHOT WATER WHEEL OF PIONEER DAYS

father Samuel, and his brother Andrew, as well as his brother-in-law, Colonel Henry Pawling, together with their families.

When the work for which they had been appointed was concluded, the members of the commission went back to Virginia, to make their report. Three of them returned, and became prominent settlers. Wallace made his home in Lincoln county, but he had not been there long when his fellow citizens drafted him for service in the legislature at Richmond. There he began his work on May 19, 1783.

Though his service was brief, the results were notable. Of the two great measures in which he interested himself, the first had to do with marriages. He presented a petition from his constituents asking, among other things, that marriages among them be made easier by the appointment of civil officers who could officiate when this was necessary. This petition would have been fruitless, for a committee tried to bury it, but the young Kentucky legislator persisted, and finally secured the passage of an act providing:

"That when it shall appear to the court of any county on the western waters that there is not a sufficient number of clergymen authorized to celebrate marriages therein, such court is hereby empowered to nominate so many sober and discreet laymen as will supply the deficiency."

Banns were to be published, and the marriages were to be performed according to the customs of the church of which the layman was a member.

One of the most important provisions of the act gave comfort to many people by providing for the legalization of marriages already performed by magistrates and others not authorized by law, but induced by the want of ministers.

MORE EDUCATIONAL SERVICES

The second major service rendered by Caleb Wallace, not only to his constituents, but to all the people of Kentucky, was the organization of Transylvania University. Thus the educational service begun in Virginia by his connection with the beginnings of Hampden-Sidney College and Washington College was crowned by an achievement even more far-reaching.

The vision of Transylvania came first to Colonel John Todd. In 1782 he persuaded the legislature to set aside eight thousand acres of land, formerly the property of British subjects, "for the purpose of a publick school or seminary of learning." But, unfortunately, the Act, in appointing members, gave them power merely to hold the property. Probably Colonel Todd would have secured further action, but he was killed at the Blue Licks in 1782.

What Todd could not do Wallace accomplished. He asked the House to amend the previous bill, and was by that body appointed to convey the measure to the Senate and seek their concurrence. Thus the trustees of the Transylvania Seminary were appointed, and were given all necessary powers. Of this board, as was eminently fitting, Caleb Wallace was a member. For, as his biographer says, "it was his own child; it bore the name which he had given it; and his affection followed it under every circumstance."

The first meeting of the board was held at John Crow's Station (Danville) in Lincoln county, in November, 1783, and Wallace became chairman, a position which he held for four years.

The institution had a precarious existence for some years. Funds were meager. "There were eight thousand acres of very good land; but very good land that was neither cleared nor enclosed was at that period one of the most plentiful and least valuable commodities in Kentucky," is the explanation of a historian of Transylvania. Yet the board clung with tenacity to their charge. Even the name was considered too precious to be relinquished when, in 1788, the school was moved to Lexington, which was outside of Transylvania proper. The new location was made permanent when a two-story brick building was presented to the school.

Better days came in consequence of an event which seemed to threaten disaster. This was the organization of a rival by the Presbyterians. This was called Kentucky Academy. Caleb Wallace, one of the trustees, saw how the endowment of the academy, and its union with his pet, Transylvania, would be most fortunate. So he coöperated in the effort to secure funds. President Washington, John Adams, and Aaron Burr were among the contributors of $10,000 in the East. The academy prospered, but in 1798 it was consolidated with Transylvania Seminary, which thenceforth was known as Transylvania University.

But Wallace, the educated statesman, was not yet content. He had the vision of a series of academies, one in each county in the State, which should be feeders for the University. Bills providing for these institutions, and for the endowment of each with six thousand acres of land, were written by Wallace and put through the legislature by those who realized the wisdom of the steps he wished them to take.

[83]

The union of the schools which make up Transylvania University, and the provision for the feeding academies, "established the most enlightened, practical and complete system of education that could at that period be witnessed in America, or perhaps anywhere else in the civilized world." The admiring historian who wrote the words just quoted said also: "There are no brighter pages in the statute books of Kentucky than those which record these acts."

The fact that the statutes planned with such far-seeing wisdom were later modified "in such a style that much the larger portion of these endowments was either squandered or frittered away," cannot be permitted to dim the fame of Caleb Wallace. And even if some of his plans miscarried, Transylvania University still exists, and each year sends out into the state and the nation well-equipped men and women who are doing some of the things for which the originator hoped and planned.

A JURIST WHO WAS FREE FROM ATTACKS

But legislation and education do not finish the tale of Wallace's services to Kentucky. For more than thirty years he was a member of the highest courts of Kentucky. First came his service in the Supreme Court, authorized in 1782 by the Legislature of Virginia, as a court of original jurisdiction independent of all other courts except the Court of Appeals. There was delay in the beginning of this court, resignations, deaths, and Indian killings. One juror declined to serve because the "salary was too small to tempt him to surrender the practice of law." But Wallace was ready to give his best to the court, and he served from July 2, 1783, until, in 1792, the admission of

HOW THE PIONEERS SAWED LUMBER

Kentucky as a State disposed of the court. During this period the salaries of the justices mounted as high as £300 a year!

With the admission of Kentucky came the Court of Appeals. To this body Judge Wallace was appointed. At the beginning the salary was but £200 per year, but service was given without thought of gain.

One of the most important cases that came before the court had to do with land titles. A decision of the majority disturbed landowners in Kentucky, and threatened the prosperity of the state. Wallace's minority judgment seemed so fair and so reasonable that the people wished it could be law. An appeal to the legislature for the removal of the offending judges failed to receive the necessary two-thirds majority in that body. But the result was good, for one of the judges saw the light, and in May, 1796, he joined with Judge Wallace in an opinion that quieted the people, removing the dread of anarchy, for it sustained the decisions of the Land Commission of Virginia, made before the admission of the state, which the original opinion had allowed to be questioned.

Attacks were made later on two of the three judges. The charge against one of them—made during the investigation of the conspiracy of Aaron Burr in 1806—was that he was in the pay of the Spanish Government. This charge was proved, and the judge had to resign. But no real attacks were made on Judge Wallace; always his public spirit and his probity were beyond question. Among those who held the highest opinion of his wisdom and dependability was the Honorable John Breckenridge, member of the legislature, who, on more than one occasion, consulted him as to pending legislation.

The most notable instance of such consultation came

[85]

in connection with the famous Resolution of 1798, whose story is worth recalling.

In 1798 the Federalists, who were then in power, succeeded in forcing through Congress a number of ill-considered Acts, altogether for individual and party reasons. Among these were the Naturalization and Alien and Sedition Acts. Jefferson and Madison, Democrats, were bitterly opposed to these measures. By agreement Madison drafted a resolution which was presented to the Virginia Legislature, while Jefferson wrote an appeal to the Legislature of Kentucky. Madison's resolution was quite temperate when compared with that by Jefferson, which insisted that, since the acts in question passed by Congress were opposed to the Constitution, they were void, and could be declared null by action of the states. One who has commented on this judgment of Jefferson has said: "Just how this was to be done, he did not explain, but he seems to have had in mind action of a majority of States."

This beginning of the Doctrine of Nullification did not proceed very far, for the plan to have similar resolutions passed by the legislatures of other states was not carried out.

This was not necessary, for aroused public opinion decided that the Federalists were unworthy of continuing in power, since they were "moving rapidly in the direction of absolute centralization and unqualified despotism."

Proof of Judge Wallace's wisdom in advising Breckenridge that the conduct of the legislature should be "firm, spirited, and constitutional," especially with regard to the most dangerous of the acts—that affecting trial by jury, and that with regard to the freedom of the press—was justified when publishers of four of the leading daily papers of the country were charged with seditious libel, and

[86]

when a man in Dedham, Massachusetts, was fined four hundred dollars and sent to prison for eighteen months. And his offense was merely the erection of a liberty pole which bore the inscription: "No Stamp Act, No Sedition, No Alien Bills, No Land Tax; downfall to the Tyrants of America, peace and retirement to the President, long live the Vice President and the Minority; may moral virtue be the basis of civil government." Fortunately, when Jefferson became President, he was able to pardon this awful offender.

Judge Wallace, elector from Kentucky, had the privilege of voting for Jefferson. This was but one of a series of honors bestowed on him by the community in which he lived. He was a member of both Kentucky's Constitutional Conventions, and he made distinct contributions to at least four of the nine conventions which paved the way for the admission of Kentucky.

The private life of this man who was responsible for so many of the good things that came to Kentucky was worthy of his public record. His home for a time was at Triggs' Station, near Harrodsburg. There he helped in the organization of Cane Run, the oldest Presbyterian church in Kentucky. In 1786 he moved to the north side of Kentucky River, at Woodford, where he had his law office, after the manner of the day, in the corner of the yard. The mistress of the home, who was the mother of his nine children, was the sister of Colonel William Christian, whose wife was a sister of Patrick Henry. One of the interesting memorials of Judge Wallace, who was guardian of the children of Colonel Christian, is a letter written by him, to the Virginia patriot, who was the executor of the Christian will. The document may be seen at the library of the Historical Society of Pennsylvania.

[87]

Colonel Christian's name, by the way, is remembered by students of Kentucky history because, after the defeat of Blue Licks in 1782, he proposed to the Governor of Virginia that a gunboat be placed on the Ohio, for defense against the Indians. He would send an armed vessel to cruise from Limestone up and down the river. "But it ought to be light and manageable for twenty or thirty men," he added, "which number, in a properly constructed vessel, would be strong enough to attack any number of Indians in canoes." Only three years after this proposal was made, Colonel Christian was himself the victim of an Indian attack.

Perhaps a reason for Colonel Christian's choice of Judge Wallace as the guardian of his children was the fact that he was a provident man. His savings were invested in land, and when he died, in 1814, he was the owner of more than thirteen thousand acres. But there were many other reasons—for instance, the fact that the Judge was true to his convictions always. An illustration of this fact was given in 1809 when a young man, who later became Chief Justice Robertson of Kentucky, applied to him, as one of the members of the Court of Appeals, for his signature to a license to practice law. Unfortunately the visit was made on Sunday, when Judge Wallace would transact no business. The incident led to a rather caustic reference to the Judge in the autobiography of Robertson. But back of the spiteful words was a real appreciation of the sterling integrity of the man who gave more than thirty years of his life to the infant Kentucky.

CHAPTER V

CHRISTOPHER LUDWICK, THE MAN WHO BAKED THE CONTINENTAL ARMY'S BREAD

THE ARMY'S CRY FOR BREAD

THE problem of provisions for the soldiers is one of the most difficult a commander has to face. And since the staff of the soldier's life, as well as of those who live quietly at home, is bread, the chief problem is as to the supply from the bakery.

To-day it is a more simple matter to provide bread for an army than it was a century ago. Think, then, what must have been the problem confronting George Washington when he knew that there must be a pound or a pound and a quarter furnished to each man each day! The bread supply must be constant if the men were to be efficient.

In his book, *The Spirit of the Revolution,* John C. Fitzpatrick tells of the early days of the war:

"Lexington and the siege of Boston brought an army into existence almost overnight, and an army that grew in numbers daily. Food for this suddenly concentrated body of men became a monstrous problem that was met with varied skill by the train-band captains and higher officers. These were not men entirely inexperienced in such matters, for King George and the old French and Indian War had taught the colonial militiamen practical, if

[89]

severe lessons, and, though the military subsistence problems of 1775 were not easily solved, they were met with such intelligence that as long as the army remained stationary, in the lines around Boston, the food supply was not a matter of great difficulty. With the evacuation of the town by the British, and the commencement of the first march of the Continental Army from Boston to New York, came the first real test of the commissary department."

For a time flour was issued. The soldiers in a company would put their flour together, and would arrange with one of their number to bake it, or, if possible, they would trade the flour to the farmers for bread.

Of course, there were difficulties in connection with either plan. The soldiers' baker was apt to use much water in the bread he baked, so that his profits were large.

Then there was always a question as to the amount of bread to be received from the country people in exchange for the flour.

Not until May, 1777, did Congress see the necessity of taking a firm hold of the situation, which was becoming alarming. There must be a baker for the army, it was decided. But who could do the work required?

THE GINGERBREAD BAKER OF LETITIA COURT

George Washington knew the man. His name was Christopher Ludwick, a Philadelphia business man who was born on October 17, 1720, at Giessen, Hesse-Darmstadt, Germany. His father was a baker, who taught him the trade, sent him to school where he secured a meager education, and saw that he became a faithful member of the Lutheran Church. When the boy was seventeen years old, he entered the army, and for three years saw hard service against the Austrians and the Turks.

After his years in the army, Ludwick went to London, where he secured employment as baker on board the *Duke of Cumberland,* trading with the East Indies. After three years in this merchant service, he secured a small patrimony from his father's estate. This he squandered in London, within a few months, and was compelled to go to sea as a common sailor. For a time he was careless, but before long he made up his mind to be somebody in the world. After saving £25 he took passage for Philadelphia.

Not yet, however, was he ready to settle down. London saw him later in the year, this time as a confectioner's apprentice. Not only did he learn the secrets of candy-making, but he was taught the cunning of the gingerbread baker.

In 1754, when he saw that he could make a living at his trade, he sailed for Philadelphia once more. There, in Letitia Court, where William Penn built for his daughter the brick house now preserved in Fairmount Park, he invited the residents of the young city on the Delaware to buy the gingerbread he made for them daily.

For twenty years he maintained his humble establishment, and became known for his integrity and his readiness to help those who needed what he could do for them, as well as for the superior quality of his wares. His neighbors gave him the title, "The Governor of Letitia Court."

When the Declaration of Independence was adopted he was, for the day, a rich man. He owned nine houses in Philadelphia, as well as four others in Germantown. He

[91]

had also £3500 in Pennsylvania currency. And he was ready to give all that he had, if necessary, in the service of his country. Better still, he was eager to give himself. He was a member of various committees and organizations which served the colonies before the beginning of the Revolution.

At one time he was present in a gathering of citizens when General Mifflin thought it would be well to take private subscriptions for the purchase of firearms. The proposition, however, did not meet with the favor of the canny men who hesitated to pay over hard cash, until Christopher Ludwick, in broken English, but in a loud voice which showed his earnestness, said:

"Mr. President, I am but a poor gingerbread baker, but put my name down for £200."

That speech closed the debate, and the motion to buy arms was carried without a dissenting vote.

In 1776 he served as a volunteer, without pay or rations. His earnestness and fidelity to the country of his adoption had a most favorable effect on some of his fellow soldiers, who were lukewarm and even cowardly. On one occasion, when he saw with sorrow that a number of soldiers were about to take French leave, he fell on his knees before them, and pleaded:

"Brother soldiers, listen for a minute to Christopher Ludwick. When we hear the cry of fire in Philadelphia, on the hill at a distance from us, we fly there with our buckets, to keep it from our houses. So let us keep the great fire of the British army from our town."

Another incident tells of his wise proposal for dealing with Hessian prisoners:

"Let us take them to Philadelphia, and there show them our fine German churches. Let them see how our trades-

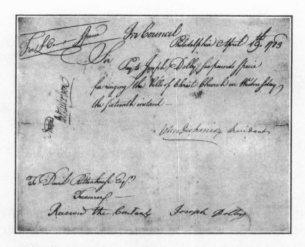

THE ORDER AND REC⸱ PT FOR THE RINGING OF THE BELLS OF
CHRIST CHURCH, PHILADELPHIA, TO CELEBRATE THE PEACE
WITH GREAT BRITAIN

THE LETITIA PENN HOUSE IN LETITIA COURT, PHILA-
DELPHIA. BUILT IN 1684. NOW IN FAIRMOUNT PARK

THE RESIDENCE OF ANTHONY BENEZET, PHILADELPHIA.
FRIEND OF CHRISTOPHER LUDWICK

men eat good beef, drink out of silver cups every day, and ride out in chaises every afternoon; and then let us send them back to their countrymen, and they will all soon run away, and come and settle in our city and be as good Whigs as any of us."

His faith in this policy of dealing with the Hessians led him to go to a Hessian camp on Long Island, where he told of the prosperity of Germans in Philadelphia. That visit, it was reported, was followed by the desertion of hundreds of soldiers; many of them became good citizens of Pennsylvania.

FROM PHILADELPHIA BAKESHOP TO FEEDING AN ARMY

This was the man on whom Washington fixed as the solution of his difficulties in supplying bread for the army. His desire was made known to Congress, and on May 3, 1777, it was

"Resolved, that Christopher Ludwick be, and he is hereby appointed Superintendent of Bakers, and Director of Baking in the Army of the United States, and that he should have power to engage, and by permission of the Commander-in-Chief, or officer commanding at any principal post, all persons to be employed in the business, and to regulate their pay, making proper report of his proceedings, and using his best endeavour to rectify all abuses in the articles of bread; . . . And that he receive for his service herein an allowance of seventy-five dollars a month, and two rations a day."

This resolution was signed by Charles Thomson, Secretary of Congress, attesting thus that it was an order of the Congress of which John Hancock was President.

Ludwick was then fifty-seven years old, had enough money for his comfort, and did not like the idea of entering on the large program proposed by Congress. But he was a patriot, and he was glad to forget his own preference in the thought that his country had need of him. Accordingly he accepted the appointment by the Continental Congress of "Superintendent of Bakers and Director of Baking in the Grand Army of the United States."

"What shall be his pay?" was the question asked by the Committee of Congress when the resolution was pending. "Suppose we allow him to supply but eighty pounds of bread for every hundred pounds of flour," was one suggestion; "then he can have as his pay the difference." But when this proposition was made to Ludwick, he said: "Is it that I shall grow rich by such ways? I will make one hundred and thirty-five pounds of bread for every hundred pounds of flour you put in my hands, and it will be good bread, and all the flour will be used, and if there is any flour over, it will also be made into bread."

DIFFICULTIES THAT WERE NOT ALLOWED TO EXIST

The work began when the army was at Morristown, New Jersey. The troops were in the field almost every day. Think of the problems to be solved by the new official! The trouble was made greater by the failure of officers to coöperate with the sturdy Ludwick. Many times "hundreds of pounds of crisp, browned bread must be sent from Ludwick's ovens to the troops in the field, and because no lieutenant or officer had been designated to receive it, it sometimes remained in the open, outside the camp, in the blazing heat of the day and the damp of the night air. The Commissioners of Issues said it was not their affair, and the quartermaster's office declined the responsibility of issuing it to the troops."

Ludwick had other difficulties. "Congress made no provision for paying the bakers which it authorized Ludwick to engage, and the old man used his private means to advance the pay of those of his bakers who were civilians. Soldiers detailed from the ranks had to remain on a different footing, but Ludwick kept them in good humour by small gratuities."

The call for advance led the Master Baker to sell some of his houses in Philadelphia. In addition to spending the amount received for them, he added the £3500 he had saved from the profits of his gingerbread bakery before the war. His biographer says that "he paid wages regularly every two months, and before he was reimbursed by the military paymaster he suffered further losses through the depreciation of the Continental currency."

At length officers were designated to receive bread, covered wagons were built for transporting it, and an inadequate fund was put at Ludwick's disposal for building bake-ovens when an army remained in one place for a time. In addition to this, large powers were given to him by Congress. In fact, Congress had such confidence in him that he was given a degree of power that was almost without a parallel for a minor officer.

Before the army moved from Morristown ovens were built there. Others were added here and there in New Jersey and Pennsylvania.

Then came the plan of having portable ovens of sheet iron, which could be transported easily. Two of these could be carried on an army wagon. But there was delay in furnishing them, and the supply of bread was at times so nearly exhausted that officers were anxious about the supply for the next meal.

Finally, in February, 1778, Congress authorized the enlistment of a company of bakers, sixty-five in all, with sixteen directors and sub-directors. This arrangement was to supplement that made by Ludwick. But it proved a failure; and it was realized that Ludwick's plan must be depended on.

In 1781 the problem was still very great. The superintendent was making Herculean efforts, but there were limits to his ability. While there was plenty of flour at the mills, there was difficulty in supplying it as it was needed. Then Ludwick was breaking down under the grueling task. He tried to resign, but Congress could not accept his resignation, in spite of his sixty-one years, his blindness in one eye, and his ill health, due to the service of his country. The thought that he had done so well, and had kept the expense of baking down to £3000 a year, influenced them to insist on his continuance.

Before long Ludwick had the help of bakers who came with the French troops. Incidentally it should be said that these French bakers served Washington a good turn. He set them to baking with all their might at Chatham, New Jersey. Henry Clinton, learning of this, thought that Washington meditated an attack on New York. When he woke up to the truth that Washington was planning to confront Cornwallis in Virginia, it was too late to save the British army.

THE VERDICT OF HIS CONTEMPORARIES

After the war Ludwick lived on his farm near Germantown. Some years were spent in poverty, for during the

HOW WOMEN OF FASHION DRESSED IN THE DAYS OF LUDWICK

THE CANNON BALL HOUSE, PHILADELPHIA, SHOWING THE MARKS OF
REVOLUTIONARY CANNON

Revolution he lost nearly all he possessed. Frequently, when he was in want, he refused to accept goods offered to him on credit, for he was unwilling to go into debt.

But while, for a season, he had little of this world's goods, he rejoiced in the possession of a letter from General Washington, written on April 25, 1785, in which his old Commander said:

"I have known Christopher Ludwick from an early period in the war, and have every reason to believe, as well from observation as from information, that he has been a true and faithful servant to the public; that he has detected and exposed many impositions, which were attempted to be practiced by others in his department; that he has been the cause of much saving in many respects; and that his deportment in public life has afforded unquestionable proof of his integrity and worth."

Fortunately, during his later years, he acquired some property and lived in greater comfort. But he did not forget the needs of others. Thus in 1797, during the yellow fever epidemic, he volunteered as a bread baker for the sufferers.

When he died, late in the year 1800, a Philadelphia paper said of him:

"In all the stations in which he acted, he was distinguished for his strong natural sense, strict probity, general benevolence, and uncommon intrepidity in assisting the cause of public and private justice."

His body was laid to rest in the cemetery of St. Michael's Church, Germantown, where a memorial service was held over his grave during the Sesqui-Centennial Exposition of 1926. Those who attended the exercises read the memorial inscription on the simple monument:

[97]

On every occasion his zeal for the relief of the oppressed was manifest; and by his last will, he bequeathed the greater part of his estate for the education of the children of the poor of all denominations, gratis. He lived and died respected for his integrity and public spirit, by all who knew him. Reader, such was Ludwick. Art thou poor, Venerate his character. Art thou rich, Imitate his example.

The story of his life, written by Dr. Benjamin Rush, was printed in Poulson's *American Daily Advertiser.* Later this brief life record was given in connection with the Proceedings of the Philadelphia Society for the Establishment and Support of Charity Schools. For the organization sought thus to do honor to the memory of "its most distinguished benefactor," which it cherished with feelings of respect and gratitude.

HOW THE GINGERBREAD BAKER PROVIDED FOR THE CHILDREN

The curious story of that benefaction by which Christopher Ludwick helped hundreds of Philadelphians during many years, should be told in connection with the life of the Gingerbread Baker. It is a story of the days when there were no free schools, when the lack of rapid transit and the telephone is brought home vividly to those who read, when eight thousand dollars was a fortune, and a benefaction of that amount something to be striven for mightily.

The best introduction to that story is the historical sketch of the society named, printed in the rare book whose title has been given.

In the winter of 1799, a few young men were in the

habit of assembling on stated evenings for the purpose of social conversation at a public house which was then a place of resort for arbitration and other business purposes. On one of these occasions, tradition relates that William Nakervie came in much later than the prescribed hour, and upon being called to account for his tardy appearance, replied that he had allowed himself to be detained to witness a most praiseworthy effort by some benevolent young women to teach gratuitously poor girls who had no other means of acquiring education, that their undertaking had greatly interested him, and he could not help thinking it would be much more creditable to himself and his friends to employ their leisure in the same way in teaching poor boys than to spend it in the indulgence of merely social intercourse.

The suggestion appealed to his friends. They determined to form a society for the purpose of teaching the rudiments of an English education to young men, especially apprentices and those beginning business. This was called "The Philadelphia Society for the Free Instruction of Indigent Boys." A night school was begun, which spent, during the first year, $9.27. Later a day school was opened, and the name of the Society was changed to "The Philadelphia Society for the Establishment and Support of Charity Schools."

Just at this time Christopher Ludwick, the gingerbread baker of Germantown, died. When his will was read it was discovered that he had left his residuary estate, estimated to be worth about eight thousand dollars, to be administered by the first society incorporated for teaching free the poor children of Philadelphia.

The young men who had found insufficient the funds which they could contribute for the purpose of carrying on their helpful educational work determined to incorporate and so secure the fund.

THE RACE OF THE UNSELFISH RIVALS

But they were not to have everything their own way. In the words of the book which told of the proceedings of the society they succeeded in incorporating:

"The magnitude of the bequest excited a desire in the trustees of the University of Pennsylvania to possess the fund, and they became formidable competitors with the society, in the endeavour to be the first to obtain a charter."

This old account goes on to tell how the two contestants ran a nip-and-tuck race, from the time they secured the necessary signatures of officials in Philadelphia. The papers so prepared had to be sent to Lancaster, the capital of the state, to be recorded officially. The Ludwick prize would belong to the organization which was first in the race. Chief Magistrate McKean of Philadelphia was absolutely fair; he "delivered the two deeds to the agents of the rival candidates, at the same moment."

There was great excitement in the city and throughout the surrounding country. Victory "depended on the despatch of the respective messengers to Lancaster," a distance of sixty-six miles over the wonderful new Lancaster Turnpike, the first turnpike in the young country.

Joseph Bennett Eves, president of the society of the young men, who bore the paper in which he and his fellows were so vitally interested, sorrowfully saw the express of the University authorities get the start. This man rushed from the courtroom with the papers, mounted a fast trotting horse which was in waiting at the door, and

CHRISTOPHER LUDWICK

was on his way in a jiffy. A light sulky had been provided for Mr. Eves, but this could not be started so early. In spite of this handicap, he overtook the trotting horse. For fourteen miles they traveled side by side, but near the famous old Spread Eagle Tavern, the rider in the sulky passed his rival, and was soon out of sight.

He could not know that the trotting horse soon gave up, exhausted, and that the rider was unable to find a substitute to carry him to the first of the relays carefully provided in anticipation of the race. So Eves did not relax his efforts. When his horse failed, he commandeered a plough-horse from a farmer in a field by the roadside. This rather poor animal enabled him to reach a town, four miles farther on, where he was able to buy from a traveler a better horse. Anxiously he looked over his shoulder to see if the rival he had distanced, he feared only for a season, was creeping up on him.

Interest in the race was intense all along the route. From time to time he passed an eager man who was holding a horse, ready for the rival racer. Here and there were groups of farmers, sometimes even crowds, who cheered him as he passed.

At Downingtown, the old settlement on the Brandywine, his heart sank as he heard the shout that the rider of the rival steed was visible in the distance. He could not know that this was an error, so he hurried on with renewed anxiety.

At last Lancaster was reached. The sixty-six miles had been covered in seven hours. Though it was evening, he routed out the Master of the Rolls, and his charter was recorded at ten minutes after eight on the evening of September 7, 1801.

Thus the funds left by the good old patriot Christopher

Ludwick passed to the hands of the Society for the Free Instruction of Indigent Boys. On the death of Mrs. Ludwick, the bequest was increased to $13,000. And for many years the savings of the gingerbread baker were used for the teaching each year of hundreds of the young people of the city where he had won fame for his honest craftsmanship as well as his sturdy patriotism.

The words of Dr. Rush on this friend of Washington, who was both in life and after his death the friend of the children, makes fitting comment on his career:

"The history of the life and character of Christopher Ludwick is calculated to show the influence of a religious education upon moral conduct; of habits of industry and economy upon success in all enterprises; and to inspire hope and exertion in young men of humble employment and scanty capital, to aspire to wealth and independence, by the only means in which they are capable of commanding respect and affording happiness."

CHAPTER VI

THE FORTUNES OF FRANCIS VIGO, THE ROBERT MORRIS OF THE NORTHWEST TERRITORY

FROM SARDINIA TO THE WESTERN WILDERNESS

GEORGE WASHINGTON was but fifteen years old and the Declaration of Independence was still twenty-nine years in the future when, at Mondovi, on the Island of Sardinia, Francis Vigo was born. Very likely his parents were Spaniards, for, though Sardinia was Italian territory, it had belonged to Spain until a little while before the birth of the boy whose life was to be so wonderfully tied up with America. It has been suggested that the Vigo family may have come from Vigo, one of the attractive old-time cities of Spain, located on Vigo Bay.

There must have been martial blood in the veins of the boy, for he was yet young when he became a private soldier in a Spanish regiment. Those were the days when Spain was the proud mistress of many colonies in the Americas, and men-at-arms were needed to keep the colonists faithful to their mother across the sea. The regiment Vigo joined was destined for service among these colonists. Tradition says that Havana saw their first service, and that, later on, they were sent to New Orleans.

At New Orleans young Vigo made the acquaintance of rough, stalwart men who came to the metropolis of the primitive South bringing with them pelts of fabulous value, as well as tales of their adventures among the Indians. The soldier handled the furs eagerly and listened with avidity to the stories of adventure in the wilderness.

With difficulty he waited for the time when he could secure a discharge from the regiment. Then he, too, started for the Arkansas country, determined to secure furs by his own prowess, and to learn how much better it was to have adventures than to hear of them from others.

From the first he prospered. He had a pleasing way that won the confidence of the Indians as well as of the frontiersmen. Gradually he worked his way north, until, in 1772, a youth of twenty-five, he found himself in the Mississippi River settlement where, in 1764, Pierre Laclède had built a trading post for Maxent, Laclède and Company, the firm which had been given a monopoly of the fur trade for all the region round about. Vigo entered on his adventure at St. Louis under the best auspices, for Lieutenant-Governor Francisco de Leyba was his silent partner. For six years fortune smiled on the genial trader in the infant city whose twentieth-century successor is still the center of the nation's fur trade.

During Vigo's long journeys in search of furs he went far up the Missouri River and the Mississippi River, as well as down the latter stream to the French villages Cahokia and Kaskaskia, and across the Illinois country to the important trading post on the Wabash River where the British controlled Fort Sackville. Everywhere he went he was a prime favorite, not only with the Spanish and the French, but with the Indians. Among those who learned to call him friend was Father Pierre Gibault, the French

THE FORTUNES OF FRANCIS VIGO

missionary who had a parish two hundred miles wide and an indefinite number of miles from north to south.

FROM VIRGINIA TO THE ILLINOIS COUNTRY

Vigo was still in Sardinia, a boy of five, when, in the home of a pioneer in Albemarle county, Virginia, George Rogers Clark was born. Thomas Jefferson, who lived less than two miles from the Clark home, was a strapping boy of fifteen when Clark was old enough to go to school. One of his later schoolmasters, by the way, was James Madison. How well some of those early heroes picked their friends and associates!

Among Clark's friends were returning travelers from the fabulous Ohio Valley region. Like Vigo, he listened to what these dauntless men had to tell, and he began to dream of going himself into the country beyond the mountains. Finally, in 1772, the year when Vigo began his experience on the site of St. Louis, Clark turned his steps westward. This was the first of a number of journeys. At length he found himself in Kentucky, where he surveyed lands, then became interested in land problems of the settlers which took him, as their emissary, to Williamsburg, the capital of Virginia. There he talked with Governor Patrick Henry, who became interested in Clark's project to defend the Kentucky country against the Indians.

The ardent patriot had not gone far with his plans to defend Kentucky against Indian aggressors before he realized that the salvation of that country lay, not merely in defeating the Indians, but in capturing the British forts at Cahokia, Kaskaskia, Vincennes, and—if possible—Detroit. Were not the Indians egged on in their warfare

[105]

against Kentucky by the insidious propaganda from these British stations?

In December, 1777, Clark told Patrick Henry of his thoughts, and of the things he had learned about the posts from spies he had sent there. Then he asked for men and supplies for the campaign he had in mind.

On January 3, 1778, a commission was given to Lieutenant-Colonel Clark which began:

"As some Indian tribes to the westward of the Mississippi have lately without any provocation massacred many of the Inhabitants of the Frontiers of the Commonwealth in the most cruel and barbarous manner, it is intended to revenge the Injury & punish the Aggression by carrying the War into their own Country. We congratulate you upon your opportunity to conduct so important an Enterprize."

This is not the tale of George Rogers Clark, so no attempt will be made to recount the absorbing story of his conquest of difficulties, his approach to Kaskaskia with one hundred and seventy-five men on July 3, 1778, and the taking over of the fort there, without bloodshed, on July 4.

The transfer of sovereignty was easy because the residents had not been satisfied with British rule. They had heard rumors of the struggle of the colonies against England, and were not averse to seeing the flag of Britain replaced by the ensign of Virginia, and to the organization, later, of Illinois as a county of Virginia.

So conditions were favorable to Clark's success at Kaskaskia. He made friends not only with the French, but with the Indians.

Yet the heart of the Virginian was filled with anxiety. He was a long way from home, and the supplies and re-enforcements which had been promised him did not come. His position was growing desperate. But difficulties were solved most unexpectedly.

SARDINIAN AND VIRGINIAN JOIN FORCES

Not long after Clark took possession of Kaskaskia, Vigo visited the settlement. Whether this visit was made in the course of his regular trading operations, or whether it was undertaken because of curiosity to see the leader of a military force from a country he admired, we do not know. We only know that soldier and trapper were soon face to face. The keen man of the forest saw at once that something was wrong with the military man; Clark looked every inch the successful leader, but it was plain that he was grievously burdened. With frontier frankness the man of furs asked the man-at-arms what was troubling him. Clark explained that, as the agent of Virginia, he was authorized to make drafts on Oliver Pollock, the agent of that state in New Orleans. But of what use to him were drafts which he could not cash for immediate needs? His soldiers were in want. True, he had some Continental currency, but this was of doubtful value, especially among people who were suspicious of anything but hard money or the peltries which were in such demand for barter.

At once Vigo saw his opportunity to help, and he grasped it. He was one of the wealthiest men in the region about Kaskaskia. He had toiled hard for his money, but he saw no better use for it than to finance Clark and his expedition.

"I will cash your drafts on New Orleans," he said. "I

will guarantee the payment of purchases here in Kaskaskia. Let me be your banker."

The offer was accepted, and Vigo became the financial
backer of Clark's campaign, much as Robert Morris was
the dependence of Washington for the colonial army.
For the time he transferred his operations from St. Louis
to Kaskaskia, conducting what was for all practical purposes a bank. He redeemed the depreciated paper money,
and was not discouraged when a dollar in silver had to be
bought with twenty dollars in paper. He continued his
advances until Virginia owed him some twelve thousand
dollars. More, he succeeded in interesting the Spanish
Commandant De Leyba at St. Louis, and Clark received
many favors from him.

No wonder a writer in the *Magazine of American History* said of this Spanish friend in need: "Without the
semblance of selfish motive, he came forward and cast
himself and his fortune into the scale of American freedom. His name is enrolled with De Kalb and Steuben and
Lafayette."

REACHING OUT TO VINCENNES

Kaskaskia was not Clark's ultimate objective; he wished
to go to Vincennes. Now that his difficulty as to funds
was solved, he had but two further troubles. If he was to
go across the Illinois country to the fort on the Wabash,
he must have reënforcements. More, he must know about
the state of affairs there; he could not look forward to as
easy a victory as he had gained at Kaskaskia.

The men he hoped would be supplied from Virginia.
But while he was waiting for them he proposed to secure
the lacking information through the friend and pastor

of Vigo, Pierre Gibault. Financed by Vigo, the Frenchman went to Vincennes, arriving during the absence of
Governor Abbott. He found that the garrison at the fort
was very small, and that the people were more ready to
listen to him than to the British officer. So, when his
little flock was gathered in the church, he made a harangue
to them, somewhat after this manner:

"It is our duty as Frenchmen and lovers of our native
land to render all the assistance we can to the struggling
colonies. Therefore I propose that we throw off all allegiance to the English nation and declare ourselves citizens of the revolted colonies. I propose that you manifest
this declaration and intention by taking the oath of allegiance to the American cause, and if you are agreed I
will now administer the oath of allegiance to you and will
assist in hauling down the English emblem over Fort Sackville."

The transfer was made without difficulty. Gibault,
after organizing a local militia to hold the fort, returned
to Kaskaskia and told Clark what he had done. Clark
at once sent to Vincennes a number of his men, led by
Captain Leonard Helms. The expedition was financed
by Vigo.

The resourceful Helms persuaded some of the residents
of the fort to join his force. Then he renamed the post
Fort Patrick Henry, and arranged for a new flag to fly
where the English colors had been. This flag contained
thirteen stripes of red and green. Madame Godare made
the crude emblem, and when Clark presented to Virginia
his statement of expenses this included "5 ells of red serge
45 cents and 3¾ ells of green serge 37½ cents." Mrs.
Godare was paid 25 cents for making the flag. A fac-

simile of this emblem may be seen to-day by visitors to the Old Cathedral Library in Vincennes. This was made by Mrs. De Lisle, a descendant of Mrs. Godare.

For a time Captain Helms prospered, but soon he began to feel the pressure of poverty. Urgent pleas were sent to Clark to come to his relief. Clark asked Vigo to go to Fort Patrick Henry. The fur trader took some supplies with him, but he depended more on his ability to persuade the residents of Vincennes to help the Americans than on what he had with him.

Though he did not know the fact, the generous Vigo was hurrying into the presence of enemies. Colonel James Hamilton at Detroit had learned with chagrin of the *coup* of Father Gibault. Realizing the importance of regaining Vincennes, he sent an expedition of six hundred men to the banks of the Wabash. He surprised the fort, with its seventy defenders, and once again found himself in control. This was on December 17, 1778, the day before Vigo's departure to take relief to Helms.

So it happened that Vigo was resting on the bank of the Embarras River, near the Wabash, when two Indians laid hands on him, announcing that he was their prisoner. Conscious that he had in his possession an incriminating note from Clark, he demanded that hands be taken from him. At the same time he promised to go with his captors.

While crossing the river, he managed to chew the note to a paste and to consign this to the water. When he stood before Colonel Hamilton there was nothing to disprove his statement that he was a Spanish trader from St. Louis. Hamilton was unwilling to release him altogether, so he told him to report every day at the fort.

These visits gave to Vigo an opportunity of which he

was not slow to take advantage. Day by day he studied the fort, its defenses, and its surroundings. He saw how he might give to the colonial cause a service even greater than money.

Again Father Gibault appeared on the scene. One Sunday morning, during the latter part of January, he went to the fort, in company with many of his congregation, and demanded the release of Vigo. If the prisoner was not sent about his business, the people would refuse to sell supplies to the English troops.

Perforce, Hamilton agreed. First, however, he asked Vigo to give his word that he would do nothing on his journey to St. Louis that would be contrary to British interests. The required pledge was given and kept—to the letter. But when St. Louis was reached, the journey was continued to Kaskaskia. He arrived there on January 29, 1779.

At once he sought Clark and told him the surprising news of the recapture of Vincennes by Colonel Hamilton. He urged that immediate departure be made for the Wabash River country, since the easiest time to capture the fort would be during the floods of the late winter, before reënforcements could come, and before the plan of Hamilton to retake Kaskaskia and to harass the friends of the colonies could be accomplished. The dream of the Englishman included even a trip up the Ohio to capture Pittsburgh!

Clark's own papers tell how important was the communication thus made. "We got every information from the gentleman that we could wish for," he said, "as he had good opportunities and had taken great pains to inform himself with a design to give intelligence."

Marshall's "Life of Washington" says that "a Spanish merchant" informed Clark that Hamilton, "who supposed himself to be in a state of perfect security at St. Vincents, had detailed Indians to block up the Ohio, and to harass the frontiers, reserving at the fort he occupied only about eighty regular troops, with three pieces of Cannon and some swivels."

Again Clark's chief concern was that he had few men and no funds. His appeals to Virginia for help had brought no response. On February 3, 1779, he wrote to Governor Patrick Henry from Kaskaskia, telling of his disappointment, speaking of Hamilton's dangerous plans, referring to Vigo's important information, and declaring his purpose to recover Vincennes or perish in the attempt. The letter contained words that must have appealed to the man who, only a little while before, had said, "Give me liberty or give me death!":

"We have the consolation that our Cause is just, and that our Country will be grateful and not condemn our Conduct, in case we fall through; if so, this country, as well as Kentucky, I believe, is lost."

Once again Vigo was the man for the emergency. He assisted in increasing Clark's force to about two hundred men, and advanced the money necessary for the expedition. Probably there were those who told him that he was throwing good money after bad, but his faith in Clark and in the cause of the colonies was firm.

The story is familiar of how Clark set out on the day after writing the letter to Patrick Henry. This was on February 4, 1779. First he divided his forces, sending a portion by river, while he led others across Illinois—at first by land, then through the overflowed country in the valleys of the Little Wabash and the Wabash. Of the sixteen days on the way, five days were required for the last nine miles to Vincennes. And on February 25, 1779, Fort Sackville surrendered to the Americans.

Thus the important fort passed to the possession of the third country to hold it. First, it is claimed, came the French Juchereau de St. Denis from Detroit in 1702, and left behind him a soldier named Leonardy who upheld the power of France in the Wabash country. In 1732 came François Marie Bissot, Sieur de Vincennes, but after four years in command he was burned at the stake by the Chickasaw Indians at the end of his ill-fated campaign conducted at the call of De Bienville, Governor of Louisiana. His successor was Saint-Ange, who was in charge when the defeat of the French on the Plains of Abraham led to the ascendancy of the British. They ruled Fort Sackville, as they called the post, for sixteen years, or until the Vigo-financed Clark made his triumphant descent.

No wonder Judge Law, in his History of Vincennes, says:

"It was, as regards the ultimate effect upon the Union, decidedly the most brilliant and useful of any undertaking during the Revolutionary War. Clark, by that campaign, added a territory embracing three of the finest States in the Union, Indiana, Illinois, and Michigan, a territory which, but for this very conquest, must now have been subject to British dominion, unless, like Louisiana, it had been acquired by purchase. For the pretence of title which our commissioners in the negotiations which resulted in the treaty of peace in 1783 set up for this immense territory was 'the capture of it by Clark and the possession of it by the Americans at the date of the conference.' "

TRANSFERS AND CLAIMS

Virginia's claim was due to the fact that she had financed Clark's expedition, and that her little army was a part of the state militia. Her claim included the country "beyond the rivers that skirted her western boundaries to the Father of Waters, from the Northwest corner of the Lake of the Woods to the Ohio River."

Virginia, therefore, was responsible to Vigo for the sums advanced to Clark. But a transfer of responsibility came in response to the resolution of the Congress of the Confederation of States, dated September 6, 1780, which considered it "advisable to press upon those States which can remove the embarrassments respecting the Western Country a liberal surrender of a portion of their territorial claims, since they cannot be possessed entire without endangering the stability of the general Confederacy." It was therefore "earnestly recommended to those States which have claim to the Western country to pass such laws, and give their delegates in Congress such powers as may effectively remove the only obstacle to a final ratification of the Articles of Confederation."

Accordingly, on October 20, 1783, Virginia passed an act authorizing the conveyance of title to the western territories. One of the conditions was "that the necessary reasonable expenses incurred by that State in subduing British forts or maintaining forts and garrisons for their defense, or in acquiring any part of the territory shall be fully reimbursed by the United States."

Provision was also made that no claims were to be allowed by the United States which had not been presented to Virginia and allowed by that state before September 24, 1788, and that bills so presented were to be paid according to a scale of depreciation which would call for the repayment of a very small per cent of the original advance.

There is no evidence that Vigo pressed for the amounts due him. Perhaps this was due to the fact that he was well-to-do. Possibly he felt that to present his account would not be patriotic, since the country was struggling hard to meet its obligations. Very likely, though, he did not have information of the invitation to tell of what was due him, or of the limiting date. He was far away, on the frontier, and news did not always penetrate so far. But even if he had been told of the opportunity he might have been discouraged when he heard of the difficulties encountered by others. For instance, General Gratiot, when arguing a case before the Indian courts, told of his father's claims against Virginia. These he took with him to New Orleans, then to Havana, then to North Carolina and Richmond; this roundabout route was much safer than a direct journey would have been. "He was engaged for two or three years in getting his pay, and but for strong friends must have been a ruined man. He received but little money, negroes and tobacco at a high price, and a quantity of land not esteemed worth looking after." When he returned to the Illinois country, other creditors of Virginia, learning of his bitter experience, decided that the game of claim presentations was hardly worth playing.

Yet Clark, the recipient of Vigo's financial favors, did not forget. When he presented his accounts to Virginia, he told of the advances made by the Spanish trader. Virginia, in turn, passed on these accounts to the United States, which made a cash allowance to the Old Dominion for all claims, including Vigo's, of about half a million dollars.

VIGO'S LATER PATRIOTIC SERVICE

But for references to Vigo buried in copies of official letters and other government archives, little information would be available covering his later career. But these official records reveal the fact that the Spaniard who had thrown in his lot with America, far from regretting the generous acts for which he had received no return, added to his deeds of devotion to his adopted country for more than a generation after the treaty of 1783 put the seal on the winning of the Northwest through Clark's skill and Vigo's generosity.

On June 20, 1790, Secretary of War Knox wrote to Vigo:

"Major Doughty has in express words given an account of the services which you have rendered him and the zeal which you have manifested for the United States in the difficult business which has been committed to your care. Your conduct therein, sir, has attracted the attention of the President, and I am directed by him to tender to you his acknowledgment thereof."

On December 30 of the same year the confidence of the Government was shown to him when he was commissioned to trade with the Chickasaws and Choctaws, and was asked to deliver to these tribes two talks signed by the President.

On May 27, 1794, General Anthony Wayne, whose services in the campaigns added to the fame won by him during the Revolution, wrote asking him, because he was "a gentleman of integrity and influence, and a sturdy and firm friend of the United States, and perfectly acquainted with all the trading people passing between Post Vincennes and Detroit, as well as from St. Louis and Cahokia

FRANCIS VIGO

Post Vincent 31 Dec. 1785

I promise to Pay to the late Copartnership of Thomas Williams & Co. of Detroit, their Executors, Administrators or Assigns or Order in all the month of May of the year One thousand Seven hundred & eighty Seven the sum of One thousand Seven hundred & twenty one Pound five shillings & nine pence New York Currency in Money for value received. ——

£1721.5.9

Vigo

ONE OF THE NOTES THAT CAUSED VIGO'S FINANCIAL DOWNFALL

OLD FORT SACKVILLE IN 1779, VINCENNES, INDIANA

to that place," to secure one or two trusty people to go
to Roche de Bout, "to discover the number and designs of
the enemy, and particularly what number of British troops
are there."

Among the manuscript treasures of the Historical Society of Pennsylvania are three letters from Vigo. One
of them, written at Vincennes, was to Wayne, evidently
an answer to the request of May 27:

"The business of the express mentioned in your first letter, is now on foot, and in the hands of one of the best
men in the United States for performing a business of that
nature, he is daily expected at this place; and I am sure, if
it is in the power of any single man to perform that business, he will do it.

"About the 22d of September an express arrived from
New Orleans to the Comdt. of St. Louis, the News he
brought is yet a secret, & the commanding officer immediately swore him to secrecy; The people of the Illinois
generally believe that the express brings a declaration of
War against the United States—previous to the express's
going to the commanding officer, he informed a gentleman
who lives in Kaskaskia that Fort Mobile was taken by
the French. Two other expresses left New Orleans at
the same time that this one did, each of which took different routs; the other two have since arrived at New
Madrid.   VIGO."

The letter was in the hand of an amanuensis, for Vigo's
education was by no means as great as his patriotism and
his generosity. But the signature was in the Sardinian's
own handwriting.

In the summer of the same year, the friend who served
as amanuensis wrote for Vigo a letter to General Clark

[117]

in which he sent an "extract from a Letter from a Gentleman of undoubted carracter in St. Louis dated May 6th 1794 to Francis Vigo of this town."

The extract follows:

"The express which was sent by the Commanding Officer of this place to Detroit returned a few days ago, and brings information that the British have made great preparation there to defend themselves against the United States.

"We are informed from New Madrid that there is three Gallies and three Galliats at that place from New Orleans Commanded by a Mr. Rausseau."

The characteristic signature, "Vigo," attested that the letter was a "True Copy."

Added to the letter was the note: "It must be observed that the Gentleman who wrote Vigo, has his reasons for not more fully explaining himself, as his property is considerable, & in the British possession."

Thus Vigo was ever showing his constancy in serving the country which was so careless of his financial claim upon it. Only once is there a hint that he sought anything for himself. On May 24, 1794, he wrote to General Clark from Fort Wayne, Indiana. After telling of going up the Wabash on an expedition to Wayne, he ventured to say, briefly and parenthetically, "I also request your Excellency (should Congress adopt the measure recommended by the President's speech of establishing Trading houses in the Indian Country) to mention my name."

A few months later, in 1795, the large-hearted man helped Wayne in his Indian campaign by advancing needed funds.

About 1800 Vigo was married to Elizabeth Shannon. For her he built a house in Vincennes, a palatial structure according to the standards of the day. This house was nearly completed when the owner learned of the coming of General William Henry Harrison, who had been appointed Governor of the Northwest Territory, with headquarters at Vincennes.

"I'll pay you twenty guineas premium if you will have the house completed when General Harrison reaches Vincennes," he said to his builder.

But when the offer of the completed house was made to the Governor, he refused to accept more than one room.

"Then he must have the best room in the house," Mr. and Mrs. Vigo agreed. And Harrison was compelled to take the parlor, a room richly panelled, with a floor laid in square blocks of white oak and black oak in alternating rows. The furnishings of this room were in keeping with the magnificence of the house, while upon the walls were pictures of note, among them an oil portrait of Thomas Jefferson.

The guest was made welcome not only to the house, but to the elegantly furnished boat—in these days it would be called a yacht—designed for voyages on the Wabash and Ohio rivers.

The completion of the Governor's own home, Grouseland, erected between 1804 and 1806—the first building of burnt brick west of the Alleghanies—enabled Harrison to repay some of the Vigos' hospitality. Since 1916 this historic mansion has been the property of the Francis Vigo Chapter of the Daughters of the American Revolution.

There is on record a statement by Harrison of his appreciation of his host. In 1834 he wrote a letter in which he said he had known Vigo for thirty-nine years, and that for thirteen years he had lived in the same town with him, and on terms of the most intimate friendship. He declared that Vigo was "utterly incapable of misrepresentation, however great his interest." Moreover, he was confident that "there were more respectable persons in Indiana who would become the guarantors of his integrity than could be induced to for any other person."

ONE HUNDRED YEARS TO PAY A DEBT

The closing words of the Harrison letter give a hint of the sorrowful events of the last years of Vigo's career:

"His whole life, as long as his circumstances were prosperous, was spent in acts of kindness and benevolence to individuals, and his public spirit and attachment to the institutions of our country were proverbial."

For the day came when the prosperous fur trader who —in the words of George Rogers Clark, penned in 1811— rendered inestimable service to his country "at a time when the cloud on which our fate hung assumed the most menacing aspect," learned the bitter experience of poverty and privation. Misfortune followed misfortune. An ill-starred partnership with the Miami Fur Company brought heavy losses. The Company promised to supply the funds with which he was to buy furs. His part of the contract was carried out, but when the day of settlement arrived, the Company charged him with the cash given him, but refused to credit him with the furs he had secured for them. The Company could force this interpretation of the accounts, and Vigo lost nearly everything he had.

In the course of his efforts to recover, he borrowed money at a ruinous rate of interest. The final blow to his fortunes was delivered when a creditor secured a judgment on one of these notes. The fatal note is reproduced with this chapter.

For the payment of this and other notes Vigo had relied on the funds which he hoped to secure from the United States. For he had presented his account to the government, asking for reimbursement of the sum so long overdue.

One of his due bills was sold to a man who had the spirit of the gambler for a very small sum. Another was destroyed by Vigo in despair of recovering anything at the hands of his country. At length, some forty years after the advance was made to Clark, Congress offered to pay the bare principal of the remaining claim for $8,616. Vigo indignantly refused this offered settlement; he felt that he had a right to interest for the long period of waiting.

The statement has been made that, during his years of poverty, Vigo was deserted by his friends, and was "cared for by a few poor, honest laborers and farmers, comrades of his in the great struggle for independence."

Fortunately this was not true. His last days were spent with Francis Vigo McKee, in Vincennes, whose brother, A. B. McKee, declares:

"He was abundantly supplied with all the comforts of life and was in his last hours watched over and nursed and cared for by kind friends, loving hearts, and no want of his was left unsupplied that was in the power of man to supply."

The tragedy of it! The old man lived more than ninety-six years, yet he did not receive one cent of his dues. The cost of the casket in which he was buried was not paid until forty years after his death!

After his death the claims were pushed in the interest of the heirs. There were no children, but others were eager to step in as parties at interest. Moreover, friends and associates whom the old man had won by his kindly, unselfish life watched with eagerness the progress of long-delayed justice. Many times they thought that a grateful country was to honor the advances made in a time of dire need. Seven times a committee of the House of Representatives reported in favor of payment. Twice bills providing funds passed the House. The Senate, too, considered bills reported out of committee, but they failed of passage until 1872, when an act passed both bodies. It was then referred to the Court of Claims. In 1873 the Court of Claims found in favor of Vigo's heirs. More delay followed, for the United States took the case to the Supreme Court.

And in 1876—ninety-eight years after the devoted acts of the Spanish pioneer—the case was decided in favor of the heirs, with provision that the principal amount of $8,616 be paid, with five per cent interest from 1788, or $41,282.60 additional.

Most of the sum went to relatives who had given no heed to Vigo during his time of need. But, fortunately, Vigo had provided by will that, when the claim was paid, $500 should go to Vigo county, Indiana, to buy a bell for the court-house in Terre Haute. This bequest was paid. And in 1887 the clear-toned bell began to proclaim—to quote the words of United States Senator Daniel W. Voorhies—that "Indiana is the last resting place of the brave, the gentle, the patriotic friend of freedom and humanity."

The school-children of Terre Haute are not allowed to forget the donor of the bell. In *Once Upon a Time in Indiana,* Charity Dye says that when the old bell tells them it is time to go to school, they say, "There goes Old Vigo." This fact led Francis Morrison to write:

"What is the story ye tell,
Old Vigo, Old Vigo?"
"I have only the tongue of a bell,
But ye know, ye know!
Look into the past if ye can,
Long ago, long ago,
And know the heart of a man.
Ye know! ye know!
Who planted the fruitful seed
That gave me unto your need,
Old Vigo, Old Vigo!"

"Whom are ye calling all day,
Old Vigo, Old Vigo?"
"Justice ye oft drive away!
Will she know? Will she know?
For the sake of the great heart who died,
Long ago, long ago . . .
What we owed him too often denied.
Ye know! ye know!
I bid her come in! Greet her well!
Oh, heed ye the song of your bell,
Old Vigo, Old Vigo!"

For many years the body of the donor of the bell lay in an unmarked grave. The enthusiasm that gave him a military funeral did not last until a monument could be erected. But to-day the people of Vincennes look on a rugged granite boulder over his dust, which bears the inscription:

FRANCIS VIGO
Patriot,
Whose devotion to the
Cause of American Liberty
Made Possible the

Capture of Fort Sackville, Feb. 25, 1779.
Born Mondovi, Sardinia, 1740.
Died in Vincennes, Indiana, March 22, 1836
Erected Oct. 1st, 1909
By the Francis Vigo Chapter, D.A.R.

The simple testimony of the patriotic Daughters should be interpreted in connection with the apostrophe of Judge Law:

"Spirit of the illustrious dead, let others judge of the matter as they may, we who have lived to see the immense advantages of that Conquest to our beloved country—so little known and so little appreciated when made—will do you justice, and we will also teach our children and our children's children who are to occupy our places when we are gone, to read, and remember, among the earliest lessons of the history of that portion of the country, which is to be also their abiding place—our own lovely valley—that its conquest and subsequent attachment to the Union, were as much owing to the councils and services of Vigo, as to the bravery and enterprise of Clark."

SITE OF THE HOME OF COL. FRANCIS VIGO

ON THE WABASH RIVER, NEAR VINCENNES, INDIANA

DEPARTMENT OF THE UNITED STATES FOR FOREIGN AFFAIRS, PHILADELPHIA.
IN THIS BUILDING WAS DRAFTED THE PROCLAMATION OF PEACE IN 1783

CHAPTER VII

HARM JAN HUIDEKOPER, THE HOLLANDER WHO BECAME A LAND BARON

THE WHY AND THE HOW OF THE HOLLAND LAND COMPANY

IT IS, of course, matter of general knowledge that France lent money to the United States for the prosecution of the war with Great Britain. But not so much has been said of the sums lent by Spain and Holland. Of a total of about $8,000,000 which came to America from Europe in America's time of need, three-fourths was from the treasury of the French Republic, but much of the balance came from Holland.

A paragraph from Paul Busti's Memorial to the Legislature of the State of New York, March 1, 1820, tells the story of Holland's financial assistance, and of the payment of the debt.

"At an early stage of the American Revolution, when the struggle for liberty and independence was yet doubtful, Dutch merchants . . . warmly espousing the cause of the infant republic, came forward, at every hazard, to furnish her with supplies in order to relieve the wants of her armies. The meritorious exertions of these individuals cannot be forgotten by the surviving patriots of the revolution. Nor will the faithful records of history cease to attest them to posterity. The government of the United States, in the enjoyment of the blessings of peace and

[125]

independence, being soon happily enabled by a wise and regular system of finance to satisfy the demand of their public creditors, the capital of part of the debt thus contracted with the merchants of Holland was thrown into their hands at a moment when the convulsions and revolutions of Europe threatened to subvert the whole fabric of civil society. Under these circumstances, they determined to reinvest their funds in American lands, and during the course of the years 1792 and 1793 the uncultivated wilds of the Genesee in New York State thus passed into the hands of the individuals who composed the Holland Land Company, and who, for the purchase and improvement of their property, formed an association."

But how were the thoughts of these Hollanders turned to American lands?

Among the associates who formed the great land company were members of banking houses like Wilhem and Jan Willink and Nicholas and Jan van Staphorst. Through these banking houses, in the winter of 1782 and 1783, John Adams arranged for the advances to America. Naturally, then, Robert Morris, who had charge of American finances during the Revolution, became acquainted, by correspondence, with these Amsterdam bankers. What more simple, then, than his explaining to them the wonderful opportunity presented by American wild lands for the investment of the large sums that would be repaid to them?

"Perhaps he already contemplated selling to them when he bought," is suggested in the Tiffany story of Huidekoper. "What steps he took to bring his lands to their notice is matter of conjecture, but a pamphlet . . . issued at Amsterdam in 1792, was doubtless one of the means employed. In the preface . . . the author states that his only reason for writing the little work is to inform the public, and principally the Holland merchants, that the purchase of uncultivated lands in America, by reason of the extreme rapidity with which they increase in value, promises greater and more certain advantages than those which their thorough business knowledge has already procured for them in the bonds of the country."

If the pamphlet was designed as a bit of advertising literature, it was abundantly successful. For on December 24, 1792, trustees Le Roy and Lincklaen bought from Robert Morris and his wife, 1,500,000 acres of the Genesee lands. Within a few months the holdings in New York were increased to 3,300,000 acres. The cost was $1,100,000. The trustees represented Wilhem Willink, Nicholas van Staphorst, Pieter van Eeghen, Hendrick Vollenhoven, and Rutger Jan Shimmelpennick, because aliens could not hold lands in this country. Later, however, the law was changed, and title was transferred.

The story of the Holland Land Company, which owned what are now Chautauqua, Cattaraugus, Erie and Niagara, as well as parts of Allegany, Wyoming, Genesee, and Orleans counties, in New York, which later bought 120,-000 acres in central New York and 499,660 acres on French Creek in Pennsylvania, is long and intricate, and of absorbing interest. But in this story of the romantic rise of Harm Jan Huidekoper only enough can be told to give background for his experience as a pioneer in America.

HARM JAN IN THE NETHERLANDS

The Hollander was born just before the adoption of the Declaration of Independence in the land which was later to give him his opportunity. April 3, 1776, was the day of joy in the home of Anne and Gesiena Huidekoper, at Hogeveen in Drenthin, which is now a part of the kingdom of the Netherlands. Harm was a sickly child, and no one thought he would ever become the out-of-door man who later helped in the conquest of American wilds. His first schooling was received in a Dame school, where he used a horn book, similar to those known in America in colonial days. Later he enjoyed a period of instruction in common school. This fact is of some importance, for it shows that his father was able to afford tuition in a school which less than one hundred pupils could attend, although the village contained six thousand people. A further indication of the state of public education is that there were few books even in the homes of the wealthy, while but two or three newspapers were taken, and these by clubs, whose members passed them on from one to another. Not until Harm Jan went to boarding-school at Crefeld in Germany did he learn the joy of having access to a library. Then he felt his mind "expanding and opening itself to new ideas."

In 1793, while the lad was at Crefeld, his brother Jan was sent to America on a mission for the Holland Land Company. It is thought the plan of the directors was that he should remain in the new country, as their agent, but his ideas changed after he left home, and he returned to Europe in less than two years. Perhaps his speedy return was due to his longing to be with the young woman to whom he was engaged, but she died soon after his return.

He was full of his experiences in America when his brother Harm Jan came home from Crefeld. The younger brother became so enthusiastic because of what he heard that, when he was given the choice of becoming a clerk in a Dutch commercial house, or of going to America, he chose America. He was attracted by the thought of making his fortune in a new land rather than joining stay-at-homes in the sorry attempt to struggle in business at home, where war was interfering with all commercial prospects. Perhaps he could become a landed proprietor in the country of opportunity! At least, this was the notion to which he clung during the year he spent with his parents after making his decision.

HARM JAN IN AMERICA

The first stage in the journey was made in August, 1796, in a *trekschuit,* or canal boat. Then came the port of Helder, where he took passage on a schooner of 120 tons. This he described as "altogether a sorry concern— old, leaky, a bad sailor, with poor rigging, and sails so old as to stand in constant need of repair." Of the five seamen one was impressed next day by an English sloop of war.

The passage required sixty-three days, a period the Dutch emigrant utilized by studying English. When he reached New York, on October 14, he was able to express his meaning in the strange tongue, but, otherwise, he had little confidence in himself. "I had little or no acquaintance with the ways of the world," he said, later; "had never been accustomed to act for myself; and my education had tended more to teach me what others had thought than to think myself."

Fortunate was this youth of twenty if he realized something of these shortcomings at the time! The trouble with most young men is not that they have shortcomings, but that they fail to realize the truth, and even think that they are fitted to go out to conquer.

The first sight of the new land made him glad. "How beautiful Long Island is, especially for a Hollander who has seen only his own country!" he exclaimed, in a letter home. "I was enchanted with all I saw. Fruit trees, grain fields, trees and shrubs—everything, almost, was new to me, and I saw here, too, that primitive state of Nature which we try with little success to imitate in our 'English gardens,' in miniature."

In New York he was dismayed as he saw the pigs and cows running down the streets. As may be imagined, he compared the New World city with the clean villages of his own land, and speedily gave the palm to Holland. But he did appreciate the perfect October weather, so in contrast with the offering of that month in his home.

His ardent desire was to become a farmer in this favored land, so he turned his steps to Cazenovia; New York, where a young cousin from Holland had established himself as a husbandman. On the way he stopped at Oldenbarneveld, the headquarters of the Holland Land Company for one of their smaller tracts, as Batavia was the location of their office for the Genesee lands.

Oldenbarneveld, now the town of Barneveld, was the home of a company of self-exiled Dutch patriots, for whom the way had been paved by Gerrit Boon. Boon traveled through the forest from Fort Schuyler, marking the way he took by blazing the trees. When he founded the village, and named it for the Dutch reformer and martyr, he was hoping to make it a center of maple sugar culture. He had learned how fruitful the trees were when they were tapped in February; why couldn't he have a vast sugar camp where trees would be tapped throughout the year? The poor man was doomed to disappointment, not only in his village, but in the dream of perennial maple sugar, by which he hoped to make large profits for the Holland Land Company, incidentally displacing the West Indian sugar, and so striking a body-blow at the immoral slave traffic.

When the journey into interior New York was extended to Cazenovia, Huidekoper very soon realized that he had been, in his way, as green as Boon. "I have since often smiled at the erroneous ideas which I, as well as other Europeans, entertained on the subject of farming. In Europe the man who owns a hundred acres of good land is rich, and can draw from it more than a competency, with little more labour than superintending the cultivation of it. Now Europeans are apt to connect the same idea with the possession of land in this country, and as they hear that very good land is to be had here at from two to four dollars per acre, they are led to believe that it requires but a few hundred dollars to make a man independent for life. I need not add that when I saw my friend De Clerq's farm covered with stumps, it did not exactly realize the beau ideal which I had formed to myself of a territorial possession; and when I learned afterwards that it had taken about $4,000 to make his farm what it was, I became sensible that I was not rich enough to become a farmer."

So, without a definite purpose in mind, Huidekoper returned to Oldenbarneveld, where he spent two years in pleasant idleness among the Dutchmen of the community. Several times he tried vainly to get into business, and it was not until the departure for Holland of a clerk in the employ of Mr. Moppa, successor of Mr. Boon as agent for the Holland Land Company at Oldenbarneveld, that his foot was placed on the ladder that led to success. "Here commenced that connection with the Holland Land Company, and with the land business, in which the whole of my subsequent life has been spent," he wrote, in his old age.

HARM JAN WINS HIS SPURS

Five hundred dollars a year, with board and lodging! That was the salary of the young clerk. The figures looked good to the man who had not yet grown away from the standards of his homeland. And it was a fine salary, according to the times. Probably it was, all told, equal to three or four thousand dollars in these expanding days. Fortunately he knew how to make splendid use of his good fortune. "I had now a competency, and lived without care," he said. "I was now not only earning my own living, but, with the rigid economy which I prescribed for myself, I was enabled to lay by the largest part of my salary, to gratify the first wish of my heart, that of being useful to my parents. My Father died before I had the means of giving effect to this wish."

This statement was not made merely for effect; throughout his life Huidekoper showed that consideration for others which has always marked the true man. Another evidence of his unselfishness was the fact that, many years after he left Oldenbarneveld, when his son Alfred visited those with whom the days of the young clerk had been spent, they could not say enough concerning him and his kindly manner of life.

A helpful glimpse of pioneer life was given by him when, in 1798, he wrote: "This settlement has never been more lively than at present; every day about twenty

IN THE KITCHEN OF THE OLD HOME

HARM JAN HUIDEKOPER'S CARRIAGE, ABOUT 1812

sleighs come laden with goods from Fort Schuyler, and they generally go back the same day laden with lime, which is burnt here. In addition, there are about fifteen or sixteen sleds engaged in hauling stone from a stone quarry."

The year 1801 brought promotion; he was asked to become the bookkeeper of the agent of the Holland Land Company at Philadelphia, with a salary of $1,200. His satisfaction was great. "The offer was too advantageous to be refused," he wrote, in his story of his life, written for his children. Soon he had even greater reason for jubilation, for he was asked to serve as secretary for the Philadelphia Population Company, another land organization, in which some of the associates in the Holland Land Company were interested. This increased his income to $1,400.

The rather sophomoric statement he made concerning his stay in Philadelphia is too good to be passed by:

"My residence in Philadelphia was of service to me, not only in a pecuniary point of view, but also as, by bringing me in contact with the world, it served to enlarge my ideas, and to improve my Manners, which latter, from my having almost continually resided in the country, had never been sufficiently attended to. But though I then endevoured to acquire the manners, and to conform to the customs of the New World into which I had been translated, I always retained my former predilections for the simple pleasures of life, and I was thus preserved from the dissipations which are but too common in large cities."

How modern residents of both city and country will smile at that rather self-satisfied conclusion!

Before long the bookkeeper's duties called him to go to Meadville, Pennsylvania, north of Pittsburgh, in the midst of the French Creek lands. A circumstantial account of the hard horseback journey is given in his journal. Perhaps the most telling observation he made was in connection with lands west of the Alleghany Mountains, for this describes something of pioneer methods as well as of the ways of careful Hollanders. These, he said, were more fertile than those near Philadelphia. "What does not please me," he added, "is the way they clear the ground here, if you call it clearing, when the greater part of the stumps are left standing. I noticed the natural result of this, for in many places the wind had blown down branches over the growing grass and injured it, and, what was worse, had in places beaten down the crops entirely and ruined them. Another thing that astonished me was that in clearing these lands the people made no use whatever of the ashes, which they left when the trees were burned. They could give no better reason for this than that every body did so and nobody cared to make potash."

At Pittsburgh he told of what proved to be an abortive attempt to make the infant city a seaport. He was astonished "to see two vessels being built, the larger of two hundred and sixty tons, the other, of one hundred and twenty tons. There was also a brigantine, . . . ready to sail as soon as the rains should have raised the Ohio, so that it could go down that river to the Mississippi. The captain of the brigantine expected to make the voyage to Europe. This will probably be the first vessel to cross the ocean which has been built two thousand five hundred miles from the sea."

At the time of this first visit to Meadville, the village was a lusty infant of fourteen years, and contained a number of log cabins, with clay chimneys. Its importance was due in part to the great lumber rafts which passed down French Creek to the Allegheny River. Salt for the entire

Ohio Valley also passed this way, the product of the salt springs at Onondaga, New York, whence oxen took it in sleds to Buffalo, when snow was on the ground. This was only the beginning of its journey, for "when the ice broke up it was taken to Erie in sailing vessels, to be carried overland to Waterford, where it was loaded upon keel boats, arks or broadhorns, canoes and bateaux, and dispatched down French Creek." Eight barrels of the commodity could be exchanged for a yoke of oxen, and one hundred barrels bought a negro boy. Nominally a barrel of salt was worth five dollars. But how many men on the frontier had five dollars in currency?

The business in Meadville called for a four weeks' stay —a short time, indeed, for a man who had made a hard trip of ten days to reach it, and who chose to return to Philadelphia by way of Niagara Falls and New York, a leisurely journey of four weeks.

Huidekoper thought he had seen the last of the crude western towns, but two years later he was asked to become agent for the Holland Land Company, with headquarters in the French Creek village. Friends urged him not to accept, but he thought the offer presented an opportunity too good to lose. It would give him a chance to make a record here, in the country of his preference, and he could then take care of his half-brother, Pieter, who had just come over from Holland. Pieter was unfitted for city life, though he was a lovable man, and a man of might. It is said that he "could take a barrel of flour in his hands, and with absolute ease run upstairs with it. He could subdue the fiercest bulldog or mastiff in full attack, for he would simply seize the animal by the throat and choke it until it became powerless."

HARM JAN, MAKER OF FARMERS

Probably in anticipation of removal to the West, Huidekoper purchased, in June, 1804, from the Holland Land Company, 22,000 acres of land. Evidently he had saved from his salary to some purpose. This was the first of many land ventures, "and it proved, in the issue, a profitable one," the purchaser noted many years later.

Two years had given ample time to a town advantageously located to develop in a marvelous fashion, so Huidekoper found in Meadville many improved houses, an academy, a church, a court-house and jail, a projected turnpike, the Erie and Waterford, and a newspaper. This journal was soon used to notify delinquent purchasers of Holland Land Company's acres that he was on the ground to collect, or, if necessary, to sue them.

But a greater problem than suits for back payments confronted the Holland Land Company at the time of the new agent's arrival. The story of this difficulty dates back to the act of the Pennsylvania General Assembly, passed in 1792, which offered all the land lying north of the Ohio River and west of the Allegheny River and Conewango Creek, to actual settlers, for seven pounds ten shillings for each one hundred acres. Title could be secured either by actual settlement, followed by a warrant, or by the giving of a warrant followed by actual settlement. Under this act the Holland Land Company took out many warrants. Settlement and improvements must be made within two years, or new warrants could be issued to actual settlers.

But there was a proviso. This, unfortunately, was not worded in clear fashion, but it seemed to many who had to become litigants against the state to indicate that, if they were prevented from making actual settlement by enemies of the United States, they should be confirmed in their title to the lands when they persisted in making settlement as soon as possible.

Now repeated Indian attacks and alarms hindered settlement. Not until 1795, when the Senate ratified the treaty of peace which followed General Anthony Wayne's campaign against the Indians, was it possible to live safely in the territory. But lands were declared forfeited, new settlers were invited in, and upstart land companies tried to take advantage of the situation. Lawsuits were the result. In the state courts the decision was against the Holland Land Company and other original holders of warrants. The associates in Holland were discouraged; they sent orders that the whole of the Pennsylvania lands should be abandoned. Huidekoper wrote to the General Agent, Paul Busti, in Philadelphia:

"I hope that you will not feel yourself obliged to follow strictly your scheme . . . a part and even a great part would be lost if the decision . . . be confirmed, but still there will be enough that will be worth saving. . . . I acknowledge that the speculation is a bad one, but now that it is made, I do not see that the whole is lost. . . . I shall take care that they have no further disbursements on this account, and that as much as possible be saved to them. To abandon would not free them from the obligations incurred, but would make them lose all the benefits that might have been reaped. If the lawsuits be completely gained, I will engage to bring everything in order in 18 months or two years; if the suits are completely lost, I shall have something worth saving."

Because the holders of Holland Company's warrants were foreigners, the case could be taken to the United

States Supreme Court. This led to the famous decision delivered by Chief Justice Marshall, in March, 1805, in favor of the litigants. He said:

"The State is in the situation of a person who holds forth to the world the conditions on which he is willing to sell his property. If he should couch his propositions in such ambiguous form that they might be understood differently in consequence of which sales were to be made, and the purchase money paid, he would come with an ill grace into Court, to insist on a latent and obscure meaning, which should give him back his property, and permit him to retain the purchase money. All those principles of equity, and of fair dealing, which constitute the basis of judicial proceedings, require that courts should lean against such a construction."

In spite of the fact that some Pennsylvanians found fault "that a decision of the national court should dominate over that of a state court in the construing of a provincial law," the decision gradually restored order. Within a few years after Huidekoper's entrance on his agency practically every case in question was settled.

Difficult matters that arose during the course of settlement of conflicting claims were handled by Huidekoper with such tact and wisdom that the name of the Company was thereafter held in even greater honor by most thoughtful people. Angry feelings survived for many years, and disputed titles were common. No personal violence was offered to the agent, though he was in danger more than once. The last remnant of feeling was shown, twenty years later, when he was fired at and his horse was wounded.

But the Company's discouragement continued, though without reason, as Huidekoper thought. The purchase price of the lands near Meadville was about $200,000, and when the suit was decided the total investment was about twice as much. But in 1809 the associates were ready to withdraw from the field. So Huidekoper went to Philadelphia to assist in the transfer of the Company's Pennsylvania lands to Griffith and Wallace. This proved an advantageous change to Huidekoper, for while his salary, under the new owner, was reduced from $2,400 to $1,000 a year, his commissions on sales and collections were increased so largely that his income became notable. He prospered to such an extent that, in 1828 and in 1836, at a cost of $234,400 he became the sole owner of the remaining lands in western Pennsylvania which had been in possession of the Holland Land Company and the Pennsylvania Population Company. By this time he was, or had been, in possession of some 80,000 acres.

HARM JAN, TRUE AMERICAN

With what judgment and thoughtfulness for the purchaser he administered these lands is evident from a statement made by his biographer:

"It was a beneficent oversight that he exercised in behalf of the pioneer settlers who procured this forest land of him with barely enough cash in hand to make the preliminary payment, and who struggled on from year to year, paying installments until the whole sum was made and the cleared and cultivated farm was their own. He kept his purchasers individually in mind; their habits of industry or of shiftlessness were known to him; the exact amount of improvement or of neglect evidenced by the state of their clearings stood on record in his books; and many were the instances in which his consideration came to the assistance of the hard-beset tillers of the soil, or in which his ingenuity devised for them ways and means of lessening their indebtedness and of keeping their land."

On one occasion—and this was a fair sample of the generous methods of the Hollander who by that time had a right to consider himself a thoroughgoing American—a settler who had bought fifty acres, promising to pay for it at the rate of three dollars an acre, was unable to meet the installments on the hundred and fifty dollars. In fact, he had paid nothing, although some years had passed since the purchase. Threatened with foreclosure, he appealed for consideration. When Huidekoper learned that he was an industrious man, but that he could not raise money, this holder of the mortgage offered to write off two thirds of the sum provided the man could pay fifty dollars. Then he showed the way to raise the fifty dollars without hardship.

Huidekoper found that the farmer had plenty of cattle, but could not dispose of the herds for the cash they required for their payments; he arranged for annual drives to market across the mountains. Steers, hogs, sheep, and turkeys even were taken, and the drive was carried on under the direction of the thoughtful landlord. The description of the traveling of cattle, pertaining to one of the drives, and of the adventures by the weary way, makes a narrative of unusual appeal and interest.

As a result of his genial, generous methods Huidekoper became a character revered in all that western region. An incident on one of his periodical visits to lands at a distance from Meadville tells of a man who sought him at the house where he was staying for the night. "Are you Mr. Huidekoper?" was the query. "Yes, sir. What can I do for you?" "Nothing, sir," the man said. "When

THE LOG CABIN OF A PIONEER SETTLER

HARM JAN HUIDEKOPER

George Washington was in this county everybody came to look at him; I wanted to look at you, sir. Good day, sir!"

Of course the financial burden carried by the proprietor of more than 80,000 acres of Pennsylvania land was great. Yet he did not for one day allow to be interrupted his thoughtfulness for his relatives in Holland. With care he made profitable investments for them, and he sent gifts on many occasions. These he did not think of as gifts, but as due recognition of past care and help received from them.

How far he carried his sense of obligation was illustrated beautifully by letters to his friend, Mrs. Susan Wallace, of Philadelphia, widow of the friend from whom he had bought much of his land. Although his obligations for the purchase of these and other lands kept him in some anxiety until all were discharged in 1840, he planned, in 1837, a grateful additional payment to Mrs. Wallace. Of this he spoke, and thought, as a right, not a gift.

The first of the series of letters—which have been examined by the author of this volume in the library of the Historical Society of Pennsylvania—was dated April 17, 1837:

"Whereas I have lately purchased from the Holland Land Company, a concern on which my deceased Friend, John B. Wallace had bestowed much labour, by which I am likely to be benefited, now as an acknowledgment of my sense of the value of his labour, and as a testimony of my regard for his memory, and of my friendship for his mourning family, I do hereby promise, covenant and engage to and with Susan Wallace, widow of said John, to pay to her the said Susan annually during her natural life the Sum of Seven hundred dollars, which Sum is to be

paid to her or her order of the first day of January in
each year. . . ."

On this letter was endorsed, years later:

"The annuity contracted for by this bond was paid with
the greatest regularity by this excellent man, up to the last
year (1849) of my mother's life.

"JOHN WM. WALLACE."

To send the specified amount was not always easy. On
December 28, 1839, when Huidekoper wished to remit,
the country was in the midst of a time of financial strin-
gency. Banks were suspending specie payments. But the
money due was sent.

On December 23, 1837, Huidekoper sent the annuity in
bills by the hand of a friend. "I have not quite so much
faith in the postoffice," he explained. On December 19,
1843, on sending check, he said: "As the close of the
year is now at hand, and as Mr. Shattuck's visit to Philadelphia affords an opportunity of saving you some postage
in these hard times, I avail myself of it to transmit it
to you."

That the money was sent gladly, always, is an indication of character: "I have once more the pleasure of
transmitting . . ." "I have once more the satisfaction . . ." "May you for many years yet continue to
enjoy this small remuneration of your husband's labours . . ." "I have cause of gratitude to God for spar-
ing me during another year, and for enabling me again
to discharge this feeble acknowledgment of the services
of one who was so deservedly dear to me."

A man who could write such letters would not have
been in sympathy with all the high-speed methods taken by
some people of these modern days to get rich. A part of

his creed was stated in a paper, "The Right and Duty of Accumulation," written in 1840, the year he completed his payments on his land:

"The tendency of a business life to develop the intellectual and moral powers must be obvious. . . . That such a life is replete with moral danger and temptation is admitted, but it is precisely this which constitutes it a school of moral discipline. . . . That . . . labour when accompanied with frugality and prudence, has a tendency to produce an excess of earnings . . . is assumed. . . . It has sometimes been contended, that though it may be lawful to earn such surplus property . . . it is our duty to dispense of it to others as fast as it accumulates. But the doing so would be destructive of its intellectual and moral influence. Under the present wise arrangement of things the increased knowledge of business is accompanied by an increase of capital calculated to give activity and a further extension to those new-born powers. . . . But if a man possesses no capital . . . a business life, instead of being a scene of constant progression, will soon become to him an irksome, unnecessary task of mere mechanical drudgery, possessing no intellectual, nor moral interest. If it be unlawful to accumulate, then there is an end of all international intercourse . . . all our manufacturing and commercial establishments must be destroyed . . . there is an end to public improvements . . . there is an end to all our colleges, hospitals, and other benevolent institutions, for all were originally founded and endowed, or are now supported by the fruits of accumulation. . . .

"I deem the . . . accumulation of property to be . . . in perfect accord with our Christian duty. It is true, that the possession of wealth imposes on us new obligations and new responsibilities. Wealth, like knowledge, is

[143]

power—power to do good and to be useful. Both came to us from God. To Him we are accountable for the use we make of them."

In accordance with his idea, so clearly expressed, Huidekoper used much of his wealth for the benefit of the community in which he lived. A great educational institution, for which he was responsible largely, has as one of its buildings Huidekoper Hall, named, however, not by him, but by others for him and his family.

One reason for the desire to do so much for the community was that he had there so many years of happiness. In 1804 he met, in Pittsburgh, Rebecca Colhoon, who was visiting there from her home in Carlisle, Pennsylvania. When he saw her he knew at once that he wished to marry her; "that moment decided my fate," he told her later. But she was not so ready to make up her mind. For a long time she kept her ardent suitor in despair. More than once she gave a regretful negative to Huidekoper's ardent pleadings. When the lover told of her rejection of his suit to his half-brother Jan, once privy councillor to the king of the Netherlands, the affectionate relative wrote in a manner that seems, perhaps, a bit startling to Americans whose relatives do not interfere in such questions as much as Europeans:

"I cannot refrain from shaking my head at the manner of her refusal; I confess that I do not understand it. Sincere, and to declare that her heart is free; sincere, and to say that respect and friendship were given to you, and sincerely to mean that she does not wish to marry. . . . Were we not so far away from each other I should come to investigate the matter in person. . . ."

On September 1, 1806, the brother's prophecies were fulfilled; Rebecca Colhoon became mistress of the spacious

ANDREW ATKINSON HUMPHREYS, 1838
(In the Absence of a Portrait of the Father of the American
Navy, This Picture of a Descendant Is Treasured Because It
- Is Said to Be Like the Ancestor.)

HAVERFORD FRIENDS' MEETING HOUSE, NEAR PHILADELPHIA.
THE LEFT OR SOUTHERN END WAS BUILT IN 1700

Huidekoper home in Meadville. There she reigned for thirty-three years. Husband and children were devoted to her.

The human quality of her husband was never revealed in a more telling manner than in the letter he wrote to Mrs. Wallace, in Philadelphia, on October 27, 1839:

"You, my kind friend, have yourself known affliction, and you will know how to sympathize with me in my bereavement. I have lost my Rebecca. She expired Yesterday after an illness of ten or twelve days, with the most perfect composure and resignation. You, my good Friend, know how happy I was in my domestic relations; and now a break has been made in them which can never be healed. But I must not complain. God has been merciful, very merciful to me. He spared my kind good wife to me while my Children were young, and has only taken her away after my children had all grown up, and when the increasing infirmities of old age began to come upon her. Besides, though much has been taken away, there is yet much left to me to bless the evening of life. I am surrounded by good affectionate children, who at all times strive to make me happy, and who, on this mournful occasion, redouble their efforts to make me feel what a treasure I have left in their love. With such around me I cannot be unhappy. My God, by his Spirit, guides me in the performance of my duties, while my life here is continued. In His own good time He will call me home to be reunited to her who for thirty-three years was the Joy and Comfort of my life."

Just such a letter as any loving husband might write about his wife! Then why print it here? Because it helps to picture as a real man one of the noble pioneers who helped in a marvelous manner to make America!

CHAPTER VIII

GLIMPSES OF JOSHUA HUMPHREYS, "FATHER OF THE AMERICAN NAVY"

A MAN WHO CAME FROM WALES

IN 1682, a little while before William Penn reached America, Daniel Humphreys came from Wales to Pennsylvania, bringing with him a letter of good character from the Quarterly Meeting of Friends. He was the pioneer, commissioned to prepare the way for his widowed mother, Elizabeth Humphreys, and her four other children. When the mother followed, in 1683, she, too, had a letter from the Society of Friends at Merionethshire, Wales. This document shows that sixteen Friends vouched for her as "a woman worthy of our recommendation, for an honest, faithful woman, that has been serviceable in her place, and praiseworthy in her Conversation among us." The four children were described as "of honest parents and whom we have known as tender Plants, growing in that work, the knowledge of which is the truth and grace of God."

The letter refers also to Daniel, "already gone into Pennsylvania, about twelve months since." This dutiful son had made ready a home for his mother and his brothers and sisters, on a farm seven miles west of the Schuylkill River. The successor of the original shelter he built for them may still be seen on the Haverford Road, near Ardmore Junction, Pennsylvania. This humble log cabin, built about 1730, is the smallest portion of the attractive Pont Reading House. The middle portion, with its stately pillars, was built about 1760. The third part, the front, was erected in 1813 by Joshua Humphreys, grandson of the original Daniel. Much of the furniture for this historic house was made from the forest near by, or was brought from France where Joshua's son Clement was sent on a mission by John Adams.

When the Friends wished to build, near the Humphreys farm, Daniel gave them the land where they erected, in 1700, the quaint stone Haverford Meeting House, which still attracts the attention of those who travel along the Eagle Road. In the burying-ground close by, along the wall, are graves of various members of the Humphreys family, in double rows.

For generations the family was prominent among the Friends, but during the Revolution the connection was broken, Joshua's determination to give his assistance to the colonies in the War of Independence leading the advocates of peace at any price to read him out of meeting. Yet the name of the family is written indelibly in the history of the Society and its memorials. For many years a town long associated with the Quakers bore their name; only within recent years did Humphreysville become Bryn Mawr.

When Daniel sought a wife he succeeded in persuading Mary, daughter of Thomas Wynne, the first Speaker of the Provincial Assembly of Pennsylvania, to enter his home. Among their six or seven children was Charles, who was a member of the Provincial Assembly from 1763 to 1776. He was one of the seven men who represented

Pennsylvania in the first Continental Congress in 1774, and he became a member of the congresses of 1775 and 1776. He did not, however, sign the Declaration of Independence, for he did not think that separation of the colonies from the Crown was the best method to solve the difficulties of which the people complained. With him in this belief were several others from Pennsylvania, who felt themselves bound by their instructions from the legislature not to sanction or support any such measure. Though these instructions were withdrawn on June 8, 1776, Humphreys did not change his own views. These were based, in part, on the fact that Pennsylvania had won from the Crown certain recognitions of popular rights, and the charter given to William Penn provided definitely for taxation without consent.

A MAN WHO COULD KEEP SECRETS

The Humphreys family is the proud possessor of a document which tells of the brief service of Charles Humphreys in the Continental Congress. This is dated, "In Congress, November 9, 1775." It reads:

"Resolved, That every member of this Congress considers himself, under the ties of virtue, honour, & love of his Country not to divulge directly or indirectly any matter or thing agitated or debated in Congress before the same shall have been determined, without leave of Congress; nor any matter or thing determined in Congress which a Majority of the Congress shall order to be kept secret, and that if any member shall violate this agreement he shall be expelled this Congress, & deemed an enemy to the liberties of America & liable to be treated as such

& that every member signify his consent to this agreement by signing the same."

Then followed twenty-eight names. John Hancock's characteristic signature was placed prominently, while Robert Morris, Samuel Adams, John Adams, and Benjamin Franklin also had place. Each signer received a copy in manuscript. Strictly speaking, however, there were no copies; each document was a duplicate, written in full, and signed in person.

It is of interest to know that the copy preserved so long in the Humphreys family is framed in wood taken from the frigate *Constitution*, when she was repaired at Boston, in 1836. The propriety of this use of the wood of the old ship will become apparent to readers of this chapter.

Daniel Humphreys's oldest son was Joshua, whose chief claim to fame is that he was the father of another Joshua, who became the Father of the American Navy.

Joshua was born June 7, 1751. In 1765, when his parents moved to Philadelphia, he was apprenticed to Jonathan Penrose, shipbuilder, who is described as "a gentleman of the highest respectability." He had not served his full term when Mr. Penrose died, but he knew the business of ship construction so well that the widow turned to him as the best man available to complete a ship then on the stocks.

When he became his own master he began to build vessels on his own account, in partnership with John Wharton. When he was still in his early twenties the Philadelphia Committee of Safety asked him to build a galley, the first armed vessel built in the Revolution. Later he was asked to build, "at the continental ship-yard," the frigate *Randolph*, "that gallant little American ship"—to quote the words of Hampton L. Carson—"which, carrying the flag under Captain Nicholas Biddle, in September, 1777, was attacked by the *Yarmouth,* a British ship twice her size. In a desperate battle when Biddle found himself doomed to defeat, because overpowered by a more powerful adversary, rather than strike his flag, he blew up his ship and perished with all his crew."

The fleet which sailed in 1776 under the guidance of Commodore Ezek Hopkins was built by Humphreys for "the Marine Committee." The Rattlesnake Flag was the ensign of this fleet, and Paul Jones was one of the officers who received orders from Hopkins, a pioneer in the glorious naval activities during the Revolution when more than eight hundred British vessels were captured, together with five thousand prisoners!

A MAN WHO COULD BUILD SHIPS

But the greatest service rendered by Joshua Humphreys to his country came in the year following 1793. In January of that year there was endless debate in Congress as to the necessity of a navy for the young country.

There were those who felt that ships must be provided which would challenge the supremacy of Great Britain on the sea. Others declared that, since it was impossible for the infant country to have a large navy, it was useless to think of doing anything.

Joshua Humphreys, who had won greater skill than ever by commercial shipbuilding during the ten years after the close of the Revolution, wrote a letter to Robert Morris which offered a simple and wise solution of the difficulty:

Southwark, January 6, 1793.

Robert Morris, Esq.

Sir:

From the present appearance of affairs, I believe it is time this country was possessed of a Navy; but as that is yet to be raised, I have ventured a few ideas on that subject.

Ships that compose the European Navys are generally distinguished by their rates; but as the situations and depths of water of our coast and Harbours are different in some degree from those in Europe, & as our navy must for a considerable time be inferior in numbers we are to consider what size ships will be most formidable and be an over match for those of an Enemy, such Frigates as in blowing weather would be an over match for double deck Ships, & in light winds, to evade coming to action, or double deck Ships as would be an over match for common double deck Ships, and in blowing Weather superior to Ships of three Decks, or in calm weather or light winds to outsail them. Ships built on those principles will render those of an Enemy in a degree useless, or require a greater number before they dare attack our Ships.

Frigates I suppose will be the first object and none ought to be built less than 150 feet Keel to carry 28.32 pounders or 30.24 pounders on the main gun deck and 12 pounders on the quarter deck. Those ships should have scantling equal to 74s and I believe may be built of Red cedar & live oak for about twenty four pounds per Ton. . . .

As such Ships will cost a large sum of money they should be built of the best materials, that could possibly be procured, the beams for the decks should be of the best Carolina pine & the lower Futtocks & Knees if possible of Live Oak. . . . All timbers should be Framed and bolted together before they are raised.

Further suggestions were made in this letter. When this was brought to the attention of those interested, there was, of course, vigorous opposition. What folly to talk of 24 pounders on a single deck! George W. Custis, Martha Washington's grandson, wrote a letter in 1844 which told of the surprise and opposition the proposal called forth. But Humphreys persisted and gave such excellent and forcible reasons for his plan that the same was adopted by the Government in all its extent.

General Knox, Secretary of War, sought a conference with the writer. This led to the message from General Knox, on April 12, 1794, asking Humphreys to prepare, immediately, "the models for the frames of the frigates proposed." On June 21, 1794, he was asked to lose no time in erecting the building for making the molds. He was to "negotiate with several of the most eminent carpenters" and win them to "engage with the Cheapest."

One week later a further letter announced his appointment as "Constructor or Master Builder of a forty-four Gun Ship, to be built at the port of Philadelphia, at the rate of compensation of Two thousand dollars per annum."

On July 24 the "Constructor of the Navy of the United States" was asked to send the molds for five other frigates to Norfolk, Baltimore, New York, Boston, and Portsmouth.

The first frigate, built in Philadelphia, was the *United States*. An incident of the building was told by George Washington Custis, years later:

"I well remember visiting with Washington the *United States* Frigate at Southwark, when her keel was laid, & stern & stern Foot only up. The Chief expressed his admiration at the great size of the Vessell that was to be. Commodore Barry was present, & Mr. Humphreys explained to the President, several of his Cabinet, and other persons who were present, the great principles which he had originated & was now by consent of the authorities putting into successful practice, all of which met with Washington's approbation & he expressed himself on his

[152]

return to his Coach much gratified with all he had seen & heard in this, his *First visit to an American Navy Yard*."

Just before the launching of the frigate, the *Aurora*, a Philadelphia newspaper, made a furious attack on President Washington. Clement Humphreys, the nineteen-year-old son of the Constructor of the Navy, saw the publisher of the paper, Benjamin Franklin Bache, at the launching. The boy attacked the libeler, on April 14, 1797, and thrashed him soundly. Of course he was arrested for his act, but when he appeared in court, he refused to plead "not guilty." Proudly he owned his conduct: "Yes, I am guilty. I caned the editor, undoubtedly." When he was convicted and fined $50 and required to give bond for $2,000 for keeping the peace, admiring citizens of Philadelphia paid the fine and supplied the bond.

A MAN WHO COULD SPEAK PLAINLY

One of the letters sent to Constructor Humphreys by Secretary Knox spoke of a "Mr. Fox who is under your direction." This Josiah Fox, an Englishman, appears later, in connection with the construction of the *Chesapeake*, one of the four frigates authorized by the Act of 1797. When it was found that there was no one at Norfolk competent to build the vessel, Fox, who was with Humphreys in the mold loft, was appointed. Before he reached Norfolk, "the keel had been spliced & laid for the 44 gun ship to be built there," Joshua Humphreys wrote. Yet "the keel was afterwards cut to that of a 36 gun ship, on a new draft drawn by Mr. Fox, differing from the one I had forwarded. By what authority the alteration was made I never could ascertain."

Perhaps it was due to jealousy. That Fox claimed to be Constructor of the Navy, and that Humphreys tried to make him realize the folly of the claim, is apparent from a letter to him written from Philadelphia on July 25, 1797.

"Sir: I rec'd your letter of yesterday purporting the Secty of War 'being very desirous that the frigate *Constellation* should be launched in the safest manner and with as little expence to the United States as possible, and judging that your [my] advice may be necessary to assist Mr. Stoddard in performing that service, desires me &c.'

"I have waited on him. It is with pleasure & with alacrity I shall always receive and obey while in the service of the United States any order of the Secretary of War, but, Sir, I cannot receive hereafter or attend to any directions from you, altho directed by the Secr. of War. While you style yourself Naval Constructor, you must know that my station in the Service of the United States requires no direction from a *Naval Constructor.* You also know that *I am at the head of that Department,* and when you direct a letter to me let it be done in Style as *Clerk of the Marine* Department. Whenever the Secretary deems my Services no longer necessary, you may then to other persons assume such title as your Vanity may suggest."

The letter was addressed most carefully to "Mr. Josiah Fox, Clerk in the Marine Department, War Office."

While, naturally, Contractor Humphreys was, theoretically, gratified to learn of the fine performances of the vessels constructed strictly in accordance with his proposal, which never lost a battle in single combat, it would have been in keeping with human nature if he had felt like saying "I told you so!" when he heard that the *Chesapeake* under Lawrence in the encounter with the *Shannon*

Phil.a July 25 – 1797

Sir

I rec.d your letter of Yesterday purporting the Sec.y of War, "being very desirous that the frigate Constitution should be launched in the safest manner and with as little expence to the United States as possible and judging that your advice may be necessary to assist Mr Stoddard in performing that service, desires me &.c:

I have waited on him, It is with pleasure & with alacrity I shall always receive and obey while in the service of the United States any orders of the Secretary of War, but Sir, I cannot receive hereafter or attend to any directions from you, altho' directed by the Sec.y of War – while, yourself Naval Constructor, you must know, that my station in the service of the United States require no directions from a Naval Constructor, you also know that I am at the head of that department – and when you direct a letter to me let it be done in Style as Clerk of the Marine department; Whenever the Secretary my services no longer necessary, you may to other persons assume such title as your Vanity may suggest –

                    I am &

                              J. H. me

Mr Josiah Fox
Clerk in the Marine department
        War Office

War Department
April 12 1794

Sir

    I request that you would please imme-
diately to prepare the models for the frame of the
frigates proposed by you in your letter of this date
and also that you would please to prepare an
accurate draft, and models of the same. the latter
to have the frame accurately described —

    I am
        Sir
          Your obed't Servant
            H Knox.

Mr Joshua Humphreys

GLIMPSES OF JOSHUA HUMPHREYS

was captured. Some such verdict as the following might
have been given: "The natural consequence of interference with my plan by a bumptious clerk, whose conceit led
him to turn a forty-four gun frigate into a thirty-six!"

But what joy he had in thinking of the performances of
the other five vessels—*Constitution,* or *Old Ironsides,
Congress, United States, Constellation* and *President!*
Their first service was in the war with Tripoli, when they
were guided to glorious victory by Decatur, Truxton,
Bainbridge, Hull, Stewart and Jones. Then came the
War of 1812 when these vessels, already ten to fifteen
years old, had their wonderful part in sea conflicts which
resulted in the capture of some fifteen hundred British
ships and twelve thousand prisoners.

Lord Nelson was indeed a prophet when, after noting
the performance of Humphreys's ships on their visit to
European waters, he said: "Those American ships will
cost the British navy very anxious thought in the future."

A MAN WHOSE SHIPS WERE CONQUERORS

The first shot in the War of 1812 was fired by the
President, commanded by John Rodgers. Until 1814
she went on her triumphant way. Once, under the leadership of Truxton, she made the *Insurgent* lower her flag,
and was captured at length only after a fierce contest with
four attacking British frigates. When the vessel was
taken to London for exhibit as a trophy of war, she advertised the glories of the American Navy as well as the
prowess of the British heroes.

After surviving the War of 1812, and taking part in
many contests in future years, the *Congress* met her death
from the Confederate ram *Merrimac,* in March, 1862,

in Hampton Roads, Virginia. There the vessel which had heralded a new day in naval construction, sank beneath the waves only at the birth of ironclads which were to transform the navies of the world.

The *United States* was triumphant over all foes, and met her end only when old age made necessary the demolition of the vessel which, under Decatur, fought the *Macedonian* to a standstill, and finally won a signal triumph.

The *Constellation's* final service was as a receiving ship at Newport. There thousands of new-born sailors became enthusiastic for their country as they trod the wooden decks of the frigate that justified the faith of Washington in plans so revolutionary that many wise leaders shook their heads when they were told of Humphreys's proposals.

And the *Constitution,* or *Old Ironsides,* as she was soon rechristened by popular approval! From the days of her conflict with the *Guerrière* the mere mention of her name was enough to arouse enthusiasm. Read what Hampton L. Carson, in an address on the Humphreys family, says of one incident in her triumphant career which showed how clearly Humphreys judged the needs of the Navy when he designed her:

"When the *Constitution* first encountered the *Guerrière,* the *Guerrière* was part of an English squadron of six large ships. Captain Isaac Hull, who then commanded her, saw at a glance that he could not fight a squadron, so he determined to put the sailing qualities of his vessel to the test. He drew off and ran away from them. They pursued in line. Soon they were spread out. He saw then that he could pick his antagonist if he could get the British ships at a sufficient distance from each other so as to give him the advantage of the wind. Think of what it was

[156]

to command a ship in those days. I am talking of sailing vessels, not of steam. There is comparatively little merit now in selecting positions for a battleship because steam will put a ship against wind and waves in any position desired, but before the days of steam, when the wind blew hard and a captain had to get the weather gauge of his enemy and maneuver in such a way as to rake him with a broadside and not be raked in turn, it required the supremest degree of seamanship. Hull had it, and he had the ship, and he had the builder of Philadelphia behind him who had planned it all. The result was that he was drawing away from the British squadron just to his own taste, when a dead calm fell upon him. Of course, even swift ships cannot sail in a calm, and the difficulty was double, for the calm had not struck the pursuing squadron; the British began to overtake him. Hull, with quick thought, looked ahead and saw rough water, indicating a breeze, ahead of him a mile away; instantly he put out his boats, put strong men in them carrying anchors and long ropes; the boats were rowed until the lines were taut, anchors were dropped, and the ship was then kedged or pulled right up to the anchors; the operation was repeated and the ship was drawn through the smooth water before the British got on to the device. Hull got into the ruffled water and began to recover the wind. By that time the British squadron was becalmed. Later, when the *Guerriére* was far ahead, Hull wheeled and in less than an hour knocked the British frigate all to pieces. *'Old Ironsides'* had achieved her first victory."

In the letter from which quotation has been made already, written by George Washington Parke Custis, to Colonel Humphreys, grandson of Joshua Humphreys, he closed his paragraph about the frigate by saying: "Let Victory tell the rest." Victory has told the rest!

A MAN WHO HAD A RIGHT TO BE PROUD

But the crowning glory of the career of this veteran of forty-two battles, which never knew defeat, was won on the day when her construction as well as the masterly seamanship of her commander, Captain Charles Stewart, enabled him to triumph over the two British ships, the *Cyane* and the *Levant.* The tale of how Stewart sailed his vessel between them, firing a withering broadside into the *Cyane,* then another into the *Levant,* while these surprised and more unwieldy opponents could not maneuver so as to get in a return broadside, is a classic in the annals of the American navy.

Long may the *Constitution* survive to inspire Americans as they enjoy the peace that makes necessary no longer a monster program of navy-building!

Humphreys's service in naval construction continued through the administrations of Washington and John Adams, and for a part of that of Thomas Jefferson. Jefferson, who was opposed to the government's naval policy, sent him into retirement. He lived until 1838, rejoicing in the evidence that his work was successful. Two years before his death he wrote an interesting letter to Josiah Barker, Naval Constructor at Charlestown Navy Yard:

"On my son Samuel's return from Boston, he presented me with a very handsome walking cane made out of a part of the frigate *Constitution* (*Old Ironsides*) which was taken out of her while under your repairs. This cane is of double value to me on account of its having been taken from one of the frigates I constructed in the year 1794, forty-two years ago. . . . The great mark of attention you have shown me in sending me so beautiful a present has made me proud, although in my eighty-sixth year of age, a time of life when I ought to be more humble."

A later gift came to the Humphreys family after the Naval Constructor's death. A model for a frigate, carved with a pen-knife by Joshua Humphreys, was discovered in the mold-loft of the Philadelphia Navy Yard. This was sent to Pont Reading, where it was a treasured possession until it was sent by the family to Independence Hall, Philadelphia. There visitors look with pride on this early evidence of Humphrey's genius for when they examine it they find on the board to which the model is fastened the lettering, "J. H. fecit, 1777."

But Joshua Humphreys's gifts to his country did not end with the frigates which were to transform the navies of the world, nor even with the work done in later years. He gave to the nation a son Samuel, who inherited his father's tastes and abilities.

A MAN WHO COULD NOT BE BOUGHT

As Chief of Construction in the Navy Yards of the United States from 1816 to 1846 he planned and superintended the building of a number of fine ships. Chief among them was the *Franklin,* a vessel that attracted wide attention by reason of its size and seaworthy qualities.

The brilliant work done by Samuel Humphreys led to an incident that reflected even greater credit on him than did his vessels. In 1824 a Russian emissary named Zaskoff asked Richard Peters of Philadelphia:

"How is it that American ships are superior to those

of any other navy in the world so far as their sailing qualities are concerned?"

Of course the answer was simple: "They are better built and better planned."

This gave the Russian his opportunity: "The Czar, Alexander, who sent me here, is very anxious to build up a navy, and has commissioned me to find the finest shipbuilder in the world. He wishes vessels which are fast sailors, and are capable of inflicting serious injury within a short time, notwithstanding heavy pounding by the waves."

The result of this conversation was an interview between the Russian emissary and Samuel Humphreys, arranged for by Mr. Peters. After a brief conversation, Humphreys was offered an engagement in Russia with a salary of $60,000 a year, with town and country residences to be maintained by the Emperor, together with carriages, horses, and servants. If this was not sufficient, Mr. Humphreys was to name his own terms.

The American asked for a day to consider this offer. Then he returned, and replied:

"The salary is greater than I could earn, more than I need, more than I want, more than I could use; as to town and country houses, I need but one, and that should be near my business. As to the coaches and servants, I always walk and wait on myself, and should find myself unable to control a multitude of servants; I do not know that I possess the talents my friend Mr. Peters ascribes to me, but I do know, and feel, that whether my merit be great or small, I owe it all to the flag of my country, and that is the debt I must pay."

The answer was heard by Joseph Hopkinson. His face

GENERAL PUTNAM LANDING AT MARIETTA, OHIO

JONATHAN DAYTON

lighted up, his right hand was waved about his head, and he exclaimed:

"Had he done otherwise, he would not have been his father's child. Mr. Adams must hear of this."

That President Adams did hear of it, is evident from his visit to Mr. Humphreys's office several weeks later, when the President informed him that he was to be the head of the Bureau of Construction and Repairs, which was to displace the "Commissioners of the Navy."

CHAPTER IX

JOHN CLEVES SYMMES, LAND KING OF THE MIAMI PURCHASE

IN THE days when the United States was young and the settlements had progressed westward to what seemed the frontier, the Alleghany Mountains, the people were looking for homes beyond these barriers. The government had millions of acres for them, so, with lavish prodigality, whole townships and future counties by the dozen and the score were offered to them in the most absurd fashion.

This era in the country's history produced a number of men who dreamed of planting cities, building towns and clearing forests for hungry homeseekers—men, for instance, like Moses Cleaveland, who founded the city that bears his name, though minus one unnecessary letter; General Rufus Putnam, of Marietta fame; and Robert Morris, the financier of the Revolution.

Here is the story of the strange career of John Cleves Symmes, who bargained for a little kingdom on the banks of the Ohio, held it for a season, then saw it slip from his grasp as he was overwhelmed by the debts that came because he had attempted more than any one man could accomplish.

THE MAKING OF A PATRIOT

Southold, Long Island, was the birthplace, on July 21, 172, of John Cleves Symmes, descendant of a long line

JOHN CLEVES SYMMES

of colonial worthies, among whom was numbered a man appointed by King Charles II to examine into the conduct of Governor Winthrop of Boston, and a captain in the Pequot Indian War against the Narragansett, King Philip. Little is known of his youth, but that he became a schoolteacher at an early age, and later was a surveyor, as were so many of the pioneers, George Washington included. In 1770 he secured a farm in the frontier county of Sussex, in New Jersey, where he built a home which he called "Solitude." There he spent years of quiet, and there he returned for peace and rest during the troubled period of the Revolution.

Sometimes this John Cleves Symmes has been confused with another man of the same name, his uncle, who did the country a favor, in the midst of the fevered days of war, by giving it a good chance to laugh. For this Symmes wrote a book on the "History of Concentric Spheres, Polar Voids, and Open Poles." And in 1813 he issued a card addressed "To all the world," in which he said:

"I declare the earth is hollow and habitable within: containing a number of hollow, Concentrik spheres, one within the other, and that it is open at the poles, twelve or sixteen degrees. I pledge my life in support of this truth, and I am ready to explore the hollow if the world will support and aid me in the undertaking."

This card, dated from Ohio, he signed "John Cleves Symmes, late Captain of Infantry."

"Symmes' Hole" was the name given by the wits of the day to the fantastic location which Symmes offered to explore. "As deep as Symmes' Hole" became a byword.

The nephew of this patron of terrestrial oddities was too well-balanced to go off on any such tangent. He became a lawyer of ability, and he used his knowledge of

[163]

the law for the benefit of his country. One who has written of his life says that he was "a real jurist, an enlightened legislator, and a sturdy patriot. From the beginning of the struggle with the Mother Country he was an unwavering friend of the Colonies, and contributed in no small degree to the success of the cause."

For fourteen years, beginning in 1774, his varied service continued. First he was chairman of Sussex county's committee of safety. In 1776 he was sent with a battalion of militia, of which he was colonel, to intercept the British who were marching to interfere with Washington as he retreated across New Jersey. In this mission he succeeded; the British were compelled to take the back-track. He helped to erect fortifications in Manhattan and Long Island; he had much to do with the fortifications on the Delaware River; he made four incursions into Long Island when the British were in possession, and on one of these occasions, with four men to help him, he captured a British schooner, taking ten prisoners. He was a member of New Jersey's Provincial Congress in June, 1776, which, at Burlington, adopted a constitution, and he was chairman of the committee charged to report the paper. This was passed on July 2, two days before Congress adopted the Declaration of Independence. This constitution was so well framed that it "remained the fundamental law of the state for sixty-eight years."

It is of interest to note, in passing, that this legislator's pay for the time spent at Burlington that year amounted to six shillings per day. "Quite economical when viewed in the light of modern legislation!" was the remark of a student of Symmes's career. "And then compare the brains with the price."

In August, 1776, when there was a contest for the

governorship of the new state between Richard Stockton and William Livingston, he cast the deciding vote which gave to Livingston the prize. It was probably an accident that, years later, when financial difficulties crowded upon him, the executors of the estate of Richard Stockton helped put on the screws that made him writhe in torture. Even more interesting, however, is the fact that Symmes's third wife was the daughter of Governor Livingston. She was called "Pretty Susan" by André in his poem, "The Cow Chase."

Service in the legislature did not interfere with military usefulness. When there was anxiety because the New Jersey soldiers at Fort Ticonderoga, disgruntled by reason of trying conditions, were determined to leave for home instead of reënlisting, he was asked to make an investigation on the ground, and to do his best to persuade them to remain in the army. Later he reported:

"Your Commissioner found the soldiers destitute of money, articles of dress; supplies of every kind they want, but shoes and stockings they are in the last necessity, for many have neither to their feet."

Then he went on to tell of the "unvanquished ardour" of these heroes, most of whom told him that they would reënlist at the expiration of their time.

As Justice of the Supreme Court of New Jersey, a position he held for many years after 1777, he was entrusted with important cases. Among the most famous of these was that of James Morgan, on trial for the murder of the Rev. James Caldwell, the patriot parson, "who fell a victim to a Continental soldier who was thought to have been bribed by those whose enmity the chaplain had earned during the conflict."

After Symmes removed to Morris county in 1785, he

was sent once again to the legislature, but his term was interrupted when, later in the same year, he was sent to Congress at Philadelphia.

THE MAKING OF A MIGHTY LANDHOLDER

While he was in Congress the stage was set for the first act in the drama of his later years.

But before the first act came, of course, the prelude. Of this the hero was Major Benjamin Stites, a New Jerseyman, who, in 1786, led a party of men from Kentucky over the Ohio in pursuit of Indians who had stolen horses from the settlements there. At least one result of the expedition was to reveal the delightful country between the Great Miami and the Little Miami rivers, tributaries of the Ohio, north of that river. This favorite country of the Indians had been seen by Captain Byrd who in June, 1780, with 600 British and Indians, came down the Great Miami and crossed into Kentucky. George Rogers Clark also had seen it in the same year, when he was on his way to destroy the Shawnee towns on the Little Miami.

Both of these men were captivated by the country, but the British commander was not in position to think of colonization, and Clark's interests were elsewhere. So it was left to Stites to bear to the East the tidings of the new-found paradise. When he was in New Jersey he told his story to Symmes, and had little difficulty in persuading that careful legislator to become as enthusiastic as he was himself.

Why not found a state between the Miamis? Symmes knew that he could not do this without assistance. But he was familiar with the manner in which New Jersey had been exploited by the absentee landlords who made up the East Jersey and West Jersey Proprietors. Why not have a modification of their organization for the vast country in Ohio of which Stites persuaded him to seek control? He, therefore, asked a number of his friends to join him in the purchase from Congress of a million or two acres in the Northwest Territory. These friends told him to submit a plan for the holding company he had in mind.

Symmes proposed that twenty-four men join in the purchase. Among them were Elias Boudinot, General Jonathan Dayton, Dr. Witherspoon and Major Stites. He, Symmes, was to be their agent, and he was to have 40,000 acres for himself. For these he was to pay the proprietors the exact sum which would be paid by them to the government. His pay for his toil and skill in engineering the Miami Purchase was to be any surplus received for these lands. Until May 1, 1788, lands were to be offered to all who would buy at the price paid to the United States for the acreage. But after that time the price would be increased one-third, the profits to be deposited with a special officer appointed by the association, these to be used later in building roads.

The reservation of these lands for Symmes's benefit endangered the enterprise at the very outset. Of course there was bitter criticism. "The proprietors have taken the best for themselves!" was the accusation. Once the New Jersey *Journal* spoke of the emigration to distant countries, "to the Emolument of certain Gentlemen who have a particular genius for landjobbing." The criticisms made Symmes impatient. "This is my affair," he said. He declared that he felt under no obligations to explain, and added, "I am sorry that I cannot please everybody." Another reservation was made for Major Stites—a sort of Discoverer's Share. To him were sold 10,000 acres of the choicest land in the district, near the mouth of the Little Miami, where, in November, 1788, the new proprietor laid out the city of Columbia.

These various plans were made before the request to Congress, on August 29, 1787, for 2,000,000 acres, extending between the Great and Little Miami rivers, and extending above the Ohio River as far as necessary. The request was approved by the Board of the Treasury and $82,000 was paid on account by the associates in the Company.

For this magnificent section of the Northwest Territory, the Company was to pay, nominally, one dollar per acre. But there was to be an allowance of one-third for inferior lands. Payment was to be in specie, or in public certificates. One-seventh might be paid in Revolutionary land warrants given to soldiers by a grateful country. Many soldiers were glad to dispose of these warrants for a nominal sum, and Symmes and his associates procured for themselves a lucrative return for handling them.

The agreement, which was never kept, was made to pay $200,000 down, and $200,000 more within a month after the receipt of a survey. A deed for 600,000 acres was to be given when the second payment was made.

Unfortunately Symmes was too impatient to wait until the survey had been made before issuing warrants to purchasers. Stites, as already related, secured one of the first of these, while others were given deeds for thousands of acres. Thus was presented the excuse for the coming of future trouble.

The haste of the land speculator was evidenced also by Symmes's departure to what he viewed as a field of triumph. In the summer of 1788, before the contract with the government had been reduced to writing, he began his journey to the West, which a facetious pamphleteer described as a jaunt to take intending emigrants on a balloon trip to the moon, which would undoubtedly discover fertile lands beyond the Alleghanies!

After three weeks, Symmes was at Bedford, Pennsylvania. There we have a glimpse of him and his company from the pen of the Rev. Manasseh Cutler, himself one of the heroes of the Marietta settlement, to the east of the Miami, and also on the Ohio. The clergyman wrote:

"Judge Symmes—John Cleves—had taken lodgings at the best tavern [in Bedford]; we, however, made shift to get lodgings in the same house. . . . Judge Symmes was complaisant . . . and had his daughter Anna with him, one or two women with husbands, six heavy wagons, one stage wagon, and a chair—a two-wheeled covered carriage for two persons, thirty-one horses, three carpenters, and one mason."

On July 18, 1788, Judge Symmes told of the difficulty of sending off his first company:

"I have even contracted several fitts of the ague and fever merely from fatigue. I have at length started off eight four-horse waggons, and thirty people, and have now twenty-five horses and as many people feeding dayly at my private expense."

At length the little company of pioneers reached Devours Ferry on the Monongahela, and from there went thirty-five miles to Pittsburgh. Symmes embarked his people and baggage on the river, but his horses he sent overland to Wheeling. There he was to overtake them and load them on the flatboats which were used for transportation on the Ohio. These boats were "made of green oak plank, fastened by wooden pins to a frame of timber,

and caulked with tow. These were called Kentucky boats."
The materials of which they were composed were found
to be of great utility in the construction of temporary
buildings for safety, and for protection from the inclem-
ency of the weather, after they had arrived at their destination.

AN AMBITIOUS SPECULATOR MADE ANXIOUS

But Symmes was not to get away from Pittsburgh so
early as he thought. For when he left the East so pre-
cipitately, somehow the idea gained currency that he
planned to get possession of the tract on the Ohio River,
then defy Congress either to collect the price of the land
or to oust him from the territory. When the report
reached Congress, there was alarm, until his associates,
Elias Boudinot and General Dayton, who were members
of that body, succeeded in reassuring them as to the probity of Symmes.

But they thought it the part of wisdom to send a message after him, to secure for them a power of attorney,
which they might use in his absence. The messenger
found him at Pittsburgh. At first the land proprietor
thought he might have to return, but he contented himself
finally with sending the power of attorney.

This power of attorney was used in facilitating consideration of the request made by Symmes in this same year,
1788; a request which showed that the thought of 2,000,-
000 acres was making the purchaser shiver:

"I beg leave to relinquish my former purchase, upon
condition that your honours be pleased to enter into a
new contract with me for a part of the same lands, of one

million acres, fronting on the Ohio, and extending inland from the Ohio between the great Miami river and the little Miami river the whole breadth."

On October 15, 1788, the new contract was signed by the Treasury Board. Of the 1,000,000 acres in this grant, 123,297 acres were to be possessed in view of the original payment. When $82,198 more was paid, there would be a release of 246,594 acres. The total obligation was for $571,428.60 cash, and $75,238 army rights, or $666,-666.60 in all. Payment might be made in United States certificates of debt, which were worth at the time five shillings on the pound.

But the Board of the Treasury was not willing to agree to the boundaries proposed by Symmes. Why should he have the frontage on the Ohio between the two Miamis, provided with his first purchase, when he was buying but half the land? He must be content with a frontage of twenty miles on La Belle Rivière. This distance was to be measured eastward from the Great Miami. The distance between the two rivers, when measured along the Ohio, was more than thirty-four miles.

This proposal did not suit Symmes. For one thing it would not include the land of Stites on the Little Miami, for which deed had been given already. Then the dream of the New Jersey promoter had always been for land between the two rivers. He insisted that the geography of the country between the rivers was too little known to afford sufficient information to enable him to agree to the bounds proposed by the Government. His request, therefore, was that he be permitted to enter the country, with settlers, and to make a survey, as a basis for a map.

Brief investigation led him to be even more insistent on the boundaries he sought. He said that "the hunters of the country" informed him that the Ohio and the Little Miami approached each other toward the mouth. This "amazeing doubling of the Little Miami" on the Ohio made the distance between them, at a point six miles up the Ohio and ten miles up the Miami, less than a mile. Thus the space between the Miamis, close to the mouth, was but twenty-seven miles, and a limitation of the tract to twenty miles frontage on the Ohio would make necessary going too far back from the Ohio, where dangers from Indians would be increased and access to the territory would be too difficult.

Yet, for all his discontent, Symmes said he would always "have the caution not to exceed what I have their concession to"; he accepted the land they granted. "But I think I ought to have more!" were the words which showed that his consent was given with great reluctance. Another indication was his failure to confine grants to the twenty-mile frontage. That he realized the danger of at least one of these grants was shown by his statement in a letter to Jonathan Dayton, called forth probably by a proposal in Congress to dispossess Stites:

"If Mr. Stites is ousted of the settlement he has made with great danger & difficulty at the mouth of the little Miami, it cannot be either politic or just."

The dissatisfaction of the Government with conditions led to talk of giving orders to the commander of Fort Harmar, near Marietta, to use his troops to dispossess the unauthorized settlers. And on July 19, 1791, Governor St. Clair of the Northwest Territory signed a proclamation in which he warned settlers that the lands to the east of the Little Miami were the property of the United States. This proclamation was the cause of much bitterness.

VAIN EFFORTS TO PLAY THE GAME

The worried manager of the Miami Purchase, while refusing to set definite boundaries to the tract until he knew more about the land, tried to play the game fairly. He pleaded for surveyors who would make definite reports about the land. The official surveyor, Israel Ludlow, was appointed in 1787, but he did not reach Fort Harmar until 1790, and he waited there for a military escort until 1791. May, 1792, came before he was able to give much information as to the character of the country. Symmes insisted, with reason, that this delay accounted for the confusion as to the boundaries. In the meantime, on November 25, 1788, Symmes sent out his own surveyors, one to each Miami.

There was difficulty in convincing would-be settlers, without a survey, that the land was worth the price asked for it. Yet Symmes was confident. On October 12, 1788, he expressed his opinion that land, especially toward the Great Miami, was worth "a silver dollar the acre," in its present state. Once he expressed his views more fully:

"The extent of country spreading for many miles on both sides of the G. Miami, is beyond all dispute equal, I believe superior in point of soil, water & timber, to any tract of equal contents to be found in the United States. From this Egypt on Miami, in a very few years, will be poured down the stream to the Ohio, the products of the country, from two hundred miles above the mouth of G. Miami; which may be principally collected at a trading town, low down on the banks of that river; where no rival city or town can divide the trade of the river."

But there was reason for pessimism in the midst of such optimism. The second payment must be made. For this

[173]

he depended on "Doct Douner from Boston" for $59,520 for land sold to men whom he sent to the Miami; on "Col. Stelle from Rhode Island" for $26,666.60; on "Mr. Morris Witham from the Province of Main" for $17,600; as well as on a few others. Then "the Kentuckyans," or some of the settlers in Kentucky, had agreed to take ten or twelve townships. How glibly these vast measures for land were spoken by the promoter!

The ten or twelve townships became seventeen townships in another reference. No wonder Symmes said of these lavish purchasers, "They encourage me much." He told how "Major Hutchins with about 300 men has promised me to make a lodgment and piket in a station 60 miles up the Great Miami."

But there was grievous disappointment in store. The Kentuckians proved unreliable; they were captious, they were jealous of a settlement that promised to rival their own colonies south of the Ohio. And Colonel Stelle, in spite of the fact that he advertised in New Jersey papers that he had 20,000 acres for sale, did not complete his contract. He had agreed to pay six shillings and three pence per acre and the surveying and registry fees, but he was not satisfied when he was told that five sections of the land allotted to him had already been sold. He refused to accept a substitute, and accused Symmes of bad faith. "Mr. Stelle very injudiciously judges of me by himself," the proprietor wrote. "He acknowledges that I have not come up to contract, and supposes for this reason that I cannot: but in this he is mistaken: not an attom of the land which he agreed for, have I since sold or agreed to sell."

That word *since* tells the story of Stelle's grievance.

Symmes tried to take comfort from the defection of

Stelle. "The lands which Mr. Stelle negotiated for are incomparably inviting and fine, and will command an immediate sale at a higher price," was the optimistic conclusion. Yet the fact remained that by reason of various failures of land contractors, the second payment was not ready in season. In a letter of May 18, 1789, Symmes made a confession:

"Whether I was premature and rash in the attempt of so considerable a purchase and settlement, or have not made my calculations on well founded principles, or whether it is, that I have those who endeavour to defeat my views, either from Interested or envious motives—I know not, but certain it is, that I have had the mortification to conflict not only with those whose malevolent disposition I had no right to expect anything better; but from those in office and power, unexpected obstructions have been thrown in my way."

Those in authority did show to Symmes many courtesies. Perhaps the greatest of them, as well as the most unexpected, was his appointment, on February 19, 1788, as one of three Federal Judges for the Northwest Territory. Judge Symmes welcomed the appointment, for he felt that it showed the confidence in him of the Government at Washington, and it helped to rehabilitate him in the good opinion of some who had been his critics. "I hope my conduct in my judicial capacity will extinguish their unfavourable sentiments," was his longing statement.

Of course, along with the sense of privilege was a deep feeling of obligation. This was all the greater by reason of the delicacy of the situation created by his appointment. For, in the words of American State Papers, I, 116:

"By the act establishing the government of the North-west Territory, the supreme judicial authority was vested in three judges, two of whom were necessary to form a Court. Their decrees were not appealable. The most of the Settlements and Forts were made on the lands purchased of the Ohio Company [headquarters at Marietta], and Judge Symmes. In the Ohio Company General Putnam was an active director, and in the Miami Purchase Judge Symmes was the principal if not the sole agent. They both were judges. Every land dispute was almost necessarily traced to some act of one or the other of these gentlemen, and they were to sit in judgment on them. Against this condition of things the people protested."

The fact that Judge Symmes continued on the court until 1803, when Ohio became a state, is evidence that the fears of the people proved groundless. He acquitted himself with credit in a place where there was unlimited opportunity for prejudicial decisions.

Not least among his qualifications for the trying post was his unfailing sense of humor. This was brought to bear at one time on the very question of the court's existence. Congress at one time proposed to increase the number of the judges. His comment to General Dayton was that, if a Chief Justice proved necessary, Congress should consider the propriety of having a man "with something above his cravat beside pomatum and powder."

Another instance of his dry humor was given in 1812, when the British captured Detroit. Symmes issued a card in which he said:

"Col. Symmes of the Senior Division of the Ohio Militia presents his compliments to Major General Brock, commanding his Britannic Majesty's force, *white* and *red,* in upper Canada. Colonel Symmes observing by the 4th Article of Capitulation of Detroit to Major General Brock all public arms . . . are to be delivered up; but as no

JOHN CLEVES SYMMES

place of deposit is pointed out by the capitulation, *forty thousand stand of arms,* coming within the description, are at the service of Major General Brock, if his excellency will condescend to *come down and take them."*

THE BATTLE OF THE TOWNS

The witty member of the judiciary did not lose sight of the opportunities before him. He wanted to found a city. The location for this troubled him. But at length he decided on the spot where the Ohio bends at a point farther north than anywhere else west of the Kanawha. There, in February, 1789, he laid the foundation for North Bend.

Farther west a town was laid out at South Bend, but there the situation was not regarded as favorable to a large town. So efforts were concentrated at North Bend, by an enlargement on January 1, 1790, in spite of his feeling, just at first, that this site, too, was unfavorable. Lots could be sold across the point from the Ohio to the Little Miami, and those who moved goods down the latter river would be able to transport them by land across the point, then reship on the Ohio, so as to save sixteen miles of rather difficult navigation.

So far, good. But there seemed to be little chance to build a city there, "unless you raise her like Venice out of the water, or get on the hill with the town." However, in spite of this difficulty, the determination was made to have the site for "Symmes City," between the rivers. "Montock-point on Long Island, invaluable as it has always been to the inhabitants of East Hampton, may be in a few years rivalled by Miami point."

It seemed best to Symmes and his associates, who advised with him from New Jersey, to retain the site at the point as a manor, for their own benefit. Every other one of the lots Symmes hoped to give away, retaining "one for each proprietor, upon condition only of the donees building immediately thereon."

Complaint was made soon that the plans for the new city had not been furthered by the lot holders, in accordance with these agreements. "Not one in six had made any provision for building or for defence. . . . The success of the City depends on the rapidity of the first, and the whole settlement on the spirit of the last. If the proprietors do not begin to build stranger men will."

The formation on January 2, 1790, of Hamilton county, the second in the Northwest Territory, led to rivalry between Losantiville and Symmes City for the location of the county seat. This was never so keen as in the desire of Symmes it should have been. He thought that the choice of his town, not only for the seat of government, but for the fort authorized by the Government, would be the making of his location. But Symmes City missed the fort, and its fate was sealed. Most of the inhabitants removed to the more fortunate center, attracted by the fort with its promised protection from the Indians. Symmes City disappeared; North Bend only remained. To-day one of the chief attractions of that little community is the grave of William Henry Harrison, son-in-law of Symmes, who was Governor of the Northwest Territory, and, later, President of the United States.

Within a year after the organization of Hamilton county, Symmes wrote, sadly, from Cincinnata (Symmes chose this spelling because he thought the feminine form was more fitting in the name of the home of the Cincinnati):

[178]

"The advantage is prodigious which this town is gaining over Northbend, upwards of forty framed and hewed log two-story houses have been and are building since last spring, one builder sets the example for another, and the place already assumes the appearance of a town of some respect—the inhabitants have doubled here within nine months past—while at Northbend we have received but three new families . . . owing to two reasons, principally —the residence of the Army here, and the great demand for labour on buildings is such as to give employment to every class from the Carpenter to the treading of Morter."

THE UNDOING OF A PATRIOTIC VISIONARY

The absence of the troops and the danger of an Indian attack at any moment filled Symmes with anxiety. Of course, he tried his best to reassure those who might be interested in his lands that the Indians were friendly, since Wyandots, Delawares, Ottawas, and Chippewas had united in making a treaty when Governor St. Clair called them into conference at Fort Harmar on December 15, 1788. But the fact remains that the Miami Purchase was looked on as a dangerous country. "The Miami Slaughter House" was the name given it by Kentuckians, who were, in fact, responsible for much of the unfriendliness of the Indians to the whites.

At first the Indians seemed friendly. "They visited the blockhouses freely, spending there whole days and nights." Then the white traders and hunters were welcome in the quarters of the savages when they were overtaken by darkness.

Symmes was not deceived by these events, though he

was eager to minimize the danger. " 'Tis true the Indian has been unexpectedly pacific, but who can vouch for a continuance of peace?" he wrote. One reason for his fear was the fact that the Shawnees had not joined with other tribes in the treaty at Fort Harmar.

Untoward incidents occurred frequently. Once an Indian attempted to collect twenty dollars, owing to him from some white man. He wished to make trouble when those from whom he would collect the amount told him that they knew nothing of debt or debtor. Their position seemed unreasonable to the savage, who felt that "what one white man owed another should pay."

More than once surveying and hunting parties were attacked by Indians. Among the telling stories of Ohio pioneers is that of the death of John Filson, who fell a victim to savage hate when he strayed a short distance from a party of those who were making investigations in the Purchase.

The anxiety of Symmes was increased by the failure of United States troops to come to his assistance, in accordance with the promises on which he counted.

Altogether the burden on the mind of the Pioneer of the Purchase was greater than he could bear. Although, on May 5, 1792, the Government patented to him 311,682 acres, the Board of the Treasury informed him that they considered themselves absolved from the contract of October 15, 1788. This was because of his failure to meet the terms agreed on.

When the limited patent was secured, Symmes found that the larger part of the sales he had made were outside its bounds. He could not give the titles he had promised.

Yet he continued to sell lands outside of his grant, for he thought he would be able to take care of the titles in

THE MEMORIAL CHAPEL AT VALLEY FORGE, PENNSYLVANIA

MODEL OF JOHN FITCH'S FIRST STEAMBOAT. IN THE
SMITHSONIAN INSTITUTION, WASHINGTON, D. C.

good time. But in 1796 a further grant was refused by the Government. "The contract has been forfeited," he was told.

Congress gave relief to those who had purchased lands for which Symmes could not give title. In 1799 they were told they might purchase them from the United States for $2 per acre additional!

Of course the first impression of readers is that Symmes was a rascal. But the judgment of those who knew him well was more favorable. "However censurable the Judge may have been in those transactions," one wrote, "it is generally conceded that he candidly and honestly believed he was entitled to the fulfilment of his contract."

The end was near. There were suits and judgments. In 1802, when he was on a visit to New Jersey, he was arrested by reason of three suits against him in the Supreme Court. Two of these actions were those of Elias Boudinot, executor of Philip Stockton, and Simeon Broadwell. Bail was given by Colonel Henry. Symmes left the state to avoid further difficulty. In a letter he defended his course:

"If my business at the Court in Marietta and next week at the City of Washington did not compel me to evade these arrests, I would give myself up at once that I might the sooner know the worst they can do against me, but at present it is very inconvenient."

But he looked after the interests of the man who had given bail for him. On February 27, 1802, he authorized his son-in-law to indemnify Colonel Henry, and to take for his own satisfaction, a deed for "Solitude," the beloved home of Symmes in New Jersey. He was asked, however, to refrain from putting the deed on record. "It had better be kept a secret," he was told, that the place might still pass for his, for this would make easier the collection of the rents by him.

Even then Symmes was not utterly cast down. "I am a philosopher, and an honest man," he wrote. "My enemies may scare me, but they will never break my spirit, nor convict me of the smallest fraud against any of them." He felt that the prosecutors were persecutors, and he believed that eventually he would pay every honest debt.

In his will he said:

"I hope I need make no apology to my children for not having so much property to leave them as might have been expected from the savings of a long, industrious, frugal and adventurous life, when they recollect the undue methods taken as well by the Government of the United States as by many individuals."

He spoke also of his sadness at the necessity of "making sacrifice of my hardly earned property at the shrine of their avarice." It had been his fortune "to be treated with the blackest ingratitude by some who now laugh at my calamity, but who would at this day have been toiling in poverty had not my enterprise to the country, my benevolence, as the property which they have purchased from me has made them rich."

The close of Symmes's life came on February 26, 1814, in Cincinnati. The funeral was held at the home of William Henry Harrison, and the body was taken for burial to North Bend. This was in accordance with his desire, expressed in his will, for at North Bend he had spent the last twenty-five years of his life.

The grave of the Pioneer of the Purchase is close to that of President Harrison, who—against the father's will, it is said—became the husband of Anna Symmes.

The inscription is simple. In addition to the date of birth and death it says:

"Here rest the remains of John Cleve Symmes, who at the foot of these hills made the first settlement between the Miami Rivers."

CHAPTER X

THE CURIOUS STORY OF JOHN FITCH, HIS MAP AND HIS STEAMBOAT

ONE of the rarest of the early maps of portions of the United States is John Fitch's Map of the Northwest, published in 1785. There is a copy in the Harvard Library, while two imperfect copies may be seen in the library of the Historical Society of Pennsylvania. But two or three more copies are known of the map that has perhaps a stranger story than any other map in existence.

A few years ago the Chief of the Division of Maps and Charts of the Library of Congress told of the map, in a book of which but two hundred copies were sold. With his book went a reproduction of the map.

John Fitch, who made the strange yet—all things considered—marvelously accurate map, was a Connecticut boy. Born in 1743, on January 21, Old Style, or February 2, according to the revised calendar, he was allowed to go to school until he was ten years old, though he was frequently taken from school to work on his father's farm. But he managed to secure an old arithmetic, and by the use of this in private he soon became quite perfect in figures. When he was eleven years old he was startled on being told that if he could secure a copy of Salmond's Geography, he could learn about the whole world. He asked his father to buy a copy for him; but instead of buying the book, his father gave John the use of a small piece of land, on which to raise potatoes. On the next holiday the boy stayed at home, dug the ground by hand, and planted the seed. The crop was sold for ten shillings, but the desired book cost twelve shillings. So John had to do more work, in order to earn the other two shillings still due on the book (for which the merchant gave him credit) and enough money besides to pay his father for the seed. But he had the geography, and he studied it thoroughly. Before long he had a good knowledge of the countries of the world. He became interested in surveying, and when his father gave him a pair of dividers and a scale, he was a happy boy.

FROM PILLAR TO POST

At seventeen, discouraged by the outlook on the farm, he resolved to go to sea. His capital was twenty-three shillings, of which his father had given him twenty. On his return he apprenticed himself to a clockmaker, who, being also a farmer, demanded that one-half of the apprentice's time should be devoted to farm work. Unfortunately the master did not carry out the terms of the indenture; he insisted on keeping young Fitch at work on the farm most of the time, and gave him little instruction in his trade.

The apprentice's experience was equally unfortunate when his services were transferred to another clockmaker, with whom he remained until he was twenty. Then he secured his release on payment of £8, for which he had to go in debt, deciding that it was wiser to contract the debt than to waste more time with a man who refused to teach him according to promise. So he went out into the world, "a clockmaker who had never made a clock, a watchmaker who had never taken a watch apart or put one together, and who had never seen the tools necessary for such delicate operations."

But of brass work he had some knowledge. He borrowed twenty shillings and announced himself ready to do business as a brass-founder. So well did he succeed that in two years he had paid off his entire indebtedness of £20, and had saved £50. More than this, he was known as a successful clockmaker; he had taught himself by experimenting on every clock he could get for the purpose.

In consequence of business misfortunes the young manufacturer decided to leave home. For some time he tramped through New York and New Jersey, earning his way by mending clocks. At Trenton he found employment at the shop of a silversmith, whose trade he soon picked up. However, business was so poor that he long lived on threepence a day. But, business gradually increasing, he was able to buy out the silversmith, and became himself an employer, doing more work than the best of Philadelphia's silversmiths. By the beginning of the Revolutionary War he had saved £800.

For a time he served as lieutenant in a New Jersey company, but when his services were desired as a gunsmith, he felt that he could be of more use at his shop than in the field. His establishment soon became a small arsenal, and his apprentices gave their entire attention to supplying the needs of the soldiers. This continued until the advance of the British made necessary the closing of the armory.

His further career during the war is clouded. He was accused of being a deserter, but the charge was answered by the statement that armorers were excluded from military service. He sought to make money by selling provisions to the army at Valley Forge, but the rapid depreciation of Continental currency took most of his savings from him.

All that was left of his savings he invested in land warrants, which he surveyed for himself. Next he visited Virginia, where he arranged to have his surveys recorded. The return to the West was made by way of Fort Pitt, where he invested in flour, which he proposed to take to New Orleans for sale. When close to Marietta, Ohio, he was taken prisoner by the Indians and carried across country to Detroit.

MAKING GAIN OUT OF HIS DISASTER

Most men would have felt that such a misadventure would put an end to all activity. But Fitch was not like most men. How he put his captivity to good use has been told by Charles Whittlesey, in his book, *Justice to the Memory of John Fitch.* The taste for geography cultivated through the textbook secured when a boy at cost of many holidays, led him to gain by observation all sorts of geographical information. But in addition he succeeded in drawing from the Indians a description of the principal rivers of the West, and the form, position, and magnitude of the northern lakes. Mr. Whittlesey goes on to say:

"It should be remembered that, as yet, no surveys had been made north of the Ohio and west of Pennsylvania. In this forlorn condition, his inquisitive mind employed itself, in tracing the various rivers whose future consequence he at once foresaw, to their sources. No traveler takes closer observation upon the topography of a country

than a Western Indian. He can mark out upon the ground
a rude map of every lake and river along which the print
of his moccasins has been made. His memory in regard
to places never fails. From the most intelligent chiefs and
warriors Fitch obtained rough outlines of that broad domain which to him appeared to be the principal seat of em-
pire. He was heard afterward to remark, that in our
country the west would be the center and the Atlantic
States the suburbs of the nation."

For a time the prisoner lived on an island near the
mouth of the St. Lawrence. Even in this unlikely place
the Yankee silversmith contrived to make money. He had
no tools except a single engraving implement, but he made
others. An old brass kettle, bought from a soldier, furnished material for brass buttons. In seven months nine
wooden clocks, three hundred pairs of brass sleeve-buttons,
and eighty pairs of silver buttons were made. Prices were
low, but the ingenious man was able to buy many comforts,
as well as to spend a dollar each week on sick prisoners.
The industry was interrupted only by an exchange of
prisoners.

After his return to Philadelphia, by way of Quebec,
Fitch made other efforts to get possession of western lands,
but new regulations by Congress, and the order by Governor Harrison, of Virginia, that there be no more private
surveys of land, once more brought him disappointment.
But, as before, he was not dismayed. He set to work to
capitalize his knowledge of the country by making a map
on a scale of two hundred miles to five and a half inches.
In his manuscript autobiography, which is now in possession of the Library Company of Philadelphia, he said:

"Having nothing to do, and for my own amusement

THE FALLS OF ST. ANTHONY, MINNESOTA, DESCRIBED BY JOHN FITCH

set to and made a Draft of that Country from Hutchin's and Murrows [McMurray's Map], with the addition of my knowledge. This was more to keep the Idea of the Country in my own mind than for any other purpose when I had this done I thought a map of this Sort would be useful to the World as I knew mine to be more accurate than any before now and Hutchin's and Morreys [McMurray's] was too large and expensive for men to Carry into the Wood and thinking that a great part of the Continent at that time turned their attention to the Western Country and wished larger information I thought that the general outline of that Country would be acceptable and got a sheet of copper and hammered it Polished it and engraved it and then made a Press and Printed it. It is true it was but cours done it was cheap Portable to any who wanted to go to the Woods and more to be relyed upon than any then Published this paid me reasonably for the time I was about it and I hope my country will not think they purchased my information too dear."

"Engraved in Abe Scout's Wheelwright shop, and printed on Charles Harrison's cider press by the author," would have been a true description.

The maps were colored by Margaret Patterson at Tom Watts's house. In the collection of the Library Company of Philadelphia is a letter from Fitch in which he says, "Pegg Patterson has been at me for painting 100 maps." This painting done by Pegg "was merely a line of color marking the boundaries and rivers and a thin wash on the lakes." On some copies these markings were quite heavy, while on others they were very light. The copy in Harvard University Library is colored heavily. Colors used varied on the different copies that have been preserved.

In his dedication of the map, "To Thomas Hutchins, Esqr. Geographer of the United States," Fitch spoke of the variations:

"It is with the greatest diffidence I beg leave to lay at your feet a very humble attempt to promote a science of which you are so bright an ornament. I wish it were more worthy of your patronage. Unaccustomed to the business of engraving, I could not render it as pleasing to the eye as I would have wished. But, as I flatter myself will be easily forgiven by a gentleman who knows how to distinguish between form and substance in all things."

Fitch followed the example of other mapmakers of the time by printing here and there on the surface such messages as the following:

"The falls of St. Anthony exhibit one of the grandest spectacles in nature; the waters dashing over tremendous rocks from a height of about forty feet perpendicular."

"The Kentucky country is not so level as it is generally represented to be, there being a range of hilly land running through it. . . ."

On June 30, 1785, the *Pennsylvania Packet* printed an advertisement as follows:

"John Fitch, having traversed the Country N.W. of the Ohio, in the several capacities of a captive, surveyor and a traveller—as the result of his labours and remarks, has completed and now wishes to sell, a new accurate Map of that Country, generally distinguished by the term New States, including Kentucky, which opens immense sources of wealth and advantageous speculation to the citizens of the United States, and therefore is an object of general attention, and having performed the engraving and printing himself, is enabled to sell at the very small price of a

French Crown.[1] To be sold by William Prestard, on the north side of Market Street, opposite Letitia Court."

THE STORY OF THE FIRST STEAMBOAT

By this time Fitch had another dream. One Sunday in 1785, while on his way home from Neshaminy of Warwick Church—which is still standing near Philadelphia—he was walking with difficulty, because of rheumatism, the reminder of his trying experiences in the West. An acquaintance, with his wife, passed him swiftly in a "chair" —a two-wheeled chaise. "I wish I could invent a way to travel on the roads by steam," Fitch said to a companion.

But when he tried to work out a plan for a steam carriage, he had so many difficulties that he turned to the construction of a model for a steamboat—a great rowboat whose oars were to be propelled by steam. The machinery was made of brass, while the paddle wheels, of wood, were built by a student at the College of New Jersey, now Princeton University. When the model was tried on a pond near Fitch's home it ran so well that he wished to build a full-sized boat for river use. Needing funds for his experiments, he petitioned Congress to guarantee the sale of four thousand copies of his map, the proceeds to be used for the steamboat.

"He will obligate himself to execute sd. Machine at his own expense; and think himself happy in thus promoting the interest of his Country, and will expect no farther reward unless it arrives in practice as well as in theory, and then submit it to the Honourable Congress, to judge of its utility, and his reward."

The memorial, presented in August, 1785, was unsuccessful. A few weeks later he presented to the American

THE ROMANCE OF FORGOTTEN MEN

Philosophical Society of Philadelphia, "The Model, with a drawing and description of a machine for working a boat against the stream by means of a steam engine." At the same time he appealed to prominent men, including Benjamin Franklin, for assistance.

Later he tried to interest General Washington, but again he failed. Finding his way to Richmond, he petitioned the Legislature of Virginia for assistance. James Madison presented his request. Though a committee was appointed, nothing was done. Governor Patrick Henry was so much pleased with the idea of the steamboat that Fitch, despairing of legislative assistance, tried to sell privately sufficient copies of the map to raise the funds. The result was the giving to Patrick Henry of a bond which is preserved in the Library of Congress:

City of Richmond, Nov. 16, 1785.
Whereas, John Fitch . . . has proposed a *Machine* for promoting navigation, with other useful purposes, which has been generally approved by all men of science who have examined the same; in order to enable the said Fitch to make a full experiment of the utility of the said *Machine,* we, the Subscribers, do promise to pay to John Fitch of Bucks County, Pennsylvania, his Heirs and Assigns, the sums against our respective Names, on the 2nd Monday of Novr. next. Provided the said John Fitch shall have ready to be delivered to us, at the City of Richmond, so many of his Maps of the North West pts of the United States, at the rate of a French Crown per map, as shall answer to the Sums respectively subscribed by us, at the rate of a French crown per map. Witness our Hands . . .

Also there has been preserved a certificate as follows:

I certify that John Fitch has left in my Hands a Bond payable to the Governor of the territory, for 350£ conditioned for exe-

THE KING OF PRUSSIA TAVERN, NEAR VALLEY FORGE, PENNSYLVANIA. A RESORT OF BRITISH SPIES WHO SOUGHT INFORMATION AS TO WASHINGTON'S MOVEMENTS

cuting his Steam Boat, when he receives subscriptions for 1000 of
his Maps, at a French Crown each.

P. HENRY.

November 16, 1785.

Again Fitch was doomed to disappointment. Although
one hundred and fifteen subscription-papers were given out
to the members of the Assembly, little attention was paid
to them. But twenty subscriptions were received, through
a man in Richmond, to whom forty maps were sent, and
from whom eight crowns were received.

On his way home to Philadelphia Fitch stopped in
Maryland, where he interested Governor Smallwood, to
whom he had a letter which told of his "useful and entertaining map." "His ingenuity in this way strongly recom-
mends him," his letter of introduction to the Governor
said, "but his genius is not confined to this idea—he has
spent much thought on an improvement of the steam engine, by which to gain a first power applicable to a variety
of uses, amongst them to force vessels forward *in any
kind of water.*"

On January 9, 1786, the Legislature of Maryland replied, through a committee, "However desirable it is for
liberal and enlightened Legislators to encourage useful
arts, yet the state and condition of our finances are such
that there can be no advance of public money at present."

The first attempt with a real steamboat was made in
1785. Rembrandt Peale, an eye witness of the trial trip
of this steamer, told of the sight:

"Hearing there was something curious to be seen at the
floating bridge on the Schuylkill at Market Street, I eagerly ran to the spot, where I found a few persons collected, all eagerly gazing at a shallop at anchor below the

[193]

bridge, with about 20 persons on board. On the deck was a small furnace, and machinery connected with a coupling crank, projecting over the Stern to give motion to three or four paddles, resembling snow shovels, which hung into the water. When all was ready, and the power of steam was made to act, by means of which I was then ignorant, knowing nothing of the piston except in the common pump, the paddles began to work, pressing against the water *backward* as they rose, and the boat, to my great delight, moved against the tide, without wind or hand; but in a few minutes it ran aground at an angle of the river, owing to the difficulty of managing the unwieldy rudder which projected eight or ten feet. It was soon backed off, and proceeded slowly to its destination at Gray's Ferry. So far it must have been satisfactory to Mr. Fitch in this his first public experiment."

Because of the mechanical difficulties in the crude paddle wheels, Fitch resolved to abandon them in favor of oars or paddles to be arranged as in a boat propelled by man power, but moved in this case by steam. A boat on this principle was built in 1787, and was comparatively successful. The test on the Delaware was witnessed by nearly all the members of the Constitutional Convention then in session in Philadelphia.

In a later model, built in 1788, the position of the oars was changed to the stern, where they were made to push against the water. Although this boat made a trip to Burlington, New Jersey, twenty miles above Philadelphia, it was seen that improvements were necessary. These were incorporated in the boat which was tested in 1790; this ran a mile on the Delaware, at dead water, in twelve minutes and a half.

So great was the success of the new model that it became a regular passenger and freight boat on the Delaware, running a total of between two and three thousand miles, at a speed of from seven to eight miles an hour, whereas Fulton's *Clermont,* seventeen years later, could accomplish little more than six miles an hour.

On June 14, 1790, the *Federal Gazette* published the following announcement:

"THE STEAMBOAT is now ready to take passengers, and is intended to set off from Arch Street Ferry in Philadelphia, every Monday, Wednesday and Friday, for Burlington, Bristol, Bordentown, & Trenton, to return on Tuesdays, Thursdays, and Saturdays. Price per passenger, 2/6 to Burlington and Bristol, 3/9 to Bordentown, 5 s. to Trenton."

Plans were made immediately to build a larger boat, the *Perseverance,* so that two boats might be sent to Virginia in time to take advantage of that state's grant of exclusive rights to the transportation on the Ohio River and its tributaries. Pennsylvania had already granted a similar right for waters under her control.

The United States Patent, signed by Washington, was granted on August 20, 1791.

Vexatious delays hindered the work on the *Perseverance.* Enemies attacked Fitch, friends forsook him, rivals interfered with him, dire poverty added to his difficulties. It became impossible to complete the vessel in season to comply with the Virginia statute. Finally, hopeless, the inventor abandoned his enterprise.

After a trip to France, Fitch returned to Kentucky. There, ill and despondent, he took his own life. A friend at first proposed to put over his grave a stone with the following inscription:

While living he declared
"This will be the mode of
Crossing the Atlantic
in time,
Whether I shall bring it to perfection
or not,
Steamboats will be preferred to
all other Conveyances;
And they will be particularly
Useful in the Navy Yard, and on the
Ohio and Mississippi."

The body of John Fitch lies forgotten in Bardstown, Kentucky.   But his prophecy has been fulfilled.

AN OLD MILL WHICH JOHN FITCH PASSED FREQUENTLY

CHAPTER XI

THE SURPRISING TALE OF CONSTANTINE SAMUEL RAFINESQUE, ERRATIC GENIUS

GENESIS

THE early years of the nineteenth century brought many odd characters to America, but few of them were so startlingly original and peculiar as Constantine Samuel Rafinesque, son of a French father and a mother who was a native of Greece, though of German descent; born in Galata, suburb of Constantinople, Turkey, on October 22, 1783.

The marks of the genius were apparent to those who knew him even when he was a boy. As the years passed they increased mightily. Oddities, too, were marked when he was young, and these increased until, even by 1818, John James Audubon—himself a character so peculiar that the evidence of his appreciation of the oddity of another is all the more delicious—wrote a description of him that is one of the choice bits of the bird-lover's fascinating *Ornithological Biography*. Here is the picture:

"A long loose coat of yellow nankeen, much the worse of the many rubs it had got in its time, and stained all over with the juice of plants, hung loosely about him like a sack. A waistcoat of the same, with enormous pockets, and buttoned up to the chin, reached below over a pair of tight pantaloons, the lower parts of which were buttoned down to the ancles. His beard was as long as I have known my own to be during some of my peregrinations, and his lank, black hair hung loosely over his shoulders. His forehead was so broad and prominent that any tyro in phrenology would instantly have pronounced it the residence of a mind of strong power. His words impressed an assurance of rigid truth, and as he directed the conversation to the study of the natural sciences, I listened to him with as much delight as Telemachus could have listened to Mentor."

The father of Rafinesque was a trader from Marseilles who made so many extended voyages that the lad was left to the guidance of his mother, evidently a woman of ability much more than ordinary.

Yet the father's long absences from home made so much impression on the young Constantine that he decided when still quite young that he, too, would be a traveler. At first he was very easily satisfied by his conception of what constituted travels; a tramp in the hills became to him a journey of importance, and he looked on himself as a worthy successor of such a world-traveler as Marco Polo, by reason of just such expeditions. He made some journeys of much greater moment, but to these he seemed to attach no more importance than to the little jaunts and tramps that took him into the heart of the young American wilderness. The modest book in which, with strange pride, he told of these expeditions, long and short, bore on the title page the couplet:

> Un voyageur des le berceau,
> Je le serais jusu'au tombeau.

"I will always be a traveler from the cradle to the grave," is a fair English rendering of the motto in the book in which he made a statement which showed his very naïve appreciation of the fact that he was a wanderer:

"It appears that whoever travels by sea in the cradle or very early, is never liable afterwards to this singular disorder [seasickness]. It seems also that whoever can sit backward in a coach without difficulty is not liable to it, but whoever cannot, will suffer sadly from it."

EXODUS

From Constantinople he made a trip at an early date. He went to Scutari in Asia, to Leghorn, with a stop on the Island of Corsica on the way home, and to Marseilles.

While at Marseilles for a season he had his first taste of the work to which he was to give his life. Then he found himself, or, as he expressed it, then he became conscious of his existence. He said that this epoch in his life followed his visits to some of the numerous country-seats which surround and beautify the neighborhood of Marseilles. These country-seats were known as *bastides*. To one or another of these he resorted for rest and refreshment. "It was there among the flowers and fruits that I began to enjoy life, and I became a Botanist." According to his own account, the beginning of another branch of his work was equally simple: "The first premium I received in a school-room was a book on animals, and I became a Zoölogist and Naturalist."

The strange education of the self-conscious lad was continued as he moved back and forth between Genoa and Marseilles, with a taste of Pisa thrown in for good measure. Sometimes his mother was his guide, again his grandmother directed him. Private tutors tried to instruct him, but they did not succeed so well because the young Græco-

Frenchman seemed to prefer his own erratic courses. Evidently he was an omnivorous reader, though it is hardly likely that he read as much as he afterwards claimed: "Before twelve years of age I had read the great universal history and one thousand volumes of books on many pleasing and interesting subjects." At another time he said of this early period that he "read every kind of books, good or bad." Then he made a statement that must be taken with a grain of salt: "But fortunately I knew how to distinguish them." That boast is akin to the claim he made in later years as to his language studies:

"I have undertaken to learn the Latin and Greek, as well as the Hebrew, Sanscrit, Chinese, and other languages, as I felt the need or inclination to study them."

A further indication of the breadth of the boy's interests, as well as of his ideas of his own abilities, is to be found in his own words as to occupation in Marseilles.

"I had made to myself a small garden in a wild and remote place. I began the study of Fishes and Birds. I drew them and collected Shells and Crabs. Daudin, of Paris, who published then a natural history of Birds, was my first correspondent among the learned, and I communicated to him some observations on Birds. I drew maps, copied those of rare works, and took topographical surveys; these were my first essays in geography."

Think of the wide range of the studies and activities of this paragon among students! Certainly he was an unusually bright boy, probably a real genius in embryo.

As Call, one of his biographers, says: "It is readily believed that this period of great mental activity and developing powers of observation would have given to the world one of its greatest naturalists, had he been freely guided by some master hand." But, alas! "the lack of coördination of powers led to habits, both of thought and literary effort, that had a serious influence, in after years, on his life and work."

Vain attempts were made to tie him down to the sedate manner of life followed by his father, the traveling merchant. But terms of apprenticeship as a clerk, both in Marseilles and in Leghorn, were destined not to be completed. For a time he liked the idea of his work, for it would lead, later on, to traveling. But he was too restless to wait for the coming of the travel period, while the thought of pleasures at hand lured him from his desk. As he said: "A decided taste for Horticulture kept me in suspense, and invited me to become a Botanical Gardener."

VAGABONDAGE

A period was put to this season of hit-or-miss floundering after a vocation when his father died of yellow fever in Philadelphia, while on one of his trading voyages, and the later rascally conduct of the partners of the dead man who robbed the family of their inheritance. At the age of eighteen, in 1802, in company with his brother, Constantine took ship for Philadelphia. The voyage of forty-two days was remarkable for the study of birds and fishes by the way, as well as for the sage observation that he was crossing the ocean "which, after 4000 years, bears yet the name of the first nations who crossed it, the Atalas and the Antis." Interesting information!

On Rafinesque's arrival in Philadelphia, Dr. Benjamin Rush, one of the most famous physicians of his day, asked the young man to become a student of medicine. But he preferred to listen to the invitation of the brothers Clifford, agents for the vessel on which he had made his voyage, to take a desk in their counting-house. The prospect of travel led him to accept the desk, but yellow fever, the scourge of Philadelphia in those days, interfered with his progress. To escape the disease, he fled to Germantown, as did President Washington during his stay in Philadelphia. While there Colonel Forrest, "a friend of horticulture," urged the clerk to leave the counting-house to travel with him for the collection of plants.

With his tempter, Constantine tramped over New Jersey, and studied the strange Pine Barrens of that state, then visited the famous Botanical Gardens of Bartram near Philadelphia and of Marshall near West Chester, Pennsylvania. A period of sanity interrupted his botanical vagabondage, for in 1803 he returned to the counting-house. Yet more yellow fever, and the thought that immediate tramps over the inviting miles of the mountain wilderness were so near at hand, combined to influence a generous act of resignation: he turned over the clerkship to his brother. As he said: "I left that situation of no advantage, and gave myself up to botany and travels during the whole year."

Freed at last from the drudgery of the business office, he tramped here and there through Delaware, the western shore of Maryland, and Pennsylvania, never so happy as when on one of his vagabond tours. Offers of horses were declined respectfully, for, as he said, "I preferred my pedestrian mode, although I had often to wade through streams and swamps." On one of his journeys he found himself among the Indians, who, he decided, were "of Tartar and Siberian origin." Again he made the acquaintance of President Jefferson, who invited him to Monticello. Through the great Virginian, in all probability, he learned of the proposed expedition of Lewis and

Clark to the sources of the Missouri River and to the Pacific coast. He was told that he might become botanist to the expedition. But the offer of work in Sicily seemed to him to give promise of greater reward, and he did not apply to accompany the men who were to win lasting fame.

Ten years in Sicily resulted in the increase of the specimens in his herbal, or collection of plants, by many thousands. His knowledge was made an income producer, for he became an exporter of the squill, a medicinal plant. The squills he bought for one dollar per hundred pounds, and, after preparation, he secured for them from $20 to $30 per hundred! His venture made him rich, but after some years the Sicilians learned his secret and spoiled his market.

Other experiences on the island were his secretaryship to the United States consul and his marriage to a Catholic, which was never recognized by her church. This marriage embittered his whole life.

While on the island in the Mediterranean he published the first of his voluminous contributions to scientific literature. Later, however, when invasion by the French was feared, he was not permitted to continue these publications, because they told too much about the island. This fact, together with the results of his unfortunate marriage, disgusted him with the country which had seemed so favorable, and once more he turned his thoughts to America.

ADVENTURE

When the young scientist took passage for America on the ship *Union,* he carried with him in fifty boxes the thousands of plants which composed his herbal, as well as

[203]

his mineral specimens, and his books and manuscripts, some two thousand maps and drawings, and more than half a million specimens of shells.

The voyage was long and trying. After many weeks the Azores were reached. Then a squall struck the vessel, which lost its masts in the encounter. The autobiographical notes tell what followed:

"Having quickly repaired our damage, as well as we could, we resumed our voyage; but were two months on the way, being baffled by violent storms, in one we had to throw our guns overboard. We had also to contend against the Gulf stream, which our Maltese sailors did not know, and we crossed improperly."

Finally, when provisions were almost exhausted, another storm was encountered. The vessel was driven on Race Rocks, between Fisher's Island and Long Island. Once more let the young scientist take up the tale:

"We had merely time to escape in our boats, with some difficulty; the long boat was too heavy to be hoisted, but floated as the ship fell, entangled in the rigging for a while. Having left the wreck we rowed towards the lighthouse of New London, then in sight, and reached it at midnight; thus landing in America for a second time, but in a deplorable situation. I had lost everything, my fortune, my share of the cargo, my collection, and labour for 20 years past, my books, my manuscripts, my drawings, even my clothes . . . all that I possessed. . . ."

The shipwrecked, ruined man walked to New London, treasuring the hope that the vessel could yet be saved. He was soon to find his mistake, for the vessel sank, after exploding because of the air in the hold.

While it is true that some who have told of the life of Rafinesque have expressed disbelief of this story of mis-

BISHOP WILLIAM WHITE

fortune, Call, the chief investigator, declares his belief in
the record. The questioning of acquaintances was a keen
sorrow to the sensitive man, who wrote:

"Some hearts of stone have since dared to doubt of
these facts or rejoice at my losses! Yes, I have found men
vile enough to laugh without shame at my misfortune,
instead of condoling with me."

After walking to New York, Rafinesque found a sym-
pathizer in Chancellor Livingston, the man famous for his
activities in connection with the Erie Canal and early
steamboat navigation on the Ohio River. He was invited
to go to the Livingston country home on the Hudson, to
teach the daughter of the house. He thought his difficulties were solved, but soon the failing health of his pupil
made necessary the departure of the family for the South.
Rafinesque was asked to accompany them, but he preferred
to remain in the North, that he might resume the pedestrian tours to which he had become accustomed during his
first visit to America. One long journey up the Hudson
and through the back country, took him through what he
called "the pittoresque part of the U. States."

After a time he settled in New York, where he was successful in business undertakings. But his peace was interrupted by a "perfid Sicilian," a bankruptcy, lawsuits,
and other troubles. Still he managed to publish there
some of his scientific writings before beginning, in 1818,
a tour of two thousand miles. He directed his steps
toward Lexington, Kentucky, at the urgency of Mr. Clifford, who had been his patron and friend ever since he
first arrived in America. Mr. Clifford, who had removed
to Lexington, thought that the young man would find
prosperity there.

After an overland journey across Pennsylvania, he

stopped in Pittsburgh, where Cramer & Spear, Booksellers, expressed interest in his plan to float down the Ohio River. They explained to him their need of a reliable chart of the Ohio from Pittsburgh to Cairo, for the use of emigrants bound down the river. They explained to him that this chart should show "all the Islands, rapids, hills, villages, &c," and told him that this would be reproduced in the pages of *The Navigator,* on the scale of four miles to the inch. The booksellers were so delighted with the promise made to prepare this chart that they promised to publish for him the story of his travels in America, and to give him 500 copies for the copyright.

After many tribulations, Rafinesque fulfilled his part of the bargain. He delivered the chart, and was paid the magnificent sum of one hundred dollars! But the publishers wriggled out of the promise to publish the book.

Those who see one of the surviving copies of *The Navigator,* preserved in libraries and museums and private collections of rare books, may marvel at the crude reproduction of the charts made by Rafinesque, and may picture the eagerness of those who studied this while floating down stream, amid dangers from lurking Indians as well as from the treacherous river. With what mingled feelings of appreciation of the work of the artist and of marvel at the intrepidity of the emigrant, the author has examined a copy which bears on the margin the comments made by the owner as he threaded the dangerous stream!

A bit of Rafinesque's description of his venturesome journey should be read:

"In company with Mr. Malin and other French gentlemen going to Illinois, have bought an ark or flat covered boat, and floated slowly down the river, stopping every night. I was thus at leisure to survey and explore; we had a smaller boat to land where we pleased, botanize and buy provisions. We had for guide as far as Gallipolis a gentleman of that town, who was returning there with his family in another ark, which he lashed to ours. Thus we averted many accidents and I began to study the fishes which we caught or bought, making drawings, &c."

After passing the Falls of the Ohio and "Shippingsport" (now part of Louisville), he went on to Hendersonville, where he spent a few days with John J. Audubon, the ornithologist.

DUPED

The sorrowful story of Rafinesque's relations with Audubon were told by Audubon in his *Ornithological Biography*. He had the grace to disguise the name of the man whom he tricked; he called him "M. de T." But there can be no mistake as to the man who was meant.

Read the story:

" 'What an odd-looking fellow!' said I to myself, as, while walking by the river, I observed a man landing from a boat, with what I thought a bundle of dried clover on his back. 'How the boatmen stare at him! Surely he must be an original!' He ascended with rapid steps, and approaching me, asked if I could point out the house in which Mr. Audubon resided. 'Why, I am the man,' said I, 'and will gladly lead you to my dwelling.' The traveller rubbed his hands with delight, and drawing a letter from his pocket, handed it to me without any remark. I broke the seal and read as follows: 'My dear Audubon— I send you an odd fish, which you may prove to be undescribed, and I hope you will do so in your next letter.'

"With all the simplicity of a woodman, I asked the

bearer where the odd fish was; when M. de T. . . . smiled, rubbed his eyes, and with the greatest good humor, said, 'I am the odd fish, I presume, Mr. Audubon.'

"We soon reached the house, where I presented my learned guest to my family and was ordering a servant to go to the boat for M. de T.'s luggage, when he told me he had none but what he brought on his back. He then loosened the pack of weeds which had first drawn my attention. The ladies were a little surprised, but I checked their critical glances for the moment. The naturalist pulled off his shoes, and while engaged in drawing his stockings, not up, but down, in order to cover the holes about the heels, told me in the gayest mood imaginable that he had walked a great distance, and had only taken passage on board the ark, to be put on this shore, and that he was sorry his apparel had suffered so much from his late journey. Clean clothes were offered, but he would not accept them, and it was with evident reluctance that he performed the lavations usual on such occasions before he sat down to dinner."

More follows in the same light vein, including the story of the midnight uproar in the naturalist's room. On investigation Audubon found his guest "running round the room naked, holding the handle of my favorite violin, the body of which he had battered to pieces against the walls in attempting to kill the bats, which had entered by the open window, probably attracted by the insects flying around his castle." Audubon says that he stood in amazement, while Rafinesque continued to run after the bats. Finally, when he was completely exhausted, he begged that one of the creatures be caught for him, since he was sure he had found a new specimen, which he wished to describe.

CONSTANTINE SAMUEL RAFINESQUE

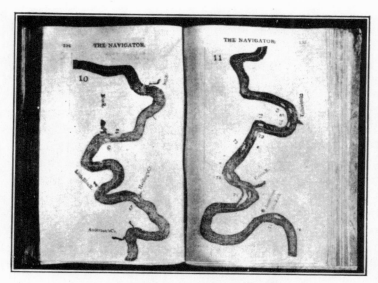

PAGES FROM "THE NAVIGATOR," 1811, PREPARED BY
CONSTANTINE SAMUEL RAFINESQUE

TRANSYLVANIA IN 1785
THE PIONEER COLLEGE OF THE WESTERN WILDERNESS

During the three weeks of the visit Audubon seized on
the craze of his guest for new species and strange birds
and fishes, as an excuse for telling him some of the most
absurd stories concerning his finds in the trees and in the
river. To these stories Rafinesque lent an eager ear.
What marvels he was hearing! How fortunate he was
to have come in touch with one whose training and reputation as a student of nature made impossible anything but
implicit belief in what he said!

So Audubon told him many things which the credulous
man incorporated, by permission, in his manuscripts. Some
of these apocryphal descriptions were published. A sample of these descriptions is that of the "Devil Jack Dia-
mond-fish," which Rafinesque called "Littolepis Adaman-
tinum":

"This may be reckoned the wonder of the Ohio. It is
only found as far up as the falls, and probably lives only
in the Mississippi. I have seen it, but only at a distance,
and have been shown some of its singular scales. Wonderful stories are related concerning this fish, but I have
principally relied upon the description and figures given
me by Mr. Audubon. Its length is from 4 to 10 feet.
One was caught which weighed four hundred pounds. It
lies sometimes asleep or motionless on the surface of the
water, and may be mistaken for a log or a snag. It is
impossible to take it in any other way than with the seine
or a very strong hook, the prongs of the gig cannot pierce
the scales which are as hard as flint, and even proof against
lead balls! Its flesh is not good to eat. It is a voracious
fish. Its vulgar names are Diamond fish (owing to its
scales being cut like diamonds), Devil fish, Jack fish, Tar
jack, &c. . . . The whole body covered with large scales
laying in oblique rows, they are conical, pentagonal and

pentahedral with equal sides, from half an inch to one inch in diameter, brown at first, but becoming of the colour of turtle shell when dry—they strike fire with steel, and are ball proof!"

Thus Audubon played on the credulity of a guest who was too evidently a harmless monomaniac, his special craze being something new and strange, for which he was always on the lookout. Perhaps the hoax was suggested by the introduction of Rafinesque as "an odd fish."

DISAPPOINTED

The unfortunate experience with Audubon was followed by seven years in Kentucky. Rafinesque taught in Transylvania University at Lexington, which, in 1819 when he became acquainted with it, was already thirty-six years old. As teacher of science—the first teacher of the subject west of the Alleghanies—he found himself in conflict with those who felt that classical culture was the only worth-while thing educationally. His really brilliant work was received with indifference which dismayed him. Soon he decided that everybody was against him, and he imagined slights when none were intended. He tried to publish books, but his efforts were in vain, for the most part. In 1821 he issued the first number of the *Western Minerva*. But the printer "dared to suppress it, at the request of some secret foes."

Several years later he tried to found a Botanic Garden. According to his plan, this was to be supported by subscribers to shares of $50 each, payable in instalments of $10. Ten acres were bought, and planting was begun. But once more there were difficulties that led to failure. His monomania asserted itself once more; he said, "I soon became aware of a secret hostility to my industry, and several subscribers did not pay their instalments."

He was instrumental in forming a literary club which he felt would give him the opportunity he longed for to pass on his ideas to others. Of this club, "The Kentucky Institute," he was secretary. Again he was doomed to disappointment. "Trifles alone were welcome," he wrote, "my communications were too learned."

In more than one instance he proposed plans that were frowned upon at the time, though the day came when they brought wealth to others. Thus, on September 6, 1820, he printed in *The Kentucky Reporter* the following communication:

"If anybody living on the banks of the Ohio, Kentucky or other streams where the Muscle Shells are common, wishes to establish a manufacture of Real Pearls, I shall be willing to communicate to them all the different processes needful to the purpose of compelling the Muscle to form these Pearls, for a small consideration, or for a share in the profits."

"The capital needed for such a Manufacture is a convenient place & from $50 to $100. The profits may amount to from $100 to $10,000 in a year, according to the size of the pearls produced."

Thus he outlined, long in advance, what is to-day one of the most profitable industries of the Ohio and Mississippi valleys.

Some comfort was found in the friendship of great men. Many times he was a guest of Henry Clay at Ashland. Thomas Jefferson continued to be a correspondent, while famous scientists of Europe, like Cuvier and Bory, welcomed his letters.

But his greatest solace was found in his travels. Kentucky, Tennessee, Ohio, and, later, Pennsylvania were examined with minute care. His observations were prepared in manuscripts and maps; these he longed to publish, but he saw no way to accomplish his purpose. He felt that he must give to the world some of the fruits of the journeys and observations that seemed to him so unusual—as, for instance, the comparison he made after his visit to Niagara Falls in 1825:

"This phenomenon of Nature excited my admiration instead of horror caused by Etna. Few scientists have seen the two great phenomena in their travels, and compared the sublime effects of water and fire."

Finally, in 1836, he managed to have printed in Philadelphia a curious little volume, *A Life of Travel,* which he sold for seventy-five cents a copy. For this book he made apology in the preface: "The style is rather familiar and neglected. I regret the egotic form of it, and should have wished to have changed it to a recital in the third person."

Later in the volume he said: "I have travelled by nearly all the possible manners except by Camels and in Balloons. By land I have travelled on foot, and on horseback, with mules and asses, in stages, coaches, carts, waggons, litters, sedan chairs, sledges, railroad cars, &c, and even on men's backs. By water I have tried canoes, boats, feluccas, sloops, schooners, brigs, ships, ships ,of war, rafts, barges, tow boats, canal boats, steam boats, keel boats, arks, scows, &c. These travels have cost me between $8000 and $10,000, which, with the interest, would now be a fortune. Since I have seldom travelled except at my own expense, altho' sometimes on business, I have never been sent nor paid by amateurs, societies or governments, like so many other learned men."

[212]

SECOND MAIN BUILDING OF TRANSYLVANIA UNIVERSITY.
ERECTED 1818

Philadelphia 25th April 1819

Sir.

I do myself the honor of acknowledging reception of your favor 7th Instant, which announces my appointment to the Professorship of Botany and Natural History in the Transylvania University, and imports the conditions and terms of said appointment; and I beg leave to advise you, as you request, of my acceptance thereof, which I hope you will be pleased to communicate to the board of Trustees.

It is my determination to be in Lexington before the end of the Summer, unless my presence should be needed before, of which I shall be apprised I hope by my friends or the usual means.

Meantime allow me to declare myself respectfully

Sir

Your most Obed St.

J. S. Rafinesque

Robert Wickliffe Esqr.
Chairman of the Board of
Trustees of the Transylvania
University.
Lexington.
Kentucky.

RAFINESQUE'S LETTER ACCEPTING THE PROFESSORSHIP IN BOTANY AND NATURAL HISTORY IN TRANSYLVANIA UNIVERSITY

It would, however, be unfair to Rafinesque to leave with readers the idea that he always wrote in such doleful vein. In his *New Flora of North America,* he told of pleasure in spite of difficulties:

"I have been welcomed under the hospitable roof of friends of knowledge and enterprise, else laughed at as a mad botanist by scornful ignorance. Such a life of travels and exertions has its pleasures and its pains, its sudden delights and deep joys, mixed with dangers, trials, difficulties, and troubles . . . The mere fatigue of a pedestrian journey is nothing compared to the gloom of solitary forests, where not a human being is met for many miles, and if met he may be mistrusted; where the food and collections must be carried in your pocket or knapsack from day to day; where the fare is not only scanty, but sometimes worse; where you must live on corn bread and salt pork, be burned and steamed by a hot sun at noon, or drenched by rain. Musquitoes and fleas will often annoy you or suck your blood if you stop or leave a hurried step. Gnats dance before the eye, and often fall in unless you shut them; insects creep on you and into your ears. Ants crawl on you whenever you sit on the ground, wasps will assail you like furies if you touch their nests . . ."

The tale was unfolded at much greater length. But after telling the whole story, the inveterate scientist spoke out:

"The pleasures of a botanical expedition fully compensate for these miseries and dangers . . . You feel an exultation, you are a conqueror, you have made a conquest over Nature, you are going to add a new object or a page to science."

The closing paragraphs of his autobiographical record revealed his naïve appreciation of his own abilities:

"Such then is the picture of my life, my labours, and my travels. I give it to the public, or rather to the learned, as an uncommon instance of perseverance and industry. May this impress youthful minds with a wish to do as well, and the friends of science with the wish to know me, or patronize the labours of my old age, permit me at last to produce under their shield, these works, fruits of my travel and research, which I desire to leave as mementoes of my life and exertions."

Throughout the book are evidences that he felt himself unjustly treated, hounded by enemies, discriminated against when he should have had position, prominence, and friends. He forgot recognition given to him by the College of New Jersey and by the Franklin Institute; it seemed easier to remember that his offerings for awards were scorned, and that the prizes went to others unjustly, or the offer was withdrawn. His inventions were stolen, or were ignored; for instance, his "Devitial Invention," which, he said, was the real basis of the modern coupon bond, was frowned upon by financiers who later appropriated the idea and deprived him of a fortune.

As a Pulmist, or an exponent of the art of curing consumption by a means he had devised, he did much, he claimed, to alleviate suffering, but his efforts were not appreciated. He was not an artist; yet he insisted that his drawings were superior to those of Audubon, and should have been published. Like Audubon, he made a trip abroad to get these printed, but he felt compelled to return to America because of the unsettled state of Europe in 1830; although he criticized America severely, he preferred the calm and security of this country.

But this is merely the beginning of his complaints. In 1832 he began to publish *The Atlantic Journal,* but this failed, because, as he said, it was too learned and too liberal. Other publications which contained only "plagiarisms and vapid travels" succeeded brilliantly. He owned that he ought to have copied them to ensure success, "but I would not thus degrade myself."

He coveted membership in learned societies. But what was election to such societies in America worth, when anyone who would pay the fee could be sure of an election? How much better the English system!

He longed for a patron; he thought of literary and scientific men in England who were supported by wealthy friends of learning. Nothing of this kind could be expected in America.

There were so many things that troubled him! He mentioned dozens, but he neglected to speak of the greatest lack of his life; he needed a wife, who might have enabled him to maintain his balance and become a real benefactor of his age. A good wife might have helped him to overcome some of the handicaps laid upon him by reason of his unregulated youth.

In spite of his limitations, and contrary to his own beliefs, he was given much recognition. In 1832 the French Society of Geography gave him a gold medal for some of his researches. Learned societies in Paris, Zurich, Vienna, Brussels and Naples, as well as many in America, honored him.

In 1854 Louis Agassiz said of him:

"From what I can learn of Rafinesque I am satisfied that he was a better man than he appeared. His misfortune was his prurient desire for novelties and his rashness in publishing them."

In spite of difficulties that prevented the publication of many of the writings of the erratic genius, the bibliography of his works as given in T. J. Fitzpatrick's story of his life contains 939 titles—papers, pamphlets, books, and other issues!

The life of the voluminous writer ended in misery. His closing days were spent in a garret in the Philadelphia slums. And in his garret he died, at the age of fifty-six, in 1840. The landlord declared that he would sell the body to a medical college, that he might secure unpaid rent. But two friends broke into the room, attached a rope to the body, and lowered it to the street through a window. Then they took it to Ronalson's Cemetery at Ninth and Catharine Streets.

When the will of the scientist—a strange document—was admitted to probate, it was found to contain the provision:

"If anybody has thought himself wronged by me, I ask their pardon. I never did anything wrong willingly, but being beset by knaves and Rivals may have compelled to act sometimes in a way not exactly as I should have chosen, had I been fairly dealt with by others."

MORRISON COLLEGE, TRANSYLVANIA
ERECTED 1830–1832

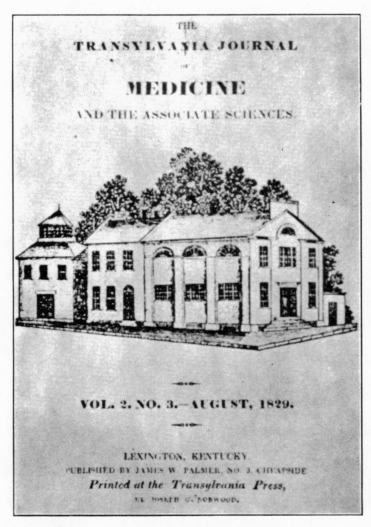

COVER PAGE OF "TRANSYLVANIA JOURNAL OF MEDICINE," SHOWING THE FIRST
MEDICAL BUILDING OF TRANSYLVANIA UNIVERSITY, ERECTED 1827

CHAPTER XII

HOW ELIHU BURRITT, THE SELF-EDUCATED BLACKSMITH, WON FAME

ELIHU BURRITT, born December 8, 1810, was a native of Connecticut. He was the son of a soldier of the Revolution, and he lived in a region from which many men had gone to fight the battles of their country. Those who returned to their little farms or their village employments delighted to gather in the evenings at the cross-roads stores or in one another's homes to talk over their experiences and to speak of the future of the land they loved.

LEARNING THE LESSONS OF PEACE

The boy Elihu was frequently an absorbed listener at these conferences, and he was early inspired to make the most of himself for the sake of that country for which the heroes whose words he heard had suffered so much. He realized that it was unlikely that there would be call for his services as a soldier—the second war with England had left the States in such an impoverished condition that a long era of peace was hoped for. But he felt that the country needed men well equipped to fight the battles of peace, and he resolved to be one of these.

Yet there was in his way a difficulty that would have seemed insurmountable to many boys. His father was poor, the entire dependence of the family being on the breadwinner's labor in winter at the shoemaker's bench and in summer on the hard-soiled Connecticut farm. School privileges were few, but the boy made the most of them, attending the local school every year for the brief winter term until his father fell ill, and he was needed at home. The death of his father when the boy was eighteen made it more than ever necessary that he work for the family at every opportunity. He became a skilled worker at many trades; when he was fifty he declared that no man in America had handled more tools in manual labor than himself.

Soon after the death of his father Elihu apprenticed himself to a blacksmith; by several years in the smithy he made of himself an expert. As he toiled at the anvil he sought to make up for deficiencies in his education, studying mathematics, not only because he wanted to become a surveyor, but because it was possible to do all the work in his mind. That his mind became exceedingly nimble and retentive is evident from the samples following of problems given in his autobiography, which was modestly written in the third person:

"How many barleycorns, at three to the inch, will it take to go around the earth at the equator?" All these figures he had to carry in his head while beating and hammering on iron . . . "How many yards of cloth, three feet in width, cut into strips an inch wide, and allowing half an inch at each end for the lap, would it require to reach from the center of the sun to the center of the earth, and how much would it cost at a shilling a yard?" He would not allow himself to make a single figure with chalk or charcoal in working out this problem, and he would carry home to his brother all the multiplications in his head, and give them off to him and his assistant, who took them down on their slates, and verified and proved each separate calculation, and found the result to be correct.

MAKING UP FOR LOST TIME

This brother, who taught a private school, encouraged him to leave the anvil for three months for mathematical study. He performed prodigies in the brief time at his disposal, for he realized that every day of absence from the smithy was costing him one dollar. Then, at the end of the quarter, he returned to his work, resolved to earn double pay for six months in order to make up for lost time. He was not too busy, however, to study Greek as he worked, a grammar carried in his hat being the reference book to which he turned at intervals during the day. At morning, noon and evening he studied Latin and French. Thus he made a beginning in acquiring the more than fifty languages of which, in later years, he was master.

The next step in his self-education must be told in his own words—modestly given in the third person:

"At the beginning of the following winter, he went to New Haven merely to reside and study in the atmosphere of Yale College; thinking that that alone, without teachers, would impart an ability which he could not acquire at home. Besides, being then naturally timid, and also half-ashamed to ask instruction in the rudiments of Greek and Hebrew at twenty-two years of age, he determined to work his way without consulting any college professor or tutor. So, the first morning in New Haven, he sat down to Homer's Iliad, without note or comment, and with a

Greek lexicon with Latin definitions. He had not, as yet, read a line in the book, and he resolved if he could make out two by hard study through the whole day, he would never ask help of any man thereafter in mastering the Greek language. By the middle of the afternoon he won a victory which made him feel strong and proud, and which greatly affected his subsequent life and pursuits. He mastered the first fifteen lines of the book, and committed the originals to memory, and walked out among the classic trees of the Elm City, and looked up at the colleges, which once had half awed him, with a kind of defiant feeling. He now divided the hours of each day between Greek and other languages, including Latin, French, Spanish, Italian, German and Hebrew, giving to Homer about half the time."

TEACHING AND MANUAL LABOR

So successful was he in the year at New Haven that he was able to teach satisfactorily in an academy not far from home, his department being languages and mathematics. Loss of health, due to confinement, led him to give up the school and go into a business that required, in part, outdoor exercise. In the financial panic of 1837 all his savings were swept away, so he walked to Boston and then to Worcester, seeking employment. At Worcester he returned to the anvil and became an ardent student at the library of the Antiquarian Society, dividing his time according to the pressure of his work. Languages especially occupied him. He translated the Icelandic sagas relating to the discovery of America.

"Among other books to which he had free access were

a Celto-Breton dictionary and grammar, to which he applied himself with great interest. And without knowing where in the dictionary to look for the words he needed, he addressed himself to the work of writing a letter, in that unique language, to the Royal Antiquarian Society of France, thanking them for the means of becoming acquainted with the original tongue of Brittany. In the course of a few months, a large volume, bearing the seal of that society, was delivered to him at the anvil, containing his letter in Celto-Breton, with an introduction by M. Audren de Kerdrel, testifying to its correctness of composition. The original letter is deposited in the Museum at Rennes, in Brittany, and is the first and only one written in America in the Celto-Breton language."

The attention of Governor Everett of Massachusetts was called to Burritt when, at thirty years of age, he applied for work in translation involving the use of Hebrew, Syrian, Chaldaic, Samaritan or Ethiopic. On behalf of some wealthy men, the Governor offered the learned blacksmith a course at Harvard University, but the independent student felt that it was best to continue as he had begun, making his own way in the world.

AN EARLY ADVOCATE OF WORLD PEACE

In 1841 he appeared as a public lecturer. His lecture of encouragement to young men to make the most of themselves was so favorably received that it was given sixty times. His lecture on universal peace was also received with acclamation. This was prepared in absolute ignorance of the writings of others, as the result of observations made while attempting to prepare a scientific lecture in which he planned to show the analogy between the anatomy of the earth and that of the human race. As he studied it dawned on him that the very structure of the earth invited and demanded universal peace.

Thus, by what seemed an accident he found his mission. He resolved to give his time and his talents to the advocacy of reform. In his own words, "he decided to forego studies which had been to him more the luxuries than the necessaries of a useful life," and devote himself to a weekly paper called *The Christian Citizen,* which advocated anti-slavery, peace, temperance and self-cultivation.

This was America's first peace organ. Soon he extended his efforts for peace by sending a short weekly article to a thousand other papers, many of which made use of his work.

The Oregon Boundary dispute, which for a time threatened war with England, led the reformer to make a visit to England, where, on the lecture platform, he advocated "The League of Universal Brotherhood." This soon gained thousands of members on both sides of the ocean. The society was pledged, among other things, to agitate the question of a reduction of international postage to a minimum, in order that letters might be sent as freely as possible between people of different nations, the idea being that the new bonds formed through the correspondence would compel peace.

Parliament was urged to take the lead in a movement for arbitration among the nations. A spirited campaign culminated in the vote of seventy members in favor of the measure and in a Peace Congress held in Paris in 1849, to which two chartered steamers carried seven hundred delegates. Enthusiasm was intense. Victor Hugo made the masterly closing speech, of which one Frenchman said, "It did not terminate, but eternized the congress."

ELIHU BURRITT

BETTER THAN A NOBEL PRIZE

There was in that day no Nobel prize to be awarded to the individual accomplishing most for the cause of international peace. If there had been it certainly would have been awarded to Elihu Burritt. But the city of Manchester, England, presented to him a testimonial inclosed in a mahogany case.

A second Peace Congress, held at Frankfort-on-the-Main in 1850, was made memorable by the effort to persuade Schleswig-Holstein and Denmark, which had just gone to war, to submit the issue to arbitration. Though the attempt miscarried because of the political interference of Austria, the world was deeply impressed.

Several more peace conferences were held before Mr. Burritt found it advisable to give his entire time to urging on the people of his own country a measure which he felt would save it from civil war, abolition of slavery by compensation of the owners. At his own expense he carried on a campaign that met with much favor in the North and some favor in the South. He had acquired no property, so it was necessary to work to pay expenses.

"During the summer he wrote most of his editorials in his shirt sleeves, on the head of a lime cask in the barn, pen and hoe alternating through the day. When soliciting signatures for the call for the Cleveland Convention (to consider his measure) he mowed an acre on a Fourth of July, and wrote about twenty letters in his barn the same day, his farm being nearly a mile from the village."

Later on, while in charge of the office of the cause in New York City, he worked without salary and tried to live on sixteen cents a day for food, eating a loaf of brown bread for breakfast and a twelve-cent cut of meat for dinner.

When the war seemed inevitable, the peace advocate settled down on his farm and devoted himself to increasing the knowledge of his neighbors in improved methods of agriculture. Later he went to England, where he walked across the island in order to visit farms and observe methods; observations made on this trip were published for the benefit of Englishmen and neighbors at home.

An appointment as American consular agent at Birmingham gave him an opportunity to do more helpful work in studying conditions of English life. During the intervals of his consular labors he wrote books on various subjects, and delivered free lectures through all the country tributary to Birmingham. As if this was not enough to occupy one man, he continued his efforts in behalf of universal peace. In fact, he was a factor in peace councils until his death.

During the administration of President Grant, he was retired from office. At home again, he wrote books on subjects as far apart as *Social Talks with Young People, The Psalms of David,* and *The Children of the Bible.* His interest in young people who were battling with difficulties and in the oppressed of every nation continued to the day of his death, March 7, 1879.

The name of Elihu Burritt, "the Learned Blacksmith," will always have a place in the roll of the world's reformers and philanthropists.

THE PARK AND CITY HALL IN NEW YORK CITY IN THE DAYS OF ELIHU BURRITT

MONUMENT TO JOHN MARSHALL, DISCOVERER OF THE GOLD WHICH BROUGHT RUIN
TO JOHN AUGUSTUS SUTTER

CHAPTER XIII

JOHN AUGUSTUS SUTTER, THE CALIFORNIA ENIGMA

EPITHETS

ONE of the greatest enigmas of history is John Augustus Sutter. It would be difficult to find a man of whom more contradictory words have been spoken. To add to the curious state of affairs, documentary evidence is cited to prove each idea!

Thus, in the minds of some, Sutter was a patriot. But others say he was a traitor. He was honest, and he was dishonest. He was open and aboveboard, and he was a schemer. He was a friend of those in need, and he had no use for anyone unless he saw the opportunity to make that person minister to his selfish ends. In short, he was a thoroughly good man, and he was a rascal.

A friend who knew him during the closing years of his life declares: "He was noted for his brave, generous, frank and confiding nature and faithful and conscientious discharge of his duties." Yet a historian says he was "an intriguer, who used every means to forward his own interests at the expense of others, an adventurer who quarreled with every associate; a merchant, who never paid a debt he could avoid; a schemer, whose energy was but a phase of reckless enthusiasm and whose executive ability did not extend beyond subjecting Indians."

Again, "he was noble-hearted, and his nobility was shown to hundreds of immigrants from the East to California. In him they found a man of cultivated interests, ready to help them and supply their needs." But note the contradiction: "In later years Sutter and his friends sought to create the impression that he aided the strangers from motives of charity, and with loss to himself, but nothing could be further from the truth."

Of all who have written unfavorably of this strange man's character, Hubert Howe Bancroft, the indefatigable historian of the Pacific coast, takes first place. According to him the pioneer was "great only in his wonderful personal magnetism and power of making friends for a time of all who could be useful to him; good only in the possession of kindly impulses. . . . He never hesitated to assume any obligation for the future without regard to his ability to meet it." . . . He was "without business capacity" . . . "Of principle, of honor, of respect for the rights of others, were found but slight traces in him" . . . He was "entitled to no admiration or sympathy" . . . "An adventurer from the first" . . . He had a "peculiar talent for inspiring confidence" . . . None of the pioneers "received so much praise from so many sources; few have deserved so little." . . . "But for the discovery of gold on his land, his name would hardly be known out of California."

These opinions of Bancroft are of great interest, because they are so opposite to the ideas of many others. The historian piles epithet on epithet, really leaving nothing for the man to stand on.

Yet the same historian—in honesty that wins his readers—is compelled to say that Sutter was "more honored with words of eulogy than any other California pioneer down to the day of his death in 1880."

Who was this strange Jekyll-and-Hyde character, and how did he win such contradictory opinions?

MAKING READY

During the closing years of the eighteenth century a family named Sooter or Sutter lived in Berne, Switzerland. But the prospect of improving their fortunes led them to migrate to the Grand Duchy of Baden. There, in the town of Kandern, on February 28, 1803, a son was born, to whom was given the name Johann August. When he was sixteen years of age his parents sent him to the land of freedom for which they longed through all their residence in Germany; even if he had been born in Germany, they were determined that he should receive his schooling in the land of Wilhelm Tell.

Those who have written fragmentary statements about his career differ as to the school he attended; one says he went to Neufchâtel, while another says he graduated from the military college at Berne. Very likely both statements are correct. At any rate he graduated from the military school when he was twenty. Before he left Basle he was made a Swiss citizen.

The duplex story of the life of Suter—or Sutter, as his name was spelled in later years—begins during the period following his acquirement of French citizenship. Both stories agree in the account of his service as a Swiss soldier, in accordance with the demand made on all young men in that country. But one story gives to him an adventurous life in France, as a member of the Swiss guard of the French Army. According to this story, "he mixed with

the élite of French society at the Court of Charles X, saw
service in the Spanish Campaign in 1823 and 1824, but
after the overthrow of the Bourbons he returned to
Switzerland." Bancroft, however, treats this French tale
as "pure fiction."

A checkered business career followed his service in the
Swiss army, coincident with his experience as an officer of
citizen soldiers who were always on call for active service in time of need. Annette Dübeld became Mrs. Sutter
in 1826. The family prospered; within six years there
were three sons and a daughter. But his business at Burg-
dorf—selling newspapers and bookbinding—did not do so
well. Soon he was a bankrupt. Bancroft seems to feel
that the result was inevitable, because "neither his capital
nor his experience was at all commensurate with his
enthusiasm."

The young Swiss was of a buoyant disposition. Why
not go to America, and there recoup his fortunes? Again
his critics say that when, in 1834, he set out for the new
venture, he left his family in straitened circumstances,
while to his creditors he left the task of settling his affairs.

His object in going to America is in dispute. "He
wanted to make a fortune" is the rather blunt and unsym-
pathetic Bancroft explanation. Others give him credit
for higher motives; they assume that he had a right to
make the statement that he did not go to America "to
retrieve a dissipated fortune," but because of his intrepid
military spirit, the traditional Swiss love of freedom, the
glowing reports of opportunities for a greater life to be
found in the rising young republic of the West. "My
object in going to America was to be a farmer," he said
once, in later life. Again he declared that he wished to
found a Swiss colony in the land of freedom.

Before landing at New York, in July, 1834, he made the acquaintance of two Germans and two Frenchmen, who agreed to join him as he went westward. The five men decided that they would learn no English while they were together, but Sutter thought best to Anglicize his given name to John Augustus. The strange partnership continued until Indiana was reached.

Sutter went on until he came to St. Louis. Later, in St. Charles, he applied for American citizenship, and bought a piece of land. He had some business success in the frontier community, where "his pleasing address, his sanguine temperament, and his personal energy" appealed to those he met. The stories of adventure and profit related in his hearing by those who had made trading expeditions on the Santa Fé trail to New Mexico, led him to look with longing to the southwest. With his usual success in approaching others, he managed to secure the coöperation of a trading company of perhaps fifty emigrants from Germany. By this time he had become master of a little English, and soon he knew enough Spanish for trading purposes. Most of his contacts were with the Indians, however. It has been charged that he was not always so careful as he might have been in his dealings with the original Americans or with his German associates. The critical Bancroft attacked him while seeming to come to his defense. He urged that too much credence should not be given to Sutter's detractors, since there were reasons "for believing that these charges were to a certain extent unfounded." This historian begs his readers to remember that "then as before and later, Sutter was an enthusiast, and he had the faculty of imparting his enthusiasm to others. His ventures were always far beyond his abilities. He rarely hesitated to incur any obligation for the future, and he was rarely able, in financial matters, to keep his promises."

But, whatever the reason, the trading company formed for operations in New Mexico was a failure, and Sutter was denounced as a swindler by some of his associates. These charges must be taken with a degree of caution, in view of the contradictory opinions of Sutter and his character.

New Mexico did not long content the restless adventurer. In the course of his work he talked with men who had been to California. They told him of the wonderful climate and the opportunities for money-making there, precisely as men from California talk to-day. Once more he succeeded in imparting to others the enthusiasm he had gained for a new venture, and before long he set out from Santa Fé with a rather mixed company—three Germans, two Americans, a Belgian, and a Mexican who went as a servant. Because he was told, by someone who seemed eager to deceive him, that the difficulties of the route across the mountains of New Mexico and beyond were too great to be considered, the company chose to return to St. Louis, and take the route to Oregon from there.

In April, 1838, the associates left St. Louis, in company with Captain Tripp, of the American Fur Company. From the Wind River rendezvous of the fur-traders, they proceeded to Fort Hall, Fort Boise, and Walla Walla. Between the Dalles and the Willamette, they joined forces with the famous pioneer missionary, Jason Lee, the story of whose journey to and experience in the Oregon country is one of the most colorful records of Western pioneering. In October they were at the Hudson's Bay Company's Fort Vancouver, where Sutter won the confidence of officials who did not hesitate to give him letters of intro-

duction to other pioneer residents of the coast with whom
he might come in contact. According to Bancroft, he was
under still greater obligations to the Hudson's Bay Company, since "his peculiar talent for inspiring confidence led
to his being given a loan by the Company which was not
repaid for many years."

Talk of California's wonderful Sacramento Valley inspired Sutter with a desire to make his venture for fortune
there. The winter season was not favorable for a journey
over the mountains, and there was no vessel bound for
Yerba Buena, as San Francisco's predecessor was known.
So he found easy the decision to go to California by way
of the Sandwich Islands. To Sutter's free and easy nature,
what was a little roundabout journey like that? And why
should a few months more or less be taken into account?

When the *Columbia* left the mouth of the Columbia
River on November 11, 1838, he was a passenger, together with one of the original party, who had remained
faithful to him. In Honolulu he spent five months, waiting
for a vessel in which he could continue his journey. These
months were by no means wasted; they gave him welcome
opportunity to meet—and sell himself to—some of the
leaders in the island community. On all he met he made,
as usual, a fine impression. He was able to choose several
new companions, as well as to secure eight or ten Kanakas,
who, he felt sure, would be useful on the ranch he proposed to start when he reached the Sacramento Valley.
For the services of each of these natives, he agreed with
the king of the Sandwich Islands to pay ten dollars per
month for a period of three years. Another picturesque
addition to the company of adventurers was an Indian lad
whom Kit Carson had sold to Sutter before his departure
for Oregon, for $100.

[231]

Among Sutter's new friends was a shipowner who agreed to send him as supercargo on the English brig *Clementine,* which sailed from Honolulu on April 30, 1839, for Sitka, Alaska. Thus another stage in the roundabout journey was begun.

Sitka brought profit in various ways, not only by trading, but by affording contact with officers of the Russian-American Trading Company. He was a favorite with these men, and he was a welcome partner in the dance with the wife of the governor, who was a Russian princess. The acquaintances made during the brief stay of the brig in Sitka bore fruit in a sheaf of letters of commendation "to whom it may concern." These were in the possession of the confidence-inspiring Sutter when the *Clementine* entered San Francisco Bay on July 1, 1839.

At last the long and involved route from Santa Fé to California was at an end. Instead of traveling a mere matter of fifteen hundred miles, as he might have done if he had not been so ready to listen to discouragers, he had made his weary way for from ten to twelve thousand miles during perhaps fifteen months!

MAKING A SETTLEMENT

Sutter's stay at Yerba Buena was brief; the rules of the port required that a foreign vessel depart after forty-eight hours' allowance for repairs. The next stage of the pilgrimage was to Monterey, the sleepy Spanish town in which Governor Alvarado was in charge of affairs for the vast region where Spanish missions, Spanish ranches, Russian traders, Hudson's Bay trappers, and a few American adventurers occupied that portion of California which had been taken from its ancient Indian possessors, or redeemed from desolation and silence.

At once he sought the Governor, made known his purpose to found a colony in California, and presented the letters of introduction from officers of the Hudson's Bay Company at Fort Vancouver and of the Russian-American Company at Sitka, as well as from merchants in Honolulu. He even bore credentials from the United States consul on Oahu, in the Sandwich Islands, who spoke of him as "a Swiss gentleman of the first class among men of honour, talent and estimation," and said that he was worthy of all confidence and support. Bancroft notes in connection with this consular letter that, in introducing Sutter as a captain who had seen service in the French army, the adventurer was lending himself to "a harmless enough deception."

Governor Alvarado, who considered himself a good judge of men, probably thought he was more impressed by the man himself than by the words of those who stood his sponsors. At any rate, "his pleasing manners, his apparent energy, his unexceptional recommendations, and the reasonable and beneficial nature of his project made his way perfectly clear."

But when Sutter made known his desire to secure a large tract of land in the Sacramento Valley which would be an "empresario de colonizaçion," Alvarado told him that this was impossible. However, he was so much impressed by the applicant that he made a suggestion:

"Why not apply to become a Mexican citizen, then go into the interior and select any tract of unoccupied land that will suit you? In a year or so, why not return to Monterey, and secure your naturalization papers, as well as a grant for the land?"

The idea appealed to Sutter. It was an easy matter to apply for citizenship. Was he not already a citizen of Switzerland! Had he not applied for American citizenship? Thus the citizenship habit had such a hold on him that he fell in at once with Alvarado's suggestion.

Another habit—the letter-of-recommendation habit—was so strong that he managed to secure a cordial note to General Vallejo, the magnate and representative of Spanish authority at Sonoma. After he paid a visit to the courtly Spanish official, Vallejo's suggestion that he make his home near him in Sonoma, or at least in the Napa or the Suisun Valley, did not appeal to him. There he would be too close to Spanish officials to carry out the purposes he had formed. Of course, he was too polite to give any such reason for refusing the Vallejo invitation; he contented himself by saying that he thought he must look until he found a home on some navigable river.

Next he sought McIntosh's Ranch, where he saw many things that increased his eagerness for the grant of land where he could be supreme. From there he went to the Russian settlements of Ross and Bodega, north of San Francisco Bay. Information gained there enabled him to find the location he sought on the Sacramento River, near the place where the American River joins forces with that stream.

During his absence from Monterey his purpose took form. He would have a trading post on the river. To this trappers from the mountains would go for supplies, and to dispose of their furs. Indians, too, would be useful to him. He would obey the laws of Mexico in his dealings with them, at least so far as proved necessary, or as suited the purpose of a man located at a point distant from the Mexican authorities. These Indians would make good

[234]

laborers. What a powerful man he could become with trappers, Indians, as well as the roving adventurers who would be attracted to such a center as he would establish!

On his return to Monterey, the privilege of citizenship was promised to him at the end of the year, as well as the future gift of a generous site for the building of a settlement, on condition that "he should maintain native Indians of the different tribes of those points in the enjoyment and liberty of their possession, without molesting them; and that he should use no other means of reducing them to civilization but those of prudence and friendly intercourse, and not make war upon them in any way without previously obtaining authority from government."

The start for the Sacramento River was made from San Francisco Bay. Enough had been learned of the program of the Swiss-American-Mexican to arouse interest. A company of his friends—already he could boast many friends in and about Yerba Buena—tendered him a farewell dinner on a ship in the harbor.

Then, on August 9, 1839, the impressive Sutter fleet started for the Sacramento River. Two chartered schooners and a four-oared pinnace—Sutter's own property—were laden with his Kanakas, three or four white men, the Indian boy from Oregon, and a bulldog which had been brought from Oahu. Then there were provisions, ammunition, agricultural tools, cattle—secured "always on credit," Bancroft says—and three small cannon from Honolulu.

For six or seven days—the vessels halted at night—the strange procession of boats threaded the channels of San Francisco Bay and Suisun Bay, avoiding the many sloughs and inlets, then ascended the Sacramento River to the site chosen for the far-reaching experiment. When

[235]

the cargoes had been unloaded and the tents pitched, the schooners started on the return trip to Yerba Buena, receiving, as they began the voyage, a salute of nine guns from the cannon which were to be the beginning of the fortification Sutter had in mind.

Of the spot where the saluting cannon were planted, Bancroft says: "No one can dispute the fact that the General [the famous California climate turns captains into generals as easily as it transforms sand into oranges!] displayed extraordinary judgment and remarkable foresight in the selection of the spot for the establishment of his colony."

Grass and tule houses for the Kanakas were occupied in September, and before winter the cannon were mounted in an adobe building, with roof of tule, forty feet long. In this Sutter lived and traded with the Indians who received his gifts, sold stolen horses to him, and more than once attempted his life.

Nueva Helvetia, or New Switzerland, as the trading post was called, was a busy place from the first. Voyages to San Francisco in the pinnace bore fruit when recruits came to the station in the wilderness, and when cattle and horses—bought, as before, on credit—were added to the herds on the grant. A road was made from the settlement to the landing-place on the Sacramento, and ambitious plans were laid for hunting, trapping and gardening operations for 1840.

Within four months of the beginning of New Helvetia, thoughtful General Vallejo wrote to the commanding officer at San José a prophetic word:

"We must not lose sight of a settlement of foreigners in the direction of the Sacramento, said to have been made with the permission of the departmental government

[236]

though contrary to law and to the latest orders from Mexico. That establishment is very suspicious."

Perhaps it did not enter the head of the courtly magnate at Sonoma that one of Alvarado's reasons for encouraging Sutter's establishment was that a rival might be created who would offset the growing influence of Vallejo!

Yet Vallejo knew how to play the game even when he was suspicious. It became his duty, in 1840, to supply soldiers for the defense of Sutter's settlement against Indians who threatened difficulty in spite of the liberal policy at first adopted by the Swiss adventurer for their pacification.

In August, 1840, when Sutter received his naturalization papers, he was authorized to represent the Monterey government at New Helvetia. As a civil magistrate he was given power to administer laws.

The trappers from New Helvetia soon came into conflict with those of the Hudson's Bay Company, and Sutter took steps to warn that company to keep off what he claimed as his trapping territory. This is but an indication of the steady increase in power of the new settlement and its proprietor, who showed his genius by taking advantage of every opportunity to increase his prestige. For example, he became the purchaser of Ross and Bodega, the posts of the Russian-American Company in northern California. The property secured was not great, but the prestige was worth the price of $30,000—especially when it is considered that the debt was to be paid in instalments during four years, and that the payments were long delayed. The property of New Helvetia was pledged for the debt.

Among the valued articles that came to Sutter from Ross were several cannon used by Bonaparte after his

[237]

disastrous expedition to Moscow; these had been presented by the Czar to the Russian-American Company. They were duly mounted in Sutter's Fort, begun in 1841, and completed in 1844, which succeeded the original adobe building.

This fort, which was to become historic, had an "adobe wall 18 feet high and three feet thick, enclosing a space of 500 by 150 feet. At the southeast and northwest corners projecting bastions or towers rose above the walls of the rectangle. Cannon commanded the gateways in the center of each side except the western. Loop-holes were pierced in the walls at different points. Guns were mounted at the main entrances on the south and elsewhere. . . . An inner wall, with the included space roofed over, furnished a large number of apartments in the California style. . . . The walls were five feet thick, and were strengthened with beams. An exterior gallery ran around the wall."

In 1841, taking a survey and map of the grant he sought, Sutter went to Monterey, and delivered a petition in which he told of his desire to cultivate a part of the many vacant lands on which he had established himself on the Sacramento River, while with him were "some industrious families who chose to follow him." This promised to be "a barrier to the incursions of the barbarous tribes to the settlements, and as a school of civilization . . . to the barbarous natives."

On June 18, 1841, Alvarado granted eleven leagues of land, since Sutter had "sufficiently accredited his laboriousness, good conduct and other qualifications required in such cases," and had shown "patriotic zeal" in favor of Mexican institutions.

Thus Captain Sutter found himself master of New

Helvetia and Fort Sutter, of which Lieutenant Wilkes, a visitor from the United States in 1841, said: "It will not be long before it becomes in some respects an American colony."

The prophecy of this officer of the United States Navy was so fully borne out by future events that one historian has been led to say:

"Captain Sutter's acts, and the progress of his establishment on the Sacramento, cannot be treated as a purely local affair, but must be presented with the current annals of the department, so closely are they connected with the general subject of immigration and the growth of foreign influence in California."

MAKING CALIFORNIA AMERICAN

In 1841 Sutter's proud position as a magnate of all he surveyed on the Sacramento River gave him a position of leadership in California that may well have ministered to his pride. To think that, only a few years before, he had come from Switzerland a penniless immigrant! Now he was "clothed with legal authority over the settlers on his estate, successful in converting the savages into laborers, owner of large herds and flocks to be paid for in the future, with a band of trappers at work for him in a region rich in furs, with a distillery yielding a profitable product of brandy, and with a constant incoming stream of immigration which was vastly increasing his strength and was soon to give great value to his land."

His prosperity led to renewed protest from General Vallejo, which angered him to such an extent that he said the annoyance must cease, or he would march on Sonoma.

A letter written to a business acquaintance on November 8, 1841, told of his dream:

"Very curious Rapports came to me from belaw; but the poor wretches don't know what they do. . . . It is too late now to drive me out of the country, the first step that they do against me is that I will make a declaration of Independence and proclaim California for a Republique independent of Mexico. . . . I am strong enough to hold me till the couriers go to the Waillamet for raise about 60 to 70 good men, another party I would despatch to the Mountains and call the hunters and Shawnees and Delawares with which I am very well acquainted. . . . If they will give me satisfaction. . . . I will be a faithful Mexican, but when the Rascle of a Castro should come here, a very warm and hearty welcome is prepared for him. . . ."

There were not lacking hints that Great Britain was ready to take advantage of Mexico's debt to her to seize the country, attach it to Oregon, and make a Pacific Coast Territory of her own. But there were many who insisted that Great Britain had no interest in a country which would probably never "become of any great importance in the history of the world, since "scarcely a country in the world is cursed with a soil more hopelessly sterile."

Loyal Mexicans, however, valued the country in spite of what were called its drawbacks. Vallejo and others wished to see Sutter dispossessed. How easily this could be managed by buying up the mortgage given to the Russian-American Company on New Helvetia when Ross and Bodega were bought! Alvarado made light of the danger when Vallejo wrote to him of his fears because Sutter exercised arbitrary and despotic power, waged war on the natives, forced them to work for him, received foreigners, not obliging them to present themselves to the authorities. "And finally he makes seditious threats," the loyal old man concluded his protest. Alvarado told him his fears were groundless, but Vallejo could not be convinced. Still he made up his mind not to use against Sutter the force by which he felt sure he could oust the dangerous man, since he disliked to interfere with such a prosperous settlement so much needed in the country.

Sir George Simpson of the Hudson's Bay Company shared Vallejo's fears. Once he wrote of Sutter:

"If he really has the talent and courage to make the most of his position he is not unlikely to make California a second Texas. . . . Captain Sutter's establishment is admirably situated. Besides lying on the direct route to San Francisco on the one hand and the Missouri and the Willamette on the other, it virtually excludes the Californians from the best parts of their own country."

Again Simpson wrote:

"The Americans, becoming masters of the interior through Sutter's establishment, would soon discover that they have a natural right to a maritime outlet; so that whatever may be the fate of Monterey and the more southerly points, San Francisco will to a moral certainty, sooner or later fall into the possession of Americans. As Texas has been wrested from Mexico on the one side of the Continent, so California will be speedily lost to her on the other. The only doubt is whether California is to fall to the British or to the Americans. The latter, whether one looks at their seizure of Texas, or at their pretensions to the Oregon, has clearly the advantage in an unscrupulous choice of weapons. We're altogether too ready to forget that the fulfilment of even the most palpable degree of providence will not justify in man the employment of unrighteous means."

Thus Simpson did not give to Sutter credit for the most patriotic motives. Yet someone who held different views said of the owner of New Helvetia that he was "determined to rear the standard of American freedom in this distant and secluded dependency of imbecile Mexico."

Perhaps it would be as well to let Sutter speak for himself as to his plans and hopes:

"Vallejo and others of the Californians, against whom rather than the Indians I kept my fort and guns in order, were jealous of my settlement. I gave passports to those entering the country, and this they did not like. I was friendly with the immigrants, of whom they were jealous. I encouraged immigration, while they discouraged it. I sympathized with the Americans, while they hated them."

Notable among the visitors to the fort were official immigrants—John C. Frémont and his party, in 1844. To them, in their need, Sutter showed great kindness. Scores, hundreds, and even thousands of less illustrious visitors to California owed to the enigma of New Helvetia assistance and encouragement, from the days of the earliest immigrants to those of the ill-fated Donner party.

Bancroft owns that "Sutter treated the immigrants well," but adds that this was "because it was to his interest to do so." Yet the kindness was not greater, "except in aiding them to evade the laws," than was that of Vallejo. "It is well that pioneers look back with gratitude to the captain's kindness, whatever may have been his motives," the historian goes on to say. "A better man would probably not have done so well; and were it not for the absurd pretensions and the unlimited flattery of later years, it would be in doubtful taste now to look too closely into Sutter's true character and merits."

It is difficult to appraise properly still other acts of

Sutter. For instance, there was his giving assistance to Micheltorena in his revolt against the authority of Alvarado, and his acceptance from the rebel of a large additional grant of land. The opera bouffe war that followed resulted in the defeat of Micheltorena, when the rebel army had dwindled from four hundred men to less than fifty. Sutter was made a prisoner, but when he explained that "he had aided Micheltorena only as a subordinate officer in obedience to orders," he was allowed to return to New Helvetia with his privileges and power as great as before.

The futile contest of Micheltorena was but the beginning of Mexico's final trouble with California. Revolts and grumblings were many and persistent. Remembering the ill-advised attempt of Commander Jones of the United States Pacific Squadron to take Monterey in 1842, when a government explanation was given that this act was absolutely without authorization, the United States Government wisely kept hands off. "In the contest between Mexico and California we can take no part, unless the former should commence hostilities against the United States," was the pronouncement of Buchanan, Polk's Secretary of State. "But should California assert and maintain her independence, we should render her all the kind offices in our power as a sister republic."

When the Frémont exploring party came to Sutter's Fort in 1846, they were given a warm welcome. The people of the territory were disturbed by the presence of so many armed men, though they professed to be a peaceable expedition. They refused to leave the country when ordered to do so. The suggestion of Sutter that Mexico buy his fort, and the revolt of the American settlers of the Sacramento and Napa valleys were events of the same year. The Bear Flag Revolt, as it was called from the ensign adopted by the rebels, was supported by Frémont. Sutter showed friendship to Frémont, and so, he claimed, turned his back on Mexico.

The events of the Bear Flag Revolt merged into those which followed the declaration of war by the United States. That declaration became vivid to California when the Stars and Stripes floated over Sonoma on July 9, 1846, and two days later over Sutter's Fort and New Helvetia, thus gratifying the commander of the strange fortress and justifying the words of Waddy Thompson in his *Recollections of Mexico*:

"Captain Suter is the real sovereign of the country if anyone is. I have no doubt his force would be more than a match for any Mexican force which will ever be sent against him."

Let Bancroft have the last word in accounting for the upheaval:

"Sutter's settlement on the Sacramento was not only the first in a broad and important territory, utilized only by trappers down to 1839; but was destined to be a leading factor in the political changes of 1846."

For a brief season after the war, the master of Sutter's Fort prospered. Growing San Francisco demanded food and lumber, and Sutter was advantageously situated for supplying the need. In time the call became so insistent that a site of a new flour mill was chosen, and, to supply material for this, a sawmill was planned on the South Fork of the American River, perhaps forty-five miles from Sutter's Fort. J. W. Marshall and some of the discharged members of the Mormon battalion which had come to California during the war, were engaged to build the mill. While the work was in progress, Marshall made the dis-

[244]

SUTTER'S FORT, SACRAMENTO, CALIFORNIA, RESTORED

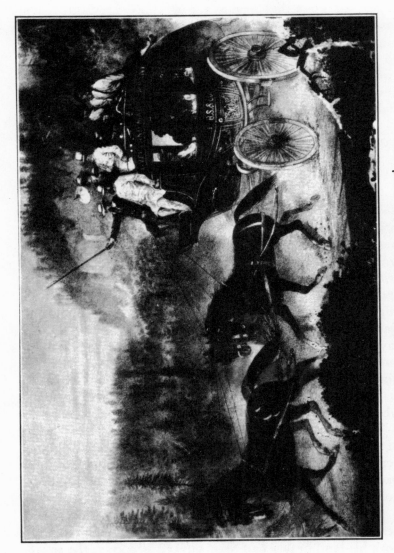

THE LIGHTNING OVERLAND MAIL. HOW SUTTER'S
LETTERS WENT TO CALIFORNIA

covery of gold that began a new epoch in California's history. In vain Sutter tried to keep the news from leaking out; he feared the desertion of the laborers who were so necessary to his agricultural operations. Yet within two months the news was known in San Francisco, and the new El Dorado was sought by every man who could possibly go into the interior.

MAKING VAIN EFFORTS TO RETRIEVE DISASTER

The discovery that brought wealth to thousands carried disaster and disappointment to Sutter. He could not secure the help he needed to care for the ranch. His herd of 13,000 horses, cattle, sheep and hogs dwindled to nothing. His responsibilities as governor of his district, under the appointment of General Stockton, and as Indian agent, by the grace of General Kearny, took his mind from some of his misfortunes. For a time he continued to live, as one of those who have written of his life says, "a simple, generous, hospitable, unostentatious life among the Americans, Irish, Germans, and civilized Indians, who were members of his household," to whom he was as a patriarch, advising and reproving, and punishing whenever punishment was necessary.

The beginning of the year 1852 saw him all but bereft of the land to which he had welcomed immigrants from the beginning of his occupation. Pretended settlers and rapacious gold diggers squatted on the broad acres, and took possession of the last of his herds.

Recourse to the courts proved vain. While the United States Land Commission found in his favor, declaring that both his land grants had been secured properly, the squatters appealed to the United States District Court of the Northern District of California. An unfavorable verdict led to a second appeal. This time the original Alvarado grant was confirmed, but that received from Micheltorena was accounted worthless.

The last of the Sutter fortune was spent in this litigation, as well as in making good titles to those who had purchased land from him in good faith. The last stand on California soil was made in the Hook Farm, on Feather River, which Sutter hoped to keep for his old age. Even this hope proved vain.

More honors were thrust on the favorite of other years by some who had not forgotten. Sutter was a member of the Constitutional Convention and he received about two thousand votes for Governor.

An example of the esteem in which he was held by many of the California pioneers was the presentation of a sword, in 1853, from the Second Ohio Regiment. To this gift he responded modestly:

"I claim no credit whatever for any service I may have rendered in the early days of California. As one of the pioneers, I could not do less than use my best exertions to promote the prosperity and contribute to the comfort and enjoyment of those who followed me to its lovely valleys. To do so was pleasure, and that alone prompted me in everything that I did. If in promoting my own pleasure I have been so fortunate as to secure the esteem of my fellow citizens, I am doubly proud."

The state of California showed its appreciation of his services to it in the past by paying to him a pension of $250 a month for fourteen years. This grant enabled him to persist in his efforts to secure justice from the national government. For many years he argued that restitution should be made to him by a grant from public lands, sufficient to replace the lands taken from him. Failing this, he felt he should receive $122,063 in cash.

Once, when he was in Washington, he learned of quaint Lititz, Pennsylvania, where associates would be congenial, while his daughter could attend a good school, and his rheumatism could be helped by the medicinal waters. For years he divided his time between the Capital and the peaceful Pennsylvania town. Once, when asked to go as far as New York City, to attend a meeting of the Pioneer Society, he wrote:

"Sick in heart and body, in vain appealing to Congress to do me justice, and to return only part of what was wrongfully taken from me, and with little hope of success, this session, unless you, my friends, by your influence will aid my cause, I could not feel cheerful as your guest at the table to-night, and I did not want to mar your pleasure by my presence."

Disappointment pursued him to the close of his life. On January 18, 1880, word was brought to him as he sat in his room in the St. Charles Hotel at Washington that, for the sixteenth time, his request to Congress had been denied. On this occasion the bill for his relief had passed the House, and was ready for the third reading in the Senate, when an overzealous member of that body, in his friendship for Sutter, talked in favor of the bill until wearied associates carried a motion to adjourn. The disappointment was too great to be borne, and Sutter's heart failed.

The funeral at Lititz was attended by delegates from the Pioneer Society of New York. General Frémont made an address, in which he said:

"The education and improvement of the people and

country of the West was his aim. His settled purpose seemed to be to live for others; his ambition was to fill the place of the American citizen to the advantage of the whole country. General Sutter was a great man, and there were many traits in his character worth imitating."

Later General Sherman said:

"To him more than to any other we are indebted for the conquest of California, with all its treasures."

Nearly thirty years after the death of the California pioneer the Moravian Cemetery Association of Lititz was told by the Native Sons of the Golden West that plans had been made to restore Sutter's Fort, and that it was the desire of California pioneers to have the body of their old friend and associate rest in the soil of that state. But when the descendants of Sutter were consulted, they would not consent to the removal of the body. So the simple stone in the quiet cemetery at Lititz still covers all that is mortal of the immigrant from Switzerland, who helped win a princely domain for the United States, while the scene of his greatest activity in California is marked by Fort Sutter Park, in which the citizens of Sacramento have restored the old structure of the pioneer. The park was the central feature of the city's celebration of the Days of Forty-nine in May, 1922.

CHAPTER XIV

JAMES L. PETIGRU, WHO WAS LOVED BY THE MEN HE OPPOSED

A STRANGE EPITAPH

IN THE churchyard of historic St. Michael's Church, Charleston, South Carolina, there is a stone which bears a remarkable inscription. The man of whom it tells died in the midst of the Civil War, when passions were at fever heat, when—as those who knew Charleston would think—no one would have been tolerated who did not shout with his fellow citizens for the Confederacy and all for which it stood. Yet this man was so opposed to the feelings and desires of his compatriots that, on one occasion, when he was asked, at a political dinner, to drink a toast to South Carolina, he said: "Certainly. To South Carolina, and may she recover her senses."

When James Lewis Petigru died, on March 10, 1863, the people of the town were aware that a hostile fleet was ready to descend on the city to bombard it. Yet they did not decide with bitterness that, since Petigru had seen fit not to think with them, but to urge teachings which were more in accordance with those of the people with whom they were at war, they would let him go to a dishonored grave. They would not do this, for they loved the man. In response to an insistent demand, the body lay in state in the court house, and was visited by thousands, rich and poor, black and white. On the day of the funeral no business was transacted.

At once there was talk of a monument to the memory of the man who had led in the opposition to some of the dearest thoughts and purposes of his neighbors. And when finally that monument was erected it bore a remarkable inscription, composed, in part, by Northern admirers, but completed and assented to by the people of Charleston:

James Lewis Petigru
Born at
Abbeville May 10th 1789
Died at Charleston March 9th 1863

Jurist   Orator   Statesman   Patriot

Future Times will hardly know
How great a Life
This simple Stone commemorates:
The tradition of his Eloquence,
His wisdom and his Wit may fade:
But he lived for Ends more durable than Fame.
His learning illuminated the principles of Law:
His eloquence was the Protection of the Poor and Wronged.
In the Admiration of his Peers;
In the Respect of his People;
In the Affection of his Family,
His was the highest Place:
The just Mead
of his Kindness and Forbearance,
His Dignity and Simplicity,
His brilliant Genius and his unwearied Industry.
Unawed by Opinion,
Unseduced by Flattery:
Undismayed by Disaster,

JAMES L. PETIGRU

He confronted life with antique courage:
and Death with Christian Hope.
In the great Civil War
He withstood his People for his Country:
But his People did homage to the Man
Who held his Conscience higher than their Praise:
And his Country
Heaped her Honours on the Grave of the Patriot,
To whom, living,
His own righteous Self-respect sufficed
Alike for Motive and Reward.

Nothing is here for tears, nothing to wail,
—Nothing but well and fair,
And what may quiet us in a life so noble.

The main source of information about the remarkable man of whom the inscription tells—a man whose name is practically unknown except in the South, and there only to a limited extent—is a biography written in war-time by an associate in Charleston, a defender of Southern institutions, whose words of appreciation were as warm as if the two men had thought alike in all essential things. Even the paper on which the facts were written—mere scraps, for paper was becoming scarce in Charleston—showed how the city was suffering because of the triumph of Petigru's views. Yet no nobler tribute has been paid by any man to another.

LIBERTY-LOVING ANCESTORS

Perhaps twenty-five years before the Revolution Petigru's grandparents, James and Mary, came to America from Ireland. Opposition to their marriage because of religious differences led them to feel that they would be

[251]

happier in this refuge of the persecuted. Naturally, their thoughts turned to Pennsylvania. After a season in Penn's Woods, they made a trying overland journey to South Carolina, where a home was selected in the Abbeville district.

From that pioneer home went out sturdy sons and daughters who had in their hearts the love for freedom and their fellows. One son was titular Bishop of North Carolina, and his son became General Johnston Petigru, of the Confederate Army. Two brothers of the Bishop served in the Revolution.

Another son, William, after campaigning with Colonel George Washington, married a member of a second perse-cuted, liberty-loving family, Louise Engevine, daughter of Jean Louis Gilbert, a Huguenot minister who had sought South Carolina when conditions in France became unsup-portable. Thus the home that welcomed James Lewis Petigru, on May 10, 1789, was prepared to give him a wonderful heritage of unselfish devotion.

The first years of James Lewis were spent on the farm on Little River, in the Flat Woods of the Albemarle Dis-trict. His parents were his first teachers, but they wel-comed the opportunity to send him to a strolling teacher from Virginia, who appeared in the neighborhood and made known his readiness to receive pupils. He said he was able to impart knowledge, but soon it became evident that he had none to impart. Years later, when in a remi-niscent mood, Petigru said that he remembered little of the would-be teacher but the rebellion of recalcitrant pu-pils who were so successful in "barring out" the master that he was compelled to seek fresh pastures.

Further attempts to secure schooling in that day when free schools had not been thought of met with indifferent

STATE CAPITOL BUILDING, SACRAMENTO, CALIFORNIA. NEAR THE SITE OF SUTTER'S FORT.

JAMES L. PETIGRU

success. But the ambitious boy, bound to keep busy, worked diligently on the farm on Buffalo Creek, twenty miles away, to which the family removed in 1800.

The boy was fifteen years old when the fame of Dr. Waddell's grammar school at Willington led James and his parents to think seriously of the possibility of his entering there. Yet how could the expenses be met? And how could James be spared?

The question was answered in a manner that brings to mind the way in which the boy Alexander Hamilton, far away in the island of St. Croix, without opportunities, was given his longed-for opportunity to go to school in the United States. Dr. Waddell was in a house near Badwill, the Petigru residence. James Lewis listened in awe to the conversation of the great man. In the course of the evening a member of the company tried to relate something that had happened in Charleston, as reported in the town paper. The narrator's inability to tell the story clearly led the boy to forget his timidity. He knew that story—so with eagerness he tried to make the whole matter plain. He succeeded so well that Dr. Waddell patted him on the head, as he said, "If I had you with me, my boy, I would make a man of you."

That settled doubts at home. Dr. Waddell must have the lad; James must have his chance!

. The school was but ten miles from the Petigru home, but the first journey was an event. "This day I go to Willington," he wrote in his diary. " 'With joy and fear I view the vast design,' " he quoted from Pope, who was even then his favorite poet.

How the brothers and sisters, as well as the parents, missed the boy! And with what joy they received him when, on Friday evenings, he returned for two days! The traits which were to make him so popular in later life were shown in the home.

A friend of many years, after listening to his tales of the school, told of it. "Willington was a sort of Eton or Rugby of American manufacture, and the doctor at the head the Carolina Dr. Arnold," he said. The Doctor had great talents for organization and government. He appealed to the honor and moral sense of the boys. So he was willing that they should do their studying far from the schoolroom. Why should they be confined within walls when the great forest invited them? Under the trees, or up in the trees they studied. On rainy days they could take shelter in log cabins. They had but two responsibilities—to make good use of their time, and to respond quickly to the signals of the school horn, which echoed periodically down the forest aisles.

Plain living was a matter of course in that primitive community. Corn bread and bacon formed the usual bill of fare, while night study was done by the light of pine torches.

At first there was much amusement because of the new pupil, whose rustic clothing and behavior made him the target of two hundred and fifty boys, many of whom came from homes of wealth. This troubled James, who longed to be on good terms with everyone. Soon, however, he won his way in consequence of an incident designed for his humiliation. While he was studying in one of the log cabins, a boy thrust a burning stick between the logs, and scorched him. Instantly James rushed outside, grasped his tormentor, and won the victory. Of course, the fighters were summoned before the master, and received condign punishment. But what mattered punishment when, by his manliness, he had won a place among his fellows which he retained by his ability, unselfishness and geniality?

After three years at Willington he was asked to become assistant teacher, but he preferred to go to Columbia. When he graduated, in 1806, he led his class. As he studied, he made his expenses by teaching in Columbia Academy. How he learned to deny himself in those anxious days! Once he had to decline a dinner invitation because he had no clothing fit to wear in exalted company!

DEBTS AND CONQUEST

On his return home after the completion of his college course he was greeted with 'hearty acclaim, not merely because he was such a favorite with all the members of the family, but because they looked to him to solve their financial difficulties that were pressing sorely upon them. His father was dead, and dependence must be placed on him. The farm home had to go. Debts were clamoring for attention.

"Better leave the family to their fate!" he was advised by some who called themselves his friends. "Go away to a new country. If you stay here you will all go down together. The circumstances are hopeless."

"I will never leave my mother," he declared. But his mother told him that his best way to help her was to go where he could make his fortune, and send something home. She would miss him, but he would be making good preparation for the future of all the family.

He made his beginning at a district school in the Eutaws. In the evenings he studied law. And whenever he could he sent to his mother money for her support. At the same time he planned for the future of his brothers and sisters. The burden he assumed so cheerfully at that time was with him for many years, until he had sent one brother to the West, another to the Navy, and a third to school in Charleston. He was slow to ask favors for himself, but for those dependent on him he was willing to seek help. But that he did this in a manly, straightforward manner was shown by a letter which he sent to Joel R. Poinsett, Member of Congress, at Washington. This letter— which is preserved by the Historical Society of Pennsylvania,—was dated at Charleston on January 25, 1822. It is worth reading, because it reveals so much of the writer's character:

"I beg to trouble you on a matter that is very unimportant, except to a few persons whom it happens to concern, and none more than myself. I have a brother (Thomas Petigru) who has been some time in the service in the Navy. Last fall he underwent his examination and passed I believe with some credit. But the number of Midshipmen examined and admitted on that occasion was such that it is possible they will not all be commissioned, and as my brother has no friends at Court, I should not be at all surprised, if I were to see him *overslawed* as they call it. I have no objection to his waiting for his turn, but he is among the oldest midshipmen of those that were present; he was not named, in the roll of those who passed, among the first, but about the middle of the list. I suppose the order in which they were named is to be considered the criterion of their degree of merit. And if that order is observed I should not complain. But I hope he may be allowed the full benefit of his place in the list; more especially as he was unavoidably absent at last year's examination, when he would have had a claim to be examined.

[256]

"I have stated the poor youth's case to you freely, and would be highly gratified if you should be able consistently with the duties of your situation to prevent his claim from being forgotten."

Promotion came soon to the young teacher. In 1811 he became tutor in Beaufort College, and when, soon afterward, the president died, the conduct of the school was left to him. Not only did he make a succes of his teaching, but he became the hero of the boys. They liked his genial humor, and they appreciated his ability to play marbles and tops with them. Yet he was a strict disciplinarian. One day he told a girl who would not study to go home and get her lesson; then he put her out of the window as a gentle hint to depart. On another occasion, when he encountered a truant pupil, he put the boy on his back and carried him to the schoolroom.

When a new president was to be elected he became a candidate for the position. What a wonderful solution to his financial difficulties would come with the new position! How earnestly he worked and planned for the preferment! His disappointment, then, was very great when he was defeated. Life seemed done. He thought he might as well give up. But before many years passed he realized that the disappointment was a blessing in disguise. If he had succeeded, he would, in all probability, have remained a teacher all his days.

The first fruit of the disappointment was his admission to the bar in Charleston in December, 1812, and the beginning of his practice in Beaufort District. He made his home at Coosawhatchie, a small town on the road between Savannah and Charleston. This town is no longer in existence; it was deserted not long after Petigru's residence there, by reason of the impossible summer climate, which drove all residents away to seek relief from pestilence in locations more salubrious. The court-house and jail were taken elsewhere, because only one man could retain his health there, and that man seemed as impervious to fever as the alligators in the stream close at hand. Prisoners so unfortunate as to be in the jail during the period of impossible weather were sure, it is said, to escape trial —they perished first.

Petigru had to contend with other difficulties than the climate. He began to practice during the War of 1812, when there was no money in the country, and little work for the lawyer. The planters could not sell the products of their farms, since England had been their best customer.

The summer of 1813 brought a summons to war service. There was fear in Port Royal and vicinity because of the presence in the harbor of the British sloops of war, *Moselle* and *Colibri*. The militia was called out for the defense of the islands, and Petigru marched to Hilton Head with the others, part of the time with a musket on his shoulder, again driving a commissary wagon. He did not believe in the war, but he was ready to do his duty.

Before he left Coosawhatchie he met, at the home of Captain James Postell, a planter whose father had been one of General Marion's officers in the Revolution, the young woman who became his bride. The site of their first home later became a camp and parade ground for Confederate soldiers.

The young lawyer won friends by his generosity; he would never take a fee from anyone who was poor. And he won the respect of all by his straightforward method of dealing with offenders. One afternoon, when there was a fight just outside his office, he strode out, picked up the biggest of the combatants, carried him by the waistband of his trousers and by the collar into his office, and seated him on the floor. "Now keep the peace!" Petigru said. And he was obeyed.

On another occasion, when he was walking on the hotel piazza, a tall, strapping man, who had been opposed in court by Petigru, followed him, calling him all kinds of offensive names. "Really, if I had a whip, I should be tempted to whip you!" the lawyer said. The loud-mouthed man thought he was bluffing. "Wait a moment," he said, "until I can bring you a whip." Soon he offered the whip to Petigru—who took it, and used it so effectually that the man was silenced, and the friendship of the people was more firmly fixed than ever.

New Orleans tempted the young lawyer, but he decided to go to Charleston instead. There he was thrown with some of the greatest lawyers of the period. The man whose partner he became, James Hamilton, went to Congress in 1822, and Petigru succeeded to his practice. Nothing seemed to be in the way of brilliant success. Perhaps this was, in part at least, the reason for the bitter enmity of an associate who could not say things too hard about him. Petigru wondered how he could win the man. The result was unexpected. The lawyer's only son, an eight-year-old lad, died by accident. At once the opponent sent to him a note of sympathy, and asked that the memory of all difficulty be swept away.

The sad accident had another sequel. For thirty-six years, on the anniversary of the event, Petigru locked himself in his room, there to live in thought of his boy. But it was characteristic of him that when he faced the world again he was more lovable and approachable than ever.

A period of service as attorney-general for South Carolina, during the era of good feeling characteristic of Monroe's administration as President, enabled him to form the acquaintance of many public men and to get his bearings for the anxious time that came to the state soon afterward.

Soon after the close of Monroe's term as President there was the beginning of turmoil in South Carolina. The trouble began with the new tariff law of 1828. This law did not please the South, especially South Carolina. John C. Calhoun, who made himself the spokesman of the discontented planters, began to talk of State Rights. Why should a state be compelled to live under a law which did not appeal to them? Surely it was their privilege to make null and void such an act, so far as their state was concerned. Why, said Calhoun, should not the malcontents have the privilege of calling a convention for the purpose of declaring the new law null and void, not to be carried into effect within their borders?

NULLIFICATION

This Nullification proposal was received in the South with various feelings. Most of the people were dumbfounded by the suggestion. Tennessee hastened to join Georgia in discountenancing it. Virginia, and even North Carolina, gave the neighboring state no sympathy. But in South Carolina many wondered if Calhoun were not pointing the way out of their difficulties.

The author of the only monograph on Petigru's life said: "In South Carolina it separated friends; it divided families; it made neighbors foes. Serious enough in its consequences throughout the State, it was charged with double hate and rage in her commercial capital. Fre-

ST. PHILIP'S PROTESTANT EPISCOPAL CHURCH, CHARLESTON, SOUTH CAROLINA

SHELDON JACKSON IN ALASKAN COSTUME

quently the adverse parties were arrayed against each other, and on the eve of coming to blows."

"Nullification means civil war," some said. "It will bring revolution with all its horrors."

"Nullification is an admirable remedy for our difficulties," was the reply. "It is safe, speedy, effectual, peaceful, having no sympathy with revolution or civil war; a preserver, not a destroyer of the Union. It is within the Constitution, not opposed to it."

Here was a mighty good chance for Petigru to keep from taking sides. That is, it would have been a good chance for a man who was not true to his convictions. The Charleston lawyer knew nothing about keeping on the fence, for policy's sake. The only policy for him was to speak plainly.

"The Union is in the balance!" he said, in effect. "Its dissolution will be an evil without remedy, and dissolution will be the child of nullification. And what excuse is there for it? The tariff is not sufficient reason for such anxiety. The declaration made by stump orators that the South is the slave of the North, that the Federal Government is a tyrant, is nothing more than the clamor of a disordered imagination."

On the platform, at barbecues, in his correspondence, he maintained his thesis boldly. "The refusal to obey a law would necessarily bring into conflict those who refuse to obey and those whose duty it is to enforce the law. To say that a State might at pleasure repeal a law of the whole Union, not only with safety, but with advantage to it, is simply an absurdity. It will end inevitably in war."

The man who could speak so plainly on a vital matter was needed in the Legislature of South Carolina, many thought. So they persuaded him to run for election.

[261]

"They have impressed me for a senator," he said. "I resisted stoutly, and bawled lustily for help, but none would help me, so nothing was to be done."

On December 15, 1830, on the night of the election, he wrote to Joel R. Poinsett at Columbia a letter, which may be seen in the collection of the Historical Society of Pennsylvania:

"The result of the election was declared about ½ after 11. I have a majority of 227 . . . a great deal of money has been lost. . . . Old Dawson won 500 dollars, betting on a majority of 200. . . . As to going up at once to take my seat, it seems unnecessary. The fatigue is not to be considered at all, but I am very anxious to go to Savannah River. I will not determine till tomorrow. I see no use in going up if the house is to adjourn on the 18th, but if I was sure it would sit until Tuesday, it would make a difference."

But on the morrow he found that the decision had been made for him. He was not elected, after all! The first announcement had been an error!

His plain speech did not make enemies for him, but it did not win enough adherents to insure his election, and a Nullification man was sent to the legislature.

However, his voice was not silenced by the verdict at the polls. He continued to give such homely messages as that reported from one gathering:

"I see some broad-shouldered and deep-chested men among you, but who of this assembly would undertake, with all his muscular power, to strip off, at a single pull, all the hair from the tail of one of yon horses that stand hitched behind you among the trees? It would be impossible for the strongest. But the weakest among you, if he takes the hairs one by one, might pull them out easily, and

leave the stump at last bare as his hand. It is thus that
dis-union will expose you to be stripped by enemies that
you now despise."

"Where did you get that horse's tail?" he was asked
by a listener who noted the effectiveness of the illustration.
"Was it the sight of the horses standing near by?"

"Not at all!" was the reply. "I got the horse's tail
from Plutarch."

Fortunately, James Hamilton, the leader on the side
of Nullification, was also a wise man. He and Petigru,
working together, managed to keep the peace. More
than once uprisings were threatened which might have led
to civil war, but better counsels prevailed. "The two leaders," it has been said, "deserved a civic crown for saving
the life, not of a citizen, but of a people."

APPRECIATION

Petigru was so full of the needs of others that he had
little time to heed his own necessities. He was so generous that his friends feared that he would have no patrimony. Both Nullificationists and Unionists were among
those who proposed that he buy a plantation, in the hope
that the necessity of providing for deferred payments on
the land would keep him from the lavish gifts which they
deprecated. But when he had the plantation his generosity
took another turn. No Negroes were so well housed or
clothed as his slaves. One result was that he became involved in debt. The plantation was lost, and he had the
choice of going through the bankruptcy court or of attempting the Herculean task of paying all claims. Of
course, he chose the latter alternative. And he succeeded
in his aim. "It required toil which few men could have

borne," a friend said of him, "toil which none but a man of high honor would have undertaken."

The character which showed itself in the days of the Nullification proposals, as well as in the time of financial adversity, enabled him to prove again his regal manhood, when the long-continued threats of trouble began to take definite form. The day came when the prophecies of Petigru, made in the season of Nullification arguments, were about to be fulfilled. Threats of withdrawal from the Union were heard on every hand. The outspoken voice of the patriot was ever lifted against the idea of a Confederation based on slavery. He endeavored at every opportunity to give the lie to the boast of the advocates of secession that "the act of dissolution would produce no effects of a serious nature; that not a drop of blood would be spilled; that no man's Negroes or houses or lands would be plundered or destroyed; that unbroken prosperity would follow the ordinance of secession." He said very plainly that war would be the result of the dissolution of the Union, . . . secession would give the abolition party a power over slavery that nothing else could give, a power to make war on Southern institutions, to proclaim freedom to Negroes, to invoke and command the sympathy and aid of the whole world in carrying on a crusade against the Southern States. He assured the people of the South that secession would unite the North, and that bankruptcy would follow war.

"But think of the election of Lincoln!" he was told. "How can we stand that?"

"The election of Lincoln is not a sufficient cause for war," was the reply. "Be patient until the next election. See if there is not a change then."

How did the people of one of the most outspoken of the

Southern States act toward the man who talked so plainly
to them, attempting to demolish all their pet ideas? In
the very midst of the tumult of war they chose him to
high office, at a large salary; he was "to codify the laws
of the State, and to give to them all possible precision and
perspicuity." And let it not be thought that this was the
result of an unexplainable impulse, to be recalled a little
later. For Petigru was reappointed to the position until
the work was completed.

For the first year of the war Petigru continued his plain
speaking on matters of vital interest. And the people who
listened to him, honored him, and continued to receive
him as their friend. Is there a parallel in American history? "I am not sure," wrote the Southerner who told of
his career, "that another example can be found in the
country of a man absolutely opposed to the will of the people, and elected by them to important and lucrative position."

What a commentary was this act, not only upon Petigru, but upon the people of South Carolina as well!

Petigru's life ended not long after the completion of
the task committed to him by an appreciative people. This
was on March 9, 1863. Before the burial in historic
St. Michael's churchyard, the body lay in state at the
court-house. There, as has been said, thousands of
mourners, rich and poor, black and white, bowed their
heads before the casket of the man of whom a life-long
friend, Alfred Huger, wrote:

"Conscientious and just in matters of truth, he would
cavil about a hair. Generous and brave, he would give
without measure, and asked nothing in return. His probity never was shaken by adversity, and his gentleness and
mercy were increased by his prosperity. Elevated in every

sentiment, he dealt lightly with those who needed his for-
giveness; uncompromising where his own rights were as-
sailed, he was sure to put those who denied them at utter
defiance; his thoughts emanated from his own mind, his
opinions became his convictions, and his convictions a part
of his belief in God. When he acted with others, it was
because they agreed with him. When he was the leader
of a party, he guided without ostentation, and controlled
without exaction."

On the day of the funeral no business was transacted in
Charleston. How could the merchants think of gain when
their friend lay dead?

Memorial services were held in Boston and New York
City.

Langdon Mitchell, who wrote incidentally of Mr. Petigru in an article in *The Atlantic Monthly,* told of a memorial meeting held soon after his death in Charleston,
when a vast crowd attended. The approach to the building, as well as the street before the doors, was occupied
by those who could not gain admission. Some of the
state's greatest men spoke. "And their eulogies appear
to have been as open, sincere, and unstrained, as we should
have expected them to be the reverse. Yet among those
who spoke there must have been some pledged to the
doctrine of Secession—life-long bitter opponents of the
man they mourned, who, doubtless, had received hard
blows at his capable hands. There was no speaker present
who did not well know that the issue of the prolonged
struggle was uncertain. Hardly a man of them but had
lost some youthful member of his family. All Charleston
was in mourning, severely impoverished, cruelly anxious,
straining nerve and courage to meet the prolonged trial
of war and the agonies of personal loss."

Soon after the close of the Civil War, the New York *Independent* printed a poem which pictured truly his glorious spirit. Of the nine stanzas five are reproduced:

No, I will not: take my answer;
    Call me traitor, think me fool;
But, by all that makes my manhood,
    Thou shalt not make me thy tool.

Play the farce out, wreak thy vengeance,
    Let me in the prison rot;
But inscribe upon my tombstone,
    "This man scorned us and our plot."

Yet unslandered by his fellows;
    For no heart, howe'er misled,
But bowed down its inner nature
    To that clearer heart and head.

Thus he lived, a man whose country
    Was not bounded by a state,
And whose uncorrupted honor
    Turned the shafts of private hate.

Thus he died, unmoved, unshaken
    By opinion's subtle art;
Now the stricken city weepeth,
    And the nation holds her heart.

CHAPTER XV

SHELDON JACKSON, THE REINDEER MAN

WHEN HUNGER CAUSED SORROW IN ALASKA

BEFORE the days of the submarine cable from America to. Europe the Western Union Telegraph Company planned to connect America with Asia by telegraph, by way of Alaska and Siberia. In 1866 linemen of the company were attracted by a party of Alaskan natives on the mountainside back of their village. About forty people of all ages were present. They were chatting and laughing as at a picnic. On a small level spot had been constructed an oblong ring of stones about six feet in length. Near by a reindeer had been killed, and a party of women were sprinkling the stones with handfuls of tobacco and choice bits of deer meat. Thinking they were making a sacrifice to the gods, the workmen asked a native who had learned a little English to explain the details. But the native said it was to be a human sacrifice. Pointing to an old man in the group, he said, "See old man— no got eyes—bym-by kill um."

Years later Captain Healy of the *Bear* was inquiring the whereabouts of a native whom he had known on a former trip. Meeting another native, he asked, "Where is George now?" "Oh," was the reply, "I shot him last year." Then the explanation was given that George was taken sick, that there seemed no hope for his recovery, and that he had been put to death.

ONE OF SHELDON JACKSON'S REINDEER HERDS

REINDEER GRAZING AT POINT BARROW, ALASKA

Dr. Jackson, hearing of many instances of this sort, made inquiries as to the reason for the heartless act. He learned that when persons have an incurable disease, or become too old to be of further service in procuring the necessaries of life, it is a common practice among the natives to put them to death. The conditions of life are so hard, the difficulties of feeding the strong are so great, that they think it best no useless man or woman should be permitted to live.

During a visit to the villages along several thousand miles of arctic and semi-arctic coast, Dr. Jackson met thousands of natives, yet he saw only one old person. He noted in his diary that this almost entire absence of aged persons among the population confirms the accounts of the custom of killing the aged and infirm.

Sometimes the children are killed because the supply of food is too scanty to care for them. One of the telegraph party already mentioned told of a famine in Alaska when, as early as October, people began to boil their deerskin bedding into soup. Many of the natives sought the advice and assistance of the strangers. One said: "You know, sir, the winter has hardly commenced. I have a wife and seven children and seven dogs to support, and not a pound of meat or fish to give them. I have some deerskins and eight fathoms of thong that I can boil up. But these are not enough to sustain the family and the dogs too until the Tchuct-chu [steamer] comes to trade, and I don't know where to get more, as my neighbors are starving too." With hesitation and a faltering voice he added: "If my children perish I will have my dogs left, but if my dogs perish, how can I go to the Tchuct-chu to get deer? Then my family will starve too, and I will have neither family nor dogs." What he wanted was for the

American to decide whether it was worse for him to let his children or his sled dogs starve, for if the latter starved it would involve the starvation of the whole family. Of course, he was advised to keep both as long as possible.

Occasionally an instance of this destitution or starvation came under the eye of an intelligent white man and was given to the world, but these periodical seasons of starvation came and went, and hundreds of human beings starved, their fate unheeded and unknown by the world.

Once there was food sufficient for the Indians and the Eskimos, but that day passed long ago. Whales, seals and sea-lions were plentiful. Just as the great herds of buffalo which roamed the plains of the United States as late as 1870 were slaughtered for their pelts, so the whales were sacrificed for the fat that encased their bodies and the bone that hung in their mouths. Soon the whales were destroyed or driven from the North Pacific. They were then followed into Bering Sea, and the slaughter went on. The remnant took refuge in the Arctic Ocean, and thither the whalers followed. Before many years the whales frequented only the inaccessible ice-fields that surround the north pole, and so were no longer within the reach of the natives. Thus one large source of food supply was cut off.

Another supply of food was derived from the walrus that once swarmed in great numbers in those northern seas. But commerce wanted more ivory, and the whalers turned their attention to hunting the walrus as well as the whale, and ten thousand of these were annually destroyed for the sake of their tusks. Where, a few years before, they were so numerous that their bellowings were heard above the roar of the waves and the grinding and crashing of the ice-fields, in 1890 Dr. Jackson cruised for weeks without seeing or hearing one. The walrus, as a source of food supply, had become all but extinct.

In like manner the seal and sea-lion, once so common in Bering Sea, had become so scarce that it is with difficulty the natives procure their skins in quantities sufficient to cover their boats. Sea-lion meat has become a luxury.

Once the natives caught and cured for winter use great quantities of salmon, but to some of the streams there came the canneries that both carried the food out of the country and destroyed the future food supply in wasteful methods.

Wild reindeer used to roam near the Eskimo villages, and it was possible to kill them in time of need. But the introduction of modern firearms frightened away these animals to the inaccessible regions of the interior.

The sad result in Alaska was apparent when deserted villages and tenantless houses were seen on all sides. Villages that once numbered thousands had been reduced to hundreds by the slow process of starvation and extermination. In one village a trader reported to Dr. Jackson that the death rate was fifteen times the birth rate.

THE MAN FOR ALASKA'S HOUR OF NEED

The sorrows of the natives in Alaska touched the heart of a man named Sheldon Jackson, who was born on May 18, 1834, at Minaville, New York. When he was twenty-five years old he became a teacher of Choctaw Indian boys in the Indian Territory. This was at a time when great buffalo herds roamed over the plains. The memory of what these animals meant to the Indians, for both food and clothing, was to influence him many years later when he was confronted by the problem in Alaska.

Jackson's next service was in the Minnesota of the pioneers. There he spent five years as a home missionary of the Presbyterian Church, caring for the needs of the scattered people. This experience prepared him for the time when, in 1869, he became "Superintendent of Missions for Western Iowa, Nebraska, Dakota, Idaho, Montana, Wyoming and Utah." Later he was asked to add Colorado and New Mexico to his territory. Before long he was known as "The Bishop of all outdoors."

His was the spirit of the true pioneer. One of his admirers, who followed his work, said of him:

"He is always on the skirmish line, where there is the most of danger and of hard work. He seems to have a good deal of the spirit of Daniel Boone, who, as soon as new settlers came near enough for him to see the smoke from their cabins, felt that it was time for him to move on."

The call to move on to greater tasks came in 1877, when he read a letter from a soldier at Fort Wrangell, Alaska, who told of the need for Christian work among the neighborhood Alaskans. When the letter was read by Sheldon Jackson, he decided to offer himself for service there.

His experiences in educating the natives led him to appeal to Congress to provide government schools. After heart-breaking effort he succeeded in securing the passage of a resolution which encouraged him to give his services in establishing and superintending schools. This he did, in connection with his regular labors. And when, in 1885, he was appointed United States Commissioner of Education for Alaska, with the privilege of superintending the expenditure of $25,000 appropriated for schools, his salary was fixed at $1200 per year. Later this salary was adjusted in such a way that the church whose servant he was paid part, while the Government paid the balance of a total that was absurdly small.

The tale of the years of service for the Government is full of absorbing interest. These were years spent in the contest for good government in Alaska. The story of how this was waged and won after seven years' relentless pursuit of friends first of no government, then of misgovernment, is a rare chapter in American history.

Enemies attacked him, and tried to make his work impossible. But he persisted in the face of obstacles, and finally was victor. Then, having won his struggle for better moral conditions for the natives, he was ready to turn to a new fight to save them from starvation.

THE DREAM AND THE RESULT

When Jackson realized the awful need, he had the vision of a remedy for the conditions that caused the death of many hundreds each year, and tempted fathers to kill their children, children their parents, and neighbors the old and decrepit about them.

He said that, of course, it was possible for the Government to feed the natives as the Indians of America are being fed. But this would cost millions of dollars annually, even if the food supplies could be transported in sufficient quantities three thousand miles from Seattle, and at last the Eskimos would be degraded, pauperized and exterminated by a slow process.

But he was hopeful as he looked across to Siberia where natives live under precisely similar conditions, yet have no difficulty in supporting themselves in comfort. They own large herds of reindeer, and from these herds they have abundant food and clothing. In time of famine, when some are in danger of starvation, there is always the possibility of the men who own the large herds of domestic reindeer hearing of their straits and coming to their relief. "Then why not make the Eskimos of Alaska self-supporting by giving them reindeer herds of their own!" was his daring thought.

So he urged that the Government, in connection with the industrial schools, should introduce the tame reindeer of Siberia and teach the young men to care for and manage them. In these schools it is of no use to teach a pupil to be a carpenter, or a shoemaker, or a tinsmith or a farmer, for there is no call for these trades. But if they are taught to handle the reindeer, the problem of the starving is solved. He said that the chief industry taught in the Alaska schools should be the reindeer culture. No good argument could be presented against this proposal, for the conditions of climate and pasturage were just what the reindeer required; there was the same degree of cold as in Siberia, and the tundras of the Arctic are covered with the moss that is ideal food for the herds. Nothing remained, then, but to go to Siberia and secure enough animals to begin the industry. For this, money, time and patience only would be necessary.

In his annual report to Washington, after returning from his tour of Alaska in 1890, Dr. Jackson made his proposition, and added:

"A moderate computation, based upon the statistics of Lapland, where similar climatic and other conditions exist, shows Northern and Central Alaska capable of supporting over nine million head of reindeer.

"To reclaim and make valuable vast areas of land, otherwise worthless; to introduce large, permanent, and wealth-producing industries, where none previously existed; to take a barbarian people on the verge of starvation and lift them up to a comfortable self-support and civilization, is certainly a work of national importance."

A storm of protest greeted Dr. Jackson's argument and suggestion. Many said that it was a visionary scheme, as impractical as other suggestions made by him. But when the objectors were challenged to point to any of his schemes which had proven impractical, they were silent. Others declared that it was foolish to spend so much thought on a few starving Eskimos who would be better off out of the world than in it. "Better let them die in peace," they said.

In spite of the clamor of the thoughtless, the report was approved by the Commissioner of Education and was referred to the Secretary of the Interior. In the Fifty-first Congress an appropriation of $15,000 was incorporated in "a bill for the introduction of domesticated reindeer into Alaska as an experiment, in connection with the industrial schools of the country." Dr. Jackson watched the bill, and used every effort to push it through, but Congress adjourned without action. However, he did not give up. Of course he might have decided to wait until the next Congress, but precious time would be lost; the delay of two years might mean the death of hundreds.

Through the newspapers he made an appeal to his friends and the friends of his work, asking for funds. He explained his plan so thoroughly that their objections were answered. He had thought out the whole scheme. He would go to Siberia, buy reindeer of the native owners, transport them to Alaska, and put them in charge of the teachers of the various schools. The schools would give them over to the care of selected young men who would be responsible for the herds. The herds would increase year by year; the increase would be given to the natives as the nucleus for herds of their own, and the beginning of the Eskimos' safety from starvation would be in sight.

He was told that the superstitious natives of Siberia would not part with their reindeer. But he insisted that he could persuade them to sell. It was objected that he could not transport the animals to Alaska, even if he succeeded in buying them. Then, convincingly, he told his plans for the voyage. He answered every objection made, and at last he had his reward. More than two thousand dollars were in his hands for the initial experiment—a small amount when compared with the fifteen thousand asked from Congress, yet enough to make a beginning.

When the announcement was made that the money given was to be spent for goods to barter with the Siberians, and that the journey would soon be undertaken with the approval of the Secretary of the Interior, the doubters smiled in anticipation of the pleasure of saying "I told you so," when Dr. Jackson should report failure.

But the little man who had successfully worked out more than one big scheme on which doubters had tried to throw cold water contented himself with smiling quietly. He knew who would be able to say, "I told you so."

BARGAINING WITH SIBERIAN HERDERS

Because of the small fund available, Dr. Jackson decided that on the trip of 1891 to Siberia he would not attempt to buy many reindeer, but would secure just enough to prove that his plans were workable. Then he could make arrangements with the owners of herds to deliver more animals to him the following year, when he hoped to make his real start in herd development.

The money contributed by his friends was carefully spent for such supplies as the natives of Siberia would desire, for he knew that all trading must be done by barter, as was the case in the days of Daniel Boone and Kit Carson.

As in previous years he was invited to make use of the U. S. S. *Bear*. The captain of the *Bear* had received these instructions from Washington:

"If you think advisable, after talking the matter over with Sheldon Jackson, you can land a small party on the Siberian shore to collect reindeer and have them ready for transportation to St. Lawrence Island on your return.

"This scheme is carried out by the Interior Department under direction of Sheldon Jackson, you will understand, you only assisting him with the work."

Before reaching the Siberian coast the voyage was full of incident. When near Ougamok Island in Bering Sea the *Bear* passed through a large school of whales. Fourteen were counted blowing at one time around the ship; they were so near that it seemed as if the ship must strike some of them. Myriads of birds darkened the surface of the water. Along the north shore of Akoutan Island the honeycombed rocks of lava formed many beautiful arches and caves, while a short distance inland lay open before the party the crater of an extinct volcano.

The morning of July 4 nearly brought a tragedy. When everyone thought there was water on all sides, the lookout who had been peering into the fog cried, "Land all around!" Rushing to the deck, Dr. Jackson found that in the fog and through an easterly set of the current, the

Bear had drifted to the westward forty-five miles in forty-one hours and was in danger of running ashore at the southeast cape of St. Lawrence Island. Another half-hour of fog would have wrecked the ship in those lonely waters. Exhausting efforts by all hands saved the vessel from disaster. The weary sailors had their reward later when they were given an extra dinner in honor of the day.

Next day anchor was cast in the midst of the whaling fleet at Port Clarence. The officers of twenty ships came aboard as soon as possible to see if there was mail for them. In their eagerness they were so nervous that it was necessary for each man to examine the large package of mail several times; each succeeding search disclosed letters which had been overlooked previously. Even then many of them left in the package plainly addressed letters, which were later handed to them by others.

When the *Bear* was ready to steam on to Cape Prince of Wales, one hundred and seventy natives who had come to Port Clarence in their umiaks were taken on board, and their eight boats were taken in tow. The sea was smooth, and the natives had an opportunity to give on deck an exhibition of some of their dances.

It was six o'clock in the evening when anchor was thrown overboard at the Cape. The natives were immediately set to work with their umiaks, taking ashore eighteen tons of coal, and the provision supplies for the mission. This work was completed at nine o'clock. The supplies were then carried from the beach to the house, the Eskimos working busily till two o'clock in the morning.

At one o'clock next afternoon, the whole village was invited off to the ship. The two men in charge of the school gave an exhibition of the children's work, in arithmetic, language and singing. After this there was a race of twelve large umiaks from the ship to the beach and return. The first boat received three pailfuls of ship's biscuit, the second boat two, and the third boat one. Later the people were assembled on deck, the officers of the ship being in full uniform, and the captain gave them a talk about the school and about the necessity of temperate habits. At the close of his address he appointed ten policemen, whose duty it was to be to assist the teachers in preserving order and looking after school attendance. The names of the ten honored young men were entered on the ship's log:

Er-a-he-na, Chief	Kar-tay-ak
Kit-mee-suk, Second Chief	Oo-tik-tok
Tiong-nok	Kal-a-whak
Ter-ed-loo-na	Wi-a-ki-se-ok
We-a-ho-na	Ma-an-a

The first chief was promised three sacks of flour as salary, while the second chief was promised two sacks. The others could look forward to one sack each. The ceremony of appointment was concluded by the presentation of an imposing cap to each of the ten officers, and the firing of three rounds of blank shells from the Dahlgren howitzer to impress the natives with the power of the ship. When the shell struck the water miles away, many were the exclamations of astonishment.

In the evening the *Bear* started across the strait to Siberia. It had been hoped to take along as interpreter a Siberian native called Shoo-Fly, who had spent several summers on a whale ship, and so knew a little English. He had agreed to go with Dr. Jackson, but he failed to keep his promise. Other attempts to secure help were likewise unsuccessful. The third mate of one of the Port

Clarence whaling fleet was recommended as an admirable
man for assisting the expedition. The mate was willing,
but his captain would not release him until the return of
the ship to San Francisco in the fall. Arrangements were
made to employ him the next season to take entire charge
of the herd which Dr. Jackson hoped to have for him.

ODD DETAILS OF THE EXPEDITION

At last an interpreter was secured who seemed quite
satisfied with these wages promised him for two weeks'
services:

1	box Pilot bread	$1.90
19	yards drill	1.61½
8	half-pint cans powder	3.00
40	pieces bar lead	1.00
3	pounds tobacco	1.35
1	iron pot	.75
	Pilot bread	.38½
		——
		$10.00

All accounts were carefully entered in the journal kept
by Dr. Jackson on the voyage. This journal showed that
he had expended for goods to be given to the Siberian
natives instead of money a total of $1,242.87. During
the season these payments were made for deer:
At Enchowankin-eu-ka, for four deer:

One rifle	$18.50
200 cartridges	6.50
	——
	$25.50

At Katiene, for four deer:

1 rifle	$18.50
200 cartridges	6.50
1 fox trap	.50
	$25.50

At Ko-nar-ri, for three deer:

1 rifle	$18.50
1 revolver	12.00
200 cartridges	6.50
1 box navy bread	1.90
	$38.90

At Senavin Straits for five deer:

1 rifle	$13.50
1 repeating rifle	18.50
200 cartridges	6.50
1 set reloading tools	3.00
1 box navy bread	1.90
	$43.40

These animals were not bought without a great deal of trouble and disappointment. The natives were suspicious and unwilling to part with their property. But Dr. Jackson was unwilling as ever to be daunted by obstacles; he was eager to continue the search long after others advised him to give up.

He had been informed that he would find "deer men" at East Cape, but when inquiry was made the information was given that the herds there were very small; if he would go to Cape Serdze Karun, one hundred miles farther on up the Arctic coast, he would find large herds.

Another informant suggested that a trip to Cape Tchaplin, one hundred and fifty miles south, might be successful. He determined to go first to the latter place. The voyage was made difficult by a field of floating ice, through which the *Bear* pushed its way.

In about twenty hours Dr. Jackson was in conference with a number of natives. A proposition was made to Quarri, the leading man, to take his whole herd of one hundred. He declined to sell, pleading as an excuse that he was keeping his herd for a time of need—some season when the walrus and the seal would fail; then the people's only protection from starvation would be the reindeer. How could he be expected to part with what might prove the salvation of his entire village? He offered to make the captain a present of two, but would not sell one animal. Dr. Jackson persisted, finally saying that he would be satisfied with ten deer. Would he not sell ten for the sake of the starving people of Alaska? The owner said he would consult his son, and hurried away.

When he did not return, Dr. Jackson went to Quarri's storehouse, whose contents were an indication of his wealth; the visitor counted two hundred sacks of flour and eighty boxes of tobacco. There was also a head of whalebone, worth from five hundred to eight hundred dollars. A second conference with the owner was as fruitless as the first. Perhaps some deer might be sold when the animals were driven down to the coast. But if Dr. Jackson would go along the shores of Holy Cross Bay at the head of Anadyr Gulf he would find large numbers, and close to the beach. Probably some of these could be bought. Yet what good would it do to buy deer? They would die on the voyage, and even if they stood the trip they would not live long in their new home.

SHELDON JACKSON

A man and a boy promised to go to Holy Cross as interpreters, but later they tried to back out. They said they were afraid to go; if no deer should be found on the beach, as promised, or if the natives would not sell from their herds, or if the bay was full of ice, then the captain would be angry and accuse them of lying to him. When the captain assured them that he would not hold them responsible, they brought off their clothes and blankets in a hair seal bag, and the voyage was resumed.

WITHIN THE ARCTIC CIRCLE

Holy Cross Bay was three hundred miles distant and Dr. Jackson realized that he must there solve the problem of finding the reindeer he hoped to buy. He had hoped to secure them so near to the island where they were to be taken for the winter that no food would be required on the journey. Now everything would be different.

An inventory of the stores on board revealed some ten or twelve pounds of oatmeal in the captain's pantry, about twenty-five pounds in the officers' mess, a few pounds in the engineers' department, and about sixty pounds in the sailors' stores. It was agreed to purchase all this. Then the meal could be mixed with the drinking water if the animals were secured.

As the northern shore of Holy Cross Bay is within the arctic circle, floating ice was looked for. But there was more ice than was anticipated. One morning, in a fog, ice suddenly appeared directly under the bows of the ship, and the heart of the officer on deck stood still; he thought he was ashore. Carefully and slowly for several hours the way was picked through the mass. When the bay was reached, floating ice still impeded progress, the night was

[283]

dark, and there was a cold, driving rainstorm. Twice the *Bear* was almost ashore.

In the morning the natives of a village of sixteen tents or yourts were surprised to see what was probably the first steamer that had entered the waters of the bay. Three or four umiaks full of natives came off from the beach. They were large, healthy and dirty. Reindeer skins, fur garments and walrus ivory were bought from them, but little information was secured.

In the afternoon Dr. Jackson went ashore. Diligent inquiries were made for reindeer, and two men were found who agreed to sell five each, but their deer were on the west side of the bay, which could not be reached till the ice should move, and the ice would not move till the wind changed.

While waiting for the wind to change a school of fifty walrus appeared near the ship. A boat was lowered, and several were killed and taken on board. The natives assisted in the capture, and were delighted with the gift of meat. As a sign of their thanksgiving for an increased food supply, they danced on the deck until late in the evening.

Finally the wind changed, the ice moved, and progress to the west side of the bay was possible. When no natives came to the ship, Dr. Jackson went ashore through a field of floating ice, and walked five miles across the country to a couple of native tents. There he found only women and children, who explained that the men had gone to the ship. The two parties had missed each other on the way.

Hastening back to the *Bear,* he found two umiak loads of natives. One of them—Lingahurigan—would not agree to sell any deer at once, but was quite willing to promise for the next year twenty-five animals, at the rate of five for a rifle, and twenty for a whale-boat. He promised, too, that he would instruct others, who would be able to increase the herd to two hundred.

At Cape Blossom, Kotzebue Sound, in the Arctic Ocean, twelve umiaks brought about three hundred natives to the ship. An active trade in skins followed, black and brown bear, white and red fox, lynx, otter and mink being exchanged for flour, powder, caps, lead and muslin drill. But no reindeer could be secured.

Other attempts were made at various places, but it was not till August 28, after cruising for several thousand miles, that the first deer was hoisted on board. Jubilantly Dr. Jackson made the entry in his diary:

"Thus it has been proved by actual experience that deer can be purchased alive."

Later fifteen deer were secured. Moss was bought from the natives that the deer might not be deprived of their accustomed food. Prophecies of failure were answered when for three weeks the sixteen animals were kept alive and in health on the moss and oatmeal water.

When these were safely landed on an island in the harbour of Unalaska, Dr. Jackson thankfully turned southward. The next season he proposed to return to Siberia and gather his herd. The experience gained during the trial trip would stand him in good stead when large funds should enable him to go ahead in earnest.

SUCCESS IN SPITE OF DIFFICULTIES

On his return from Siberia, Dr. Jackson reported his success to the Department of the Interior, and was given assurance that a government appropriation certainly would be forthcoming for the next season's work.

In the winter a bill was introduced in the Senate appropriating fifteen thousand dollars "to be expended under the direction of the Secretary of the Interior for the purpose of introducing and maintaining in the territory of Alaska reindeer for domestic purposes." This bill passed the Senate, but it failed to pass the House, so Dr. Jackson was compelled to continue the work in dependence on the public. But he was not discouraged. He was confident that the eyes of the lawmakers would be opened before long. In the meantime he proposed to do his best to show the practicability of his plan, and the absolute necessity of stocking the barren coast of Alaska with reindeer.

Accordingly, on April 28, 1892, he again sailed from San Francisco on the *Bear*. On June 1 the steamer anchored at St. Paul Island, where he bought a whale-boat rescued from the wreck of a whaler, which he knew he would need in the transportation of reindeer from the shore to the ship. At Unalaska he visited the reindeer which had been bought the year before, and found that they had passed the winter well. Several fawns had been added to the herd.

At St. Lawrence Island there was a stop while the ship's carpenter made some repairs at the mission station. Dr. Jackson learned that the man in charge of the erection of the schoolhouse and teacher's residence the previous summer had left a large number of orders for navy bread with natives who had helped in the work. These were redeemed by the distribution of three boxes of bread. An account of a different nature was to be settled with Chief Iurrison, who had persuaded the carpenter to build for him a small house from lumber left after the construction of the school. A note had been left for Dr. Jackson that the chief was to pay three hundred dollars in whalebone and ivory. The first instalment of this debt was collected, and more was promised the following year.

At Port Clarence a site. was selected for the Reindeer Station, to which deer were to be brought and from which they would be distributed to the different mission stations. The United States flag was immediately hoisted on a signal pole. Until buildings could be erected, two tents were put up to afford shelter for the supplies that were to be left behind.

The work of building was begun at once, in order that quarters might be ready for the animals to be purchased that season, and that there might be a suitable place for the instruction of the men who were to be sent out in charge of the deer.

The carpenters of the *Bear* and their assistants succeeded in finishing the buildings promptly and the station was then completed by the construction of two "dugouts," in which the superintendent and his assistants would take refuge during the severe winter weather. The final touch was given to the cluster of buildings by christening the whole the "Teller Reindeer Station."

During the summer five trips were made from Port Clarence to Siberia and return. On the first trip fifty-three reindeer were bought and four native herders were secured. On July 3 the *Bear* was back at Teller Station, but the surf was too heavy to allow the safe landing of the deer.

The delay made possible a fitting celebration of the Fourth of July by the landing on that day of the first herd of domesticated reindeer in Alaska and on the continent of America. The deer, each with the four feet tied together, were taken aboard a launch and carried ashore in litters. They were then untied, hobbled and turned loose.

Three ran away and took to the hills; the herders recovered them after a long chase.

On the second trip the ice proved a great hindrance, fog was encountered, two anchors were broken, and natives visited were unwilling to dispose of deer. Finally, however, sixteen animals were bought and transported.

A BATTLE WITH THE ICE

On one of the later trips that same season, the *Bear* encountered so much ice that it was remarkable the reindeer-seeker survived to tell the experience. For days the vessel was fastened amid the floes. Finally there was a chance to move slowly. Most of one day was spent in shifting anchor and dodging the ice floes. At noon the ice became so dense that further progress was impossible, so the ship was fastened to a floe with a grapnel. In the evening an attempt was made to force a way through the ice, but at midnight the attempt was given up. At times the ship was prevented from being pushed ashore by the ice only by constant ramming of the ice seaward.

From midnight to noon the next day the ship was drifting in heavy and closely packed ice, the engine starting and stopping at intervals. Soon after noon the ice becoming too heavy for further progress, the engine was stopped and the vessel drifted. An hour later the ice seemed to open a little to the eastward, and an effort was made to go in that direction. At midnight clear water was reached, and a little later the *Bear* came to anchor off the village of Uttan, Siberia.

On July 21 a boat was sent ashore after a noted deer man. When he came on board, it was learned that his herd was three or four days' journey distant, and that he was willing to sell only four or five animals.

As a large ice floe was seen bearing down upon the vessel, and as the captain did not relish the idea of being imprisoned another week and perhaps wrecked in the bay, he left the village at full speed. For hours there was an exciting race with the ice, which was a solid, unbroken field as far as the eye could reach. The ice was rapidly gaining upon the fugitives; large detached pieces—like scouts—were forging ahead of the *Bear* and placing themselves directly in her path. Against these she rammed and jarred. But at length the projecting cape of the bay was reached and passed just as the ice floe was swinging on it; as the cape barred the progress of the pursuing ice, the vessel was safe.

During the afternoon the fog was so dense that the passage of Bering Straits was made before anyone knew it. When the fog lifted a little the captain found he was twenty miles ahead of the place he supposed he was at. At 10:20 P.M. the vessel came to anchor off the Reindeer Station.

A fair sample of difficulties in dealing with the natives was the experience of August 6, when the *Bear* anchored near a village in Holy Cross Bay. Five umiak loads of people came aboard. Inquiries were at once made for reindeer. At first the Siberians said the deer were near; then they said they were far off. Again they said that they had been on the coast earlier in the summer, but when the ship did not come, the herders had driven them back into the country because the mosquitoes were too bad. At one time they offered to sell a ship load. When they thought bucks were wanted, they had only roes to sell, and when they found roes were desired, their herd proved to be all bucks.

Then they asked two prices for what they proposed to sell. They declared that they would lose the increase of the herd if they should sell, while the cartridges for which they traded would be used up, and they would have nothing.

Captain Healy of the *Bear* then argued that if their deer should die the next year they would have nothing and would starve, while if they had cartridges they could shoot walrus and seal and live. Or, for what they would receive for their deer they could trade with natives further back, and get two deer for one. Finally, after five hours' talk, the boat was lowered. At midnight Monday the launch returned with sixteen deer. The sailors had been nearly sixteen hours pulling against the sea and storm to reach the ship. One of the deer died the next day, another had to be killed, and two or three others were crippled, probably as the result of being tied and kept so long on the launch.

In spite of adverse circumstances, one hundred and seventy-one deer were landed at Port Clarence during the summer.

During the winter following the superintendent of the herd left at Teller Station trained twelve deer to draw sleds. With two teams selected from the twelve he made a satisfactory journey to Cape Prince of Wales, sixty miles distant, and return. As he was anxious to disprove the fears of some doubters that Eskimo dogs would molest the reindeer, he was careful to picket the deer at night in the neighborhood of villages, in which there were from one hundred to three hundred dogs. Not once was an attack made on them.

In March, 1893, Congress appropriated six thousand dollars for the purchase of further reindeer. The sum was to be given for expenditure by Dr. Jackson as Commissioner of Education for Alaska.

When he returned to Teller Station he was grateful to find that the herd had increased to two hundred and twenty-three animals, in spite of the death of twenty-seven. During the summer further purchases were made, and the herd increased rapidly.

In August, 1894, the next step was taken. One hundred and nineteen head were taken from the herd and put in charge of the missionary at Cape Prince of Wales, with the understanding that he was to look after the increase and train men to take charge of them.

CONTRACTS AND TESTS

This was the first of many divisions of the herd. Every missionary who received them was required to enter into a contract. It was agreed that the Government would furnish one hundred or more reindeer as a loan, subject to recall if the conditions of the loan were not complied with, for the term of five years. In return for this favor, the mission was required to feed, clothe and care for the native apprentices during this period, and at its close return the original number of reindeer loaned them. Of the increase year by year at least eighty per cent became the property of the mission. In some cases twenty per cent of the net increase was given to the instructors. It was found to be good policy, also, to give to each apprentice the increase of a certain part of the herd which had been assigned to him, so that at the conclusion of his term of service he might have fifty or more deer to brand as his own. In all the arrangements which were made from time to time with respect to the distribution of the several herds, it was the settled policy of the Government to give an increasingly large percentage of fawns to the natives as they became more proficient and skilful in handling the animals entrusted to their care.

In 1905 the Government still owned thirty per cent of the reindeer in Alaska; the mission stations owned twenty-one per cent; the Lapps, who had been brought to Alaska to act as herders, owned eleven per cent; while the natives had acquired thirty-eight per cent.

In 1902, when the last reindeer were imported, thirty animals were added to the herds. Then the Russian Government forbade further exportation. Up to this time twelve hundred and eighty deer had been taken into Alaska.

Soon Dr. Jackson's experiment was declared a decided success. It had been found that reindeer could be depended on to travel swiftly over long distances, drawing heavy loads; and also to secure food above ground and under the snow, over a vast extent of territory, north of the agricultural belt of Alaska.

For long journeys a reindeer team is far superior to a dog team, as the latter cannot haul sufficient provisions through an uninhabited country to feed themselves. A broken reindeer can drag two hundred pounds on a sled through country of all kinds, and instead of eating food carried on the sledges he will browse on the moss or lichen which he digs deep in the snow.

The first practical test of the endurance of reindeer in Alaska, and their adaptability to winter travel, was made in the winter of 1896-97, under the direction of the superintendent of the station at Teller. Starting from this station on December 10, with nine sleds and seventeen head of reindeer, he traveled southward to a station on the

Kuskokwim River, about a thousand miles distant. His trip was described in a government document. The course, while traveled by compass, was a zigzag over unbeaten tracks, in order to better learn the extent and abundance of moss pasturage. Scaling high mountain ranges, shooting down precipitous declivities with toboggan speed, plodding through valleys filled with deeply-drifted snow, laboriously cutting a way through the man-high underbrush in the forest or steering across the trackless tundra, never before trodden by the foot of white men; gliding over the hard-crusted snow, or wading through slush two feet deep, on imperfectly frozen rivers, unknown to geographers, were the experiences of the trip.

It is said that the journey was the most remarkable ever made by reindeer. One day there came an arctic blizzard, against which neither man nor beast could stand upright. The reindeer were blown down—one was literally swept off the mountainside—the loaded sleds were overturned, and the men, throwing themselves flat between the rocks, clung to one another, to keep from being blown away. About a week after this extraordinary experience, the party encountered a succession of blinding snow-storms and were reduced to such straits that they were obliged to cut the railing from their sleds for fuel. When the last of these storms had passed away, the temperature fell to seventy-three degrees below zero, causing even the reindeer to break loose from their tethers and tramp ceaselessly around the tents for warmth. Near the close of the journey there was one long stretch where, contrary to information, no moss was found. Hence, it was necessary to push on continuously for four days and three nights, without a morsel of food for the deer until a wooded tract was reached, where trees were cut down that the deer might feed on the black moss which hung from them. On this terrible march, five of the deer fell dead or helpless in their serious adventure.

The return journey was made to Teller without serious adventure.

Thus a round trip of two thousand miles on sledges, the longest on record, was made over an unmarked and unknown route, in the worst and most inclement season of the year. With a better knowledge of the route some of these dreadful experiences might have been avoided, but the experiment served its purpose in proving the capabilities of the deer for making such a journey, in case of necessity.

In October, 1897, word was sent to Washington that three hundred seamen on board eight ice-bound whaling ships were in danger of perishing from hunger at Point Barrow. Deer and dogs were secured, and the overland journey was begun on December 18. After a trying trip of more than three months the starving whalers were reached, and just in time. More than two hundred reindeer were slaughtered for food, and the men were in good condition when the *Bear* arrived several months later.

To-day a large herd of reindeer is maintained at the Relief Station at Point Barrow, in order that a second expedition like this will be unnecessary.

Perhaps the most important work done by the reindeer is on the post route. In 1899 Dr. Jackson secured the establishment of the first Reindeer Post Route in the United States, from St. Michael, on the coast of Bering Sea, to Kotzebue, within the arctic circle. Three round trips of more than twelve hundred miles each were to be made every winter. Other routes have since been added. It was a natural development to arrange for the transporta-

tion of freight and passengers. A chain of reindeer stations, about one hundred miles apart, on many of the
important lines of travel on the coast and in the interior
makes possible reliable and speedy transport. One writer
who knows the country declares that eventually fifty thousand teams will be needed by the people; he says the nature
of the country is such that in many sections no other known
means of transportation can displace them.

The captain of the United States revenue cutter *Corwin*
reported to Congress his idea of the natives' debt to Dr.
Jackson, when he said:

"The reindeer furnish their owners with food, clothing
and shelter, and nearly all the necessaries of life. The
flesh, blood and entrails are eaten. The skin makes the
garments, beds, and tents. The skin of the leg, which is
covered with fine short hair, makes the boots. From the
antlers are made many of their implements, drill bows for
lighting fires, knife handles, etc. The sinews of the deer
make the native thread, and a most excellent thread it is.
The bones, soaked in oil, are burned for fuel, and in addition to all this the deer furnishes his master with the
means of transportation and indeed to a large extent as-
sists in forming the character of the man."

In 1912 there were thirty-three thousand reindeer in
the country. To import the beginning of the herds cost
the Government only about two hundred thousand dollars. The cost to Dr. Jackson was far greater; his expenditure of toil and privation cannot be calculated.

But he made good on his plan, and the Eskimos were
saved from extinction. The herds have grown enormously,
and will grow far more. To-day the meat supply calls
for an outlet outside of Alaska; the exportation of dressed

[295]

reindeer to other portions of the United States is a question of time.

Dr. E. W. Wilson of the Bureau of Biological Survey of the Department of Agriculture, which has charge of the reindeer industry of Alaska, after speaking of the great increase of the herds, tells of its probabilities. The survey has available grazing area sufficient to care for between 3,000,000 and 5,000,000 reindeer. Dr. Wilson says that the annual surplus over that number will yield a meat product each year worth more than the precious metals mined in the territory and second only to the fisheries as a permanent income-producing asset.

BIBLIOGRAPHY

Address on Andrew Bradford Delivered at the Annual Meeting of
the Historical Society of Pennsylvania, Feb. 9, 1869. By Horatio Jones. *Philadelphia, 1869.*

Address Delivered at the Celebration by the New York Historical
Society, May 20, 1863, of the Two Hundredth Birthday of Mr.
William Bradford. By John William Wallace. *Albany, 1863.*

Alaskan Pathfinder, The. (Story of Sheldon Jackson.) By John
T. Faris, *New York, 1913, 1927.*

Audubon the Naturalist. By Francis Hobart Herrick. *New York,*
1917.

Biographical and Historical Sketch of Early Indiana. (Vigo) By
Woollen. *Indianapolis, 1883.*

Centennial Law Suit, A. By C. C. Baldwin. Western Reserve
and Northern Ohio Historical Tract, No. 35. *Cleveland.* December 1876.

Colonel Francis Vigo. By A. B. McKee. Indiana Magazine of
History, December 1923. *Indianapolis.*

Colonel William Bradford, The Patriot Printer of 1776. By
John William Wallace. *Philadelphia, 1884.* (One hundred
presentation copies printed.)

Conquest of the Country Northwest of the River Ohio. (Vigo)
By William H. English. *Indianapolis, 1896.*

Constitution and Laws of the Philadelphia Society for the Establishment and Support of Charity Schools. (Ludwick) *Philadelphia, 1860.*

Correspondence of John Cleves Symmes. Edited by Beverly W.

Bond, Jr. Printed for the Historical and Philosophical Society of Ohio. *New York*, 1926.

Growth of the United States. By Ralph Volney Harlow. *New York*, 1925.

Harm Jan Huidekoper. By Nina Moore Tiffany and Francis Tiffany. *Cambridge*, 1904.
History of California, Volume 5. (Sutter) By Hubert Howe Bancroft. *San Francisco*, 1886.
History of Tennessee. By James Phelan. *Boston*, 1888.
History of the American Frontier. By Frederick L. Paxson. *Boston*, 1924.
History of the City of Vincennes, A. (Vigo) By Henry S. Canthorn. *Cleveland*, 1902.
History of the Pacific States of North America. (Sutter) Volume 3 and 4. Hubert Howe Bancroft. *San Francisco*, 1886.
Humphreys Family of Haverford and Philadelphia, The. By Hampton L. Carson. *Lancaster*, 1922.

Indiana's First Settlement. (Vigo) By E. A. Bryan, Magazine of American History, Volume 21.

Life and Public Services of John Cleves Symmes. By Charles H. Winfield. Proceedings of the New Jersey Historical Society. Second Series, Volume 5, Number 1.
Life and Times of Judge Caleb Wallace. By William H. Whitsitt. Filson Club Publications. *Louisville*, 1888.
Life and Writings of John Filson, the First Historian of Kentucky. By Reuben T. Durrett. Filson Club Publications. *Louisville*, 1884.
Life and Works of General John A. Sutter. By John B. Landis. Lancaster County Historical Society Publications. Volume XVII. *Lancaster*, 1913.
Life and Writings of Benjamin Franklin. (Bradford) By Albert Henry Smythe. *New York*, 1905.

Life and Writings of Rafinesque. By Richard Ellsworth Call. Filson Club Publications. *Louisville,* 1895.

Life as It Is. By J. M. W. Breazeale. *Knoxville,* 1842.

Life of Christopher Ludwick. By Benjamin Rush, M.D. *Philadelphia,* 1801.

Life of Travels and Research in North America and Europe. By C. S. Rafinesque. *Philadelphia,* 1836.

Many Sided Franklin, The. (Bradford) By Paul Leicester Ford. *New York,* 1899.

Memorial to the Legislature of the State of New York. By Paul H. Busti. *Albany,* 1820.

Penalties of Patriotism. (Vigo) By Joseph J. Thompson. Journal of the Illinois State Historical Society, January, 1917.

Petigru, James Lewis. By William J. Grayson. *New York,* 1866.

Political and Social History of the United States. 1492-1828. By Homer C. Hackett. *New York,* 1925.

Princeton. (Wallace) By Varnum Lansing Collins. *New York,* 1914.

Rafinesque, A Sketch of His Life, with Bibliography. By T. J. Fitzpatrick. Historical Department of Iowa. *Des Moines,* 1911.

Spirit of the Revolution. (Ludwick) By John C. Fitzpatrick. *Boston,* 1924.

Stiegel Glass. By Frederick William Hunter, *Boston,* 1914. Limited Edition, 420 copies.

Story of Princeton. By Edwin M. Norris. (Wallace) *Boston,* 1917.

Transcript of Fort Sutter Papers. Dunbar. Lenox Library, *New York.* Undated.

United States, The. By W. H. Hudson and I. S. Guernsey. *New York.* Undated.

THE ROMANCE OF FORGOTTEN MEN

Who Built the First United States Navy? By Colonel William
Humphreys, Retired, U.S.A. Journal of American History.
Volume X, Number 1. *New York,* 1916.

INDEX

INDEX

Fulton, Robert, 195
Fur traders, 230

Gallipolis, Ohio, 207
Garden of John Bartram, 25
Generosity of a pioneer land-
owner, 140
Genesee lands, 126
Geography learned from the In-
dians, 187
Germantown, Pennsylvania, 96,
202
Gibault, Father Pierre, 104, 109
Gingerbread baker of Letitia
Court, 92
Girty, Simon, 79
Glassware wins fame for Henry
W. Stiegel, 21
Godare, Madame, flagmaker, 109
Gold discovered in California,
244
Goode, Lieutenant Governor Pat-
rick, 53
Grant, General U. S., 224
Gray's Ferry, Philadelphia, 194
Great Britain and California,
240
Grouselands, first burnt brick
building west of Alleghanies,
119
Guerrière, defeated by the Con-
stitution, 156
Gunboat on Ohio River proposed,
88

Hamilton, Alexander, 253;
James, 110, 257, 263
Hampden-Sidney College and Ca-
leb Wallace, 77
Hampton Roads, Virginia, 156
Hancock, John, 61, 93, 149
Hanover, Presbytery of, appeals

to Virginia House of Bur-
gesses, 74
Harmar, Fort, 172, 173, 179
Harrison, William Henry, 119,
178, 182
Harrodsburg, Kentucky, 87
Harvard University, 221
Harvard University Library, 184,
189
Haverford Meeting House, 147
Helms, Captain Leonard, at Vin-
cennes, 109
Henderson, Richard, 78
Hendersonville, Kentucky, 207
Henry, Patrick, 77, 87, 105, 106,
112, 192;
Rev. Robert, 65
Historical Society of Pennsylva-
nia, 19, 35, 87, 117, 256,
262;
of New York, 37
History of American Printing,
quoted, 56
"History of Vincennes," quoted,
113
Holland Land Company, 127,
128, 130, 136, 137, 139
Holland lends money to the
United States, 125
Holme, John, quoted, 39
Holz, Elizabeth, marries Henry
W. Stiegel, 6
Honolulu, Hawaii, 231
Honor of a pioneer, 142
Hopkins, Commodore Ezek., 150
Hopkinson, Joseph, 160
Horse Shoe Road, 5, 20
Household expenditures of Henry
William Stiegel, 10
Huber, Elizabeth, marries Henry
W. Stiegel, 5
Huber, Jacob, ironworker, 5
Hudson River, 205

Miami River, Ohio, 166
Missouri River, 104, 203
Mitchell, Langdon, 266
Model of steamboat, John Fitch's, 192
Money transport in 1839, difficulty of, 142
Monongahela River, 169
Monroe, President James, 260
Monticello, Jefferson's home, 202
Monterey, California, 232
Morris, Robert, 18, 103, 108, 126, 149, 150, 162; Mrs. Robert, 19
"Morris's Folly," 19
Morrison, Francis, quoted, 122
Morristown, New Jersey, 94
Moselle, sloop of war, 258

Nakervie, William, 99
Nancy, ship, 3
Nassau Hall, Princeton, 69, 71
Native Sons of the Golden West, 248
Navigator, The, how Rafinesque prepared, 206
Navy, American, Father of the, 146
Navy, first American proposed, 150
Navy yard, first visit to an American, 152
Nelson, Lord, on American ships of war, 155
Neshaminy Presbyterian Church, 72
New Brunswick, Presbytery of, 72
New Castle, Delaware, 35
"New Flora of North America," quoted, 213
New Haven, Connecticut, 219

New Jersey campaign in the Revolution, 164
New Jersey *Journal,* quoted, 167
New Madrid, Missouri, 117
New Mexico, 230
New Orleans, Louisiana, 103, 107, 187, 259
New Switzerland, California, 236
New York City, 43, 129, 152, 205
New York Historical Society, 44
Newport, Rhode Island, 44, 156
Niagara Falls, New York, 135, 212
Non-Conformists appeal to Virginia House of Burgesses, 74
Norfolk, Virginia, 152
Norris, Edward M., quoted, 70
North Bend, Ohio, 177, 182
Northwest Territory, 114, 167, 168, 172, 175, 178, 188
Nueva Helvetia, California, 236
Nullification, beginning of, 86
Nullification: in Kentucky, 86; in Georgia, 260; in North Carolina, 260 in South Carolina, 260; in Tennessee, 260; in Virginia, 260;

"Odd fish" for Audubon, 207
Ohio Company, 176
Ohio River, 162, 205, 206
Old Ironsides, ship, 155, 156, 158
Old people in Alaska put to death, 268
Old State House, Philadelphia, 69
"Old Vigo," the bell at Terre Haute, Indiana, 123
"Once Upon a Time in Indiana," quoted, 122

INDEX

INDEX

DATE

GAYLORD